Government Intervention
in Religious Affairs

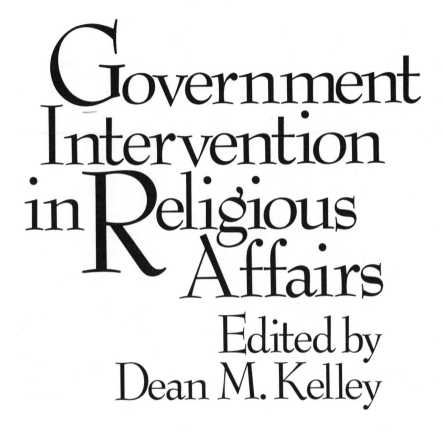

Government Intervention in Religious Affairs

Edited by
Dean M. Kelley

THE PILGRIM
PRESS | NEW YORK

Library of Congress Cataloging in Publication Data
Main entry under title:

Government intervention in religious affairs.

1. Religious liberty—United States—
Addresses, essays, lectures. 2. Church and
state—United States—Addresses, essays,
lectures. I. Kelley, Dean M.
KF4865.A75G68   342.73′0852   82–355
ISBN 0–8298–0602–4   347.302852   AACR2
ISBN 0–8298–0434–X (pbk.)

The material on pages 117–19 and 122–23 has been reproduced with permission
from the *Internal Revenue Manual* published and copyrighted by Commerce
Clearing House, Inc., 4025 West Peterson Avenue, Chicago, Illinois 60646.

The Pilgrim Press, 132 West 31 Street, New York, N.Y. 10001

It is proper to take alarm at the first experiment on our liberties.
—JAMES MADISON

Contents

Government Intervention in Religious Affairs

Introduction

There was a time not long ago when many people used the phrase "Separation of Church and State" to mean "Stop the Catholic Church." Some still use the phrase to mean "Keep (all) the churches in their place," and that "place" is thought by them to be the sanctuary, the cloister and the sacristy.

But in the past decade, more and more people have come to see that the danger of the moment is not dominance by a Church or all the churches but the increasing dominance of government and its propensity to press the churches back into ever smaller sanctums of time and space and subject. The churches are let know that if they venture out of their hallowed precincts of chapel, croft and chantry into the "real" world, they will have to brave the rigors that their "secular counterparts" (supposedly) have to meet.

(This glib equating of religious bodies with business corporations, banks, political parties, trade unions, professional associations and advertising agencies sounds fair and evenhanded until one realizes that each such category has its own unique place and function in American life with its own appropriate protections and disabilities, and that they cannot be treated as though they were interchangeable.)

A Look at History

In the three and a half centuries that the American society has been in existence on these shores, the place of religion in that society and its laws has undergone some significant changes. During the colonial period, some and perhaps many colonists left Europe for the New World seeking religious liberty. Some of them thought of that liberty as applying to the collective expressions of religion, and thus set up new sacral communities, new holy utopias, such as the Massachusetts Bay Colony, where the Word of the Lord was to be the basic canon of conduct for everyone, producing a kind of theocracy, and some would say, a pious tyranny.

Others thought of religious liberty as being primarily an attribute of individuals, and so eschewed the exclusive dominance of any ecclesiastical authorities. Among them were the radical first experiments in

3

non-establishment of religion: the Providence Plantations of Roger Williams, the Quaker commonwealth of Penn's Woods, and the latitudinarian sanctuary of the Catholic Lord Baltimore.

When the time came for the formation of the new nation over two hundred years ago, several of the colonies had established churches and others did not. Since some of the establishments were Anglican and others Congregational, neither had an uncontested claim for national hegemony, and growing numbers of dissenters (particularly Baptists and Presbyterians throughout the colonies as well as Anglicans in New England and Congregationalists—if any—in Virginia) resisted the notion of any national establishment.

The First Amendment of the new nation's Constitution made clear in 1789 that Congress was not to erect a national establishment nor disturb the state establishments where they existed: "Congress shall make no law *respecting* an establishment of religion. . . ." (Nevertheless, the existing establishments withered away, the last one—Massachusetts—being eliminated by that state in 1833.) The First Amendment continued, ". . . nor prohibiting the free exercise thereof," thus guaranteeing religious liberty, at least against federal action. The states had similar guarantees of religious liberty, though over the years their interpretations of what that meant increasingly diverged.

Judicial interpretations of those two succinct and deceptively simple clauses were very sparse during the nation's first century and a half, partly because the federal courts were unwilling to apply the federal clauses to matters within the jurisdiction of the states and partly because there was not a great deal of troubling of the church-state waters. Though there were efforts to apply the federal Bill of Rights to all citizens, these did not avail until the Fourteenth Amendment in 1868 forbade the state to "make or enforce any law which shall abridge the privileges or immunities of citizens of the United States" or to "deprive any person of life, liberty or property without due process of law," and even then the Supreme Court did not begin to incorporate portions of the federal Bill of Rights selectively into the law applicable to the states until 1925, and did not so apply the "free exercise" clause until 1940 (*Cantwell* v. *Connecticut*) or the "no establishment" clause until 1947 (*Everson* v. *Board of Education*). By these acts, it unleashed a torrent of church-state litigation that has produced in the past forty years more than five times as many significant church-state decisions by the U.S. Supreme Court as in all the years preceding![1]

Interpreting the Religious Clauses

During this eventful two centuries, the Supreme Court has discovered some often unsuspected implications in the First Amendment, including these:

1. Civil courts will not overturn the decision of appropriate ecclesiastical tribunals in deciding control of church property (*Watson* v. *Jones*, 1872);

2. Claims of religious liberty do not justify polygamy (*Reynolds* v. *U. S.*, 1878);

3. The state may purchase welfare services from a church-related hospital without violating the no-establishment clause (*Bradfield* v. *Roberts*, 1899);

4. The free exercise of religion cannot be infringed by states any more than it can by Congress (*Cantwell* v. *Conn.*, 1940);

5. The state may not infringe on the free exercise of religion unless it can show a "clear and present danger" to the public interest (*Cantwell* v. *Conn.*);

6. The free exercise of religion is a "preferred freedom" entitling it to more exacting judicial scrutiny than other rights (*Murdock* v. *Pennsylvania*, 1943);

7. The state cannot require orthodoxy of its citizens in matters of opinion (such as politics and religion) (*West Virginia State Board of Education* v. *Barnette*, 1943);

8. Religious believers cannot be required to prove the validity of their beliefs as a condition of soliciting contributions (*U. S.* v. *Ballard*, 1944);

9. "Neither a state nor the Federal Government can set up a church. Neither can pass laws which aid one religion, aid all religions, or prefer one religion over another. Neither can force nor influence a person to go to or to remain away from church against his will or force him to profess a belief or disbelief in any religion. No person can be punished for entertaining or professing religious beliefs or disbeliefs, for church attendance or nonattendance. No tax in any amount, large or small, can be levied to support any religious activities or institutions, whatever they may be called, or whatever form they may adopt to teach or practice religion. Neither a state nor the Federal Government can openly or secretly participate in the affairs of any religious organizations or groups and *vice versa*." (*Everson* v. *Board of Education*, 1947; *McCallum* v. *Board of Education*, 1948; *Torcaso* v. *Watkins*, 1961, unanimous Court);

10. Nevertheless, it is not an "establishment of religion" for the state to provide bus transportation (*Everson* v. *Board of Education*, 1947) or textbooks (*Cochran* v. *Board of Education*, 1930; *Allen* v. *Board of Education*, 1969) to children attending parochial schools;

11. Released time religious instruction violates the no-establishment

clause if held on public school premises (*McCallum* v. *Board of Education*, 1948), but not if children are released from public schools for such instruction elsewhere (*Zorach* v. *Clauson*, 1952);

12. It is not an "establishment of religion" for the state to set aside a day of rest that may coincide with the holy day of the majority (*McGowan* v. *Maryland*, 1961) even if that works a financial hardship on persons who observe another day for religious reasons (*Braunfeld* v. *Brown*, 1961);

13. Nevertheless, a Seventh-day Adventist cannot be deprived of unemployment compensation if she refuses to take a job that would require work on Saturday (*Sherbert* v. *Verner*, 1963), though an employer need not violate seniority rules or expend more than a minimal amount to accommodate a Sabbatarian (*TWA* v. *Hardison*, 1977);

14. A person otherwise qualifying cannot be barred from service as a notary public because he refuses to take an oath invoking the Deity, since this would prefer religion over non-religion and theistic religions over non-theistic ones (*Torcaso* v. *Watkins*, 1961);

15. The state cannot sponsor prayers or devotional Bible reading in public schools, even if participation therein is voluntary, since it is sponsorship even in the absence of coercion that violates the establishment clause (*Engel* v. *Vitale*, 1962; *Abington* v. *Schempp*, 1963);

16. The state may not prohibit because it is offensive to some persons for religious reasons the teaching of evolution in public schools (*Epperson* v. *Arkansas*, 1968);

17. It is not an "establishment of religion" for the state to exempt from property taxation houses of worship (along with educational and charitable property) (*Walz* v. *Tax Commission*, 1970);

18. There are three tests of "establishment": whether (1) the purpose of a law is secular and (2) its primary effect is not to advance or hinder religion (*Abington* v. *Schempp*, 1963) and (3) it does not result in excessive entanglement of government and religion (*Walz* v. *Tax Commission*, 1970);

19. Various forms of aid to parochial schools would require constant state surveillance to determine that solely secular purpose and effect were present, and such surveillance could not be carried out without excessive entanglement; therefore such aid cannot pass the tests of establishment (*Lemon* v. *Kurtzman*, 1971, *PEARL* v. *Nyquist*, 1973, *Meek* v. *Pittenger*, 1975, etc.);

20. Nevertheless, similar aid can be given to church-related colleges because their students are less susceptible to indoctrination (and for other reasons) (*Tilton* v. *Richardson*, 1971; *Roemer* v. *Board of Public Works*, 1976; *Hunt* v. *McNair*, 1973);

21. A citizen cannot be barred from public office because he is ordained (*McDaniel* v. *Paty*, 1978);

22. Congress did not authorize the National Labor Relations Board to supervise elections for labor representation among lay teachers in Roman Catholic parochial schools (*NLRB* v. *Catholic Bishop of Chicago*, 1979);

23. Any contentions that the establishment clause is not applicable to the states or that it prohibits only governmental preference of one religion over another "are of value only as academic exercises" (*Abington* v. *Schempp*, 1963);

24. The phrase "religious training and belief" in the description of conscientious objectors exempted from compulsory military service cannot be construed to exclude non-theistic religion or beliefs that occupy a place in the life of the believer parallel to the belief in God of one clearly qualifying for exemption (*U. S.* v. *Seeger*, 1965; *Welsh* v. *U.S.*, 1970).

Trends in Religion

In the same two centuries, some significant social changes pertinent to our topic occurred as well. At the beginning of that time, religious institutions and their leaders played a prominent role on the social stage, due in part to the dearth of other popular diversions, yet the proportion of actual church members was relatively small, about five percent of the population.[2] Two hundred years later, more than sixty-five percent of the population are members of one or another religious organization.[3] The clergy receives less deference but perhaps more respect—or at least so it was through the 1950's.

During the first century of disestablishment, the churches discovered the tremendous vitality of voluntaryism that enabled them to launch powerful enterprises in the nineteenth century: the foreign and home mission movements, the Sunday School movement, the abolition movement, the temperance movement, the settlement-house movement, the Freedman's Aid movement, and many others, as well as building vast arrays of colleges, hospitals, homes for orphans, foundlings, and the aged, not to mention church structures of all persuasions, styles and sizes. Many of these were lay, rather than ecclesial, organizations.

After a glorious crescendo in the 1950's, the mainline churches in the mid-1960's suddenly faltered during a time of ferment that debunked or discredited many traditions and institutions. The mighty Roman Catholic Church, which had seemed so threatening to some, after Vatican Council II was unable to hold on to the "turf" it had staked out in the lives of its members and in the social and political scene. In the latest quarter-century, the "mainline" churches (at least) have receded substantially from their salience in the nation's consciousness, and a second line or successor string of religious groups has been coming into prominence: evangelicals, charismatics, fundamentalists, and even a plethora of new religious movements (which, while not a new phenomenon, seems to have gained greater visibility than any others since the Jehovah's Witnesses in the 1930's and 1940's or the Mormons in the mid-nineteenth century). Some of the evangelical and fundamentalist groups have pressed forward in the political arena in 1980 with new assertiveness under such banners as "The Moral Majority," "Christian Voice," etc., suggesting that they may be taking up a role until recently dominated by "social gospel" types in the "mainline" traditions.

Perhaps these resurgent moralists are trying to regain some of the old Protestant dominance that was lost somewhere in the mid-twentieth century, when Roman Catholics and Jews (and others) pressed for "equal time" on center stage, and many of the marks of Protestant cultural "establishment" were overthrown, e.g., prohibition, Sunday-closing laws, prayer in public schools, bans on the teaching of evolution. The moralists themselves maintain that they are leading a Scripture-inspired crusade for the restitution of morality in American life and an end to the plague of permissiveness, deviance and corruption. But their restitutional vision has mixed with it some strange elements more closely akin to the gospel of the right wing of the Republican Party—opposition to the Panama Canal Treaty and SALT II, support for nuclear power and an expanded defense budget—than to the teachings of Old Testament or New.

Their thrust with respect to church-state relations has two aspects: one is to reinstate and amplify the symbolic evidences of religious allegiance in public life in order to demonstrate the authority of God over the nation; the other is to press back or eliminate the government's efforts to oversee, regulate, and restrict the activities of churches. In the first they are at odds with the mainline churches; in the second, they may not be.

Many people for whom religion is important have become increasingly distressed about the trends of the past few decades, which have seen the increased privatization, interiorization and "spiritualization" of religion in American life. By this is meant the commonly accepted notions that "religion is [only] a personal matter," "it is the business of the home and the church [alone]," and "it should concern itself [solely] with 'spiritual' matters"—which are considered to be (wholly) personal and psychological in character. The great religious traditions of the Western world —Judaism, Christianity and Islam—can never accede to their sequestration from the central currents and concerns of human life and activity. They insist that God is ruler over all, and that whatever significantly affects the lives of persons is of deep concern to God and to those who seek to do God's will, particularly the institutions of religion.

These trends are sometimes referred to as "secularization," and indeed there has been an increasing displacement of religious symbols, motives and considerations from people's decision-making, interests and communications. But because Christian theology has a high regard for the proper autonomy of the civil, temporal and secular, the term "secularization" may not be as useful as the more limited and precise terms used above—privatization, interiorization, "spiritualization," and perhaps "psychologization"—to describe those trends.

The decisions of the U.S. Supreme Court on church-state issues, especially prayer and devotional Bible-reading in public schools, have —for the best of reasons, e.g., justice to minority religions and nonbelievers—contributed to the reinforcing of these attitudes that have been endemic since the Enlightenment. And the classic civil-libertarian views stemming from John Stuart Mill and his ilk, which have (rightly) inspired such jurisprudence, envision the highly prized right of religious liberty to be not only a property of *persons*, which it is, but of individual persons acting (only) in dispersion, which it may not be. That is, the civil libertarian's solicitude for religious liberty is made uneasy if two or more persons gathered together seek to exercise their religious liberty in *concert*, and if they do so as a *church*, the civil libertarian becomes positively apprehensive and his/her solicitude for the "free exercise of religion" tends to be replaced by intense anxieties about "establishment." Thus the *collective* free exercise of religion by believers joined together in organizations has enjoyed a somewhat more limited recognition in American church-state law and a distinctly suspicious reception in less reflective circles.

That has long been the case, of course. Organized religion often makes people uneasy, and sometimes with good reason. As one of the more intense and elemental of human activities, it has often been perverted or distorted or exploited to the hurt of human beings. But even in its inferior or degraded forms, it is providing a function essential to human social life,[4] a consideration not generally recognized. Because religion is potentially a very powerful force in human affairs, there is a constant temptation to try to control it, exploit it, at least to "ride herd" on it, a temptation that is well-nigh irresistible in the wake of occasional scandals or atrocities, such as the tragic suicides and murders at Jonestown in Guyana. Government officials come under more pressure than usual to "do something" about unconventional religions, and this increased vigilance spills over on more conventional religions as well.

Indeed, much of the governmental intervention described in the papers that follow arises not so much from the spontaneous initiative of public servants as it does from the demands of the public they serve. Beneath the surface tolerance of the people seethes the immemorial anxiety about strange and outlandish religions which periodically bubbles over in times of stress with primal cries of hostility and fright that impel the servants of the people to a militance they otherwise might not display.

A Broadly Inclusive Conference

As a result of the trends and changes described above, a wide spectrum of religious groups has become increasingly concerned about what they view as growing governmental intervention in religious affairs. In February of 1981 they came together in what is probably the most inclusive gathering of religious bodies in American history, encompassing representatives of over 90 percent of organized religion in the country, to consider the problem and its implications for religious liberty. One of the products of their efforts is this volume, which contains in edited form the papers presented at that Conference.

Most of the papers focus on the legal issues and controversies arising from government intervention in religious affairs, since the terms of the encounter of interests between religion and government are (thus far) defined mainly by statutes and regulations, and the arena for their resolution has been (thus far) in administrative processes and the courts. The papers, by and large, however, are not unduly technical, and the interested lay reader should not find them difficult to follow.

The legal focus of this material does not mean that there are not Biblical, theological, ethical, social, political and economic aspects of the subject; some of these are touched on in the papers. The theological component has been almost entirely omitted because of the diversity of the audience. Several of the great religious traditions represented have profound and articulate treatises on the theology of church-state relations, and about many of the concrete arrangements of church and state in the United States of the twentieth century they might agree; but they reach that point by different routes, and it would take another volume just to summarize them.[5]

These papers do not attempt to survey the whole terrain of church-state law in the U.S., but only a rather limited sector of it. This introduction has outlined some of the broad strokes which frame that jurisprudence, and of course it is only one of many systems of law in the world today, each of which has its own way of relating government(s) and religion(s), though many of them imitate in one way or another the heroic institutional invention of the American Constitution: the independence of the civil covenant from the religious covenant.[6] So: this volume focuses on that portion of the church-state law of the United States where the activities of religious bodies intersect with the regulatory responsibility and authority of government.

The stage is set by the chairperson of the Conference in his opening statement, in which he lists seventeen specific areas of governmental intervention in religious affairs. The chairperson was William P. Thompson, Stated Clerk (chief executive officer) of the United Presbyterian Church in the U.S.A., former President of the National Council of the Churches of Christ in the U.S.A. and of the World Alliance of Reformed Churches, an attorney with twenty years of private practice before he was elected in 1966 to head one of the major religious bodies in the country. His firm but fair skills as presiding officer led the Conference smoothly and expeditiously through its three days of deliberations.

The volume begins with the opening statement by the chairperson, in which he makes this important point:

> No one of these developments, taken by itself, is sufficiently alarming to necessitate a convocation like this, and indeed some of them might be thought by some people to be justified. But the *pattern* that they form when viewed *together* is an alarming one. . . .

The keynote address at the Conference follows under the banner "Government as Big Brother to Religious Bodies." It was presented by William Bentley Ball, an attorney in private practice in Harrisburg, Pennsylvania. He has defended religious bodies against government encroachment in twenty states and the U.S. Supreme Court, where he was on the winning side in *Wisconsin* v. *Yoder*, upholding the right of Amish communities to educate their children in their own way after the eighth grade, and in a companion case to *NLRB* v. *Catholic Bishop of Chicago*, which held that Congress did not give the National Labor Relations Board authority to regulate elections for union representation of lay teachers in parochial schools.

One of the outstanding Constitutional scholars in the country, Laurence H. Tribe, professor of law at Harvard University, presented an illuminating paper on "Church and State in the Constitution," in which he compared the unique provisions for the protection of religious bodies to the equally unique, but different, status of Indian tribes, the family, and political parties, each of which is insulated in various ways against unfettered governmental regulation. Professor Tribe, in addition to being the author of the definitive work, *American Constitutional Law*, which has been quoted by justices of the Supreme Court in their opinions, has been active in several important appeals such as that of the Worldwide Church of God against its takeover by the State of California.

William Lee Miller, the next author, brings an unusual combination of skills to his task. He is Professor of Political Science and of Religious Studies at Indiana University, and Director of the Poynter Center on American Institutions there. During the year of the Conference, 1981, he was the Annenberg Distinguished Scholar at the Center for the Study of the American Experience at the University of Southern California, and in 1981–82, he was Visiting Scholar at the Woodrow Wilson Center of the Smithsonian Institution. He is the author of several books, including *Piety Along the Potomac* (N.Y.: Houghton Mifflin, 1964) and *Of Thee, Nevertheless, I Sing: an Essay on American Political Values* (N.Y.: Harcourt Brace Jovanovich, 1975). His task was not an easy one in this setting. He was asked to do a critique of the theme of the Conference, to present "the other side," as it were, an appreciation of the positive role of government in curbing the perversions and pretensions of religion. His thesis is summarized in the title, "Responsible Government, Not Religion, Is the Endangered Species."

One of the most trenchant and insightful papers at the Conference covers two important areas—(1) church property law and (2) the effort by some state attorneys general to exercise supervision over churches' financial affairs—which have in common a legal rationale based on the theory of trusts. This paper, "Who Owns the Churches?", analyzes the use—or mis-use—of trust theory in an attempt to render churches "accountable" to the "public" for what would otherwise be private actions. The author first sought for this topic was the former president of Brigham Young University, Dallin H. Oaks, who in November, 1980, after spending a year's study-leave researching this subject (which was published by the *Stanford University Law Review*), was appointed to the Supreme Court of Utah and thus became ineligible to accept our invitation. At that late date, the task was undertaken by Father Charles M. Whelan, S.J., the member of the Planning Committee who had suggested Oaks for the job. Father Whelan teaches Constitutional law and tax law at Fordham University Law School in New York City and is an associate editor of the Jesuit weekly magazine *America*. With Dean Kelley, he is codirector of the Project on Church, State and Taxation at the National Conference of Christians and Jews. He is of counsel to the Office of General Counsel of the U.S. Catholic Conference and a member of its Tax Advisory Committee.

A paper exploring one problem area is appropriately entitled, "Frontier Issues of Tax Exemption," and was presented by Stanley S. Weithorn, senior partner in the New York law firm of Baer, Marks and Upham. He is author of the definitive law-school text "Tax Techniques for Foundations and Other Exempt Organizations," now in seven volumes. He teaches law as a Special Professor at Hofstra University School of Law (his alma mater) and as Adjunct Professor at the University of Miami School of Law. He has chaired bar association committees, including the Subcommittee on Charitable Contributions of the American Bar Association's Section on Taxation, and he is counsel to many national not-for-profit organizations. His paper explores two subjects that are just beginning to emerge as crucial grounds for grappling between government and religious bodies: (1) the meaning of "inurement" (as in ". . . no part of the net earnings of which *inures* to the benefit of any private stockholder or individual . . ." in Section 501(c) (3) of the Internal Revenue Code), and (2) the attempt by the IRS to require compliance with "public policy" as a condition of tax exemption though there is no authority for such a requirement in the statute.

Some Case Studies

Two case studies of struggles with the Internal Revenue Service follow. One describes the Service's determination that the Board of Church and

Society of the United Methodist Church could not receive deductible contributions for coalitions which it did not control, even though they were predominantly composed of organizations entitled to deductibility in their own right. That case was to have been presented by the General Secretary of the Board of Church and Society, George Outen, a member of the Planning Committee of the Conference. Because of his tragic and untimely death of heart failure on Christmas Eve, 1980, the Planning Committee turned to John E. Stumbo, an attorney in Topeka, Kansas, who is chairman of the trustees of the Board of Church and Society, and who had been directly involved in the struggle with the IRS. He prepared a report of that experience—on rather short notice—and it is included here under the title, "The IRS Cracks Down on Coalitions."

The second case study is entitled, "Concordia College Challenges the IRS" and describes the college's refusal to file an annual informational return (Form 990) as required by the IRS, which ruled that it was not exempt from filing because it is not an "integrated auxiliary" of the Church, although the Church insists it is. This case study was presented by Philip Draheim, a partner in the law firm of Stolar, Heitzmann, Eder, Eigel & Harris in St. Louis, Missouri, which is representing the Lutheran Church—Missouri Synod in this matter.

A third case study is included, entitled, "A Baptist Seminary Resists the Equal Employment Opportunity Commission," describing the litigation under way between Southwestern Baptist Theological Seminary in Fort Worth, Texas, and the EEOC because of the seminary's refusal to file Form EEO-6, reporting the compensation, tenure, race, sex, and national origin of the seminary's employees. The Seminary, representing all six such schools of the Southern Baptist Convention, contended that as a religious institution it was exempt from the requirements of the Equal Employment Opportunity Act of 1972; the EEOC insisted that it wasn't. The Federal District Court in Fort Worth ruled against the EEOC, and the Circuit Court of Appeals ruled partly for it. This case study was presented by James E. Wood, Jr., Simon Bunn Professor of Church-State Studies at Baylor University, Waco, Texas. He is also Director of the J.M. Dawson Studies in Church and State and Editor of the *Journal of Church and State*, and he was Executive Director of the Baptist Joint Committee on Public Affairs from 1972 to 1980. He is an ordained minister of the Southern Baptist Convention.

A hitherto little-noticed problem was lifted up for the conferees under the title, "The Potential for Government Surveillance of Religious Organizations," by Sharon Worthing, who described the reporting requirements imposed on religious bodies by various statutes, including listing in the Master File maintained by the Internal Revenue Service. Miss Worthing is an attorney with a major Wall Street law firm in New York City. She attended Yale University and Barnard College, graduating from the latter *cum laude* with honors in history, and took her law degree at Fordham Law School, where she was Articles Editor of the Law

Review. She is a member of the Committee on Religious Liberty of the National Council of Churches, of the National Advisory Council of Americans United for Separation of Church and State, and of the Editorial Council of the *Journal of Church and State.*

Another very active battleground in church-state law is "Current Issues in Government Regulation of Religious Solicitation," which is written by one of the most active practitioners in this area in the country, Barry A. Fisher, who heads his own public-interest litigation law firm of eight attorneys in Los Angeles. He has won scores of church solicitation cases in all parts of the country, and he was counsel in two important cases before the U.S. Supreme Court in the 1979 term, *Heffron* v. *ISKCON* and *Larson* v. *Valente.*

A similar problem is explored by Eugene R. Scheiman in the paper entitled "Obtaining Information from Religious Bodies by Compulsory Process." This paper focuses on the use of grand jury and other subpoenas to obtain data from churches, clergy and church-workers. Mr. Scheiman, while with the New York firm of Cahill, Gordon and Reindel, prepared several briefs *amicus curiae* for the National Council of Churches in cases of this type. He has since joined the New York firm of Baer, Marks and Upham.

Another increasingly controverted area involves the use of the tax code as a device for "Government Restraint on 'Political' Activities of Religious Bodies." A paper on this subject was presented by Wilfred Caron, General Counsel of the United States Catholic Conference, and two of his colleagues, John Fliekweg and Deirdre Dessingue, the latter having come to the General Counsel's office directly from five years' work as staff attorney with the Internal Revenue Service. Their task was made more difficult by the U.S. Catholic Conference's having just been named a defendant in a suit by an organization called Abortion Rights Mobilization against the U.S. Treasury and the IRS, seeking revocation of the tax exemption of the Roman Catholic Church for alleged violation of the restrictions in Section 501(c) (3) on "political" activity because of its opposition to abortion; thus they were somewhat cautious in their presentation not to say anything that could be used against them in that litigation.

[The U.S. Catholic Conference has since filed a motion for dismissal of that action on various grounds, but it concludes with the challenge that if the Court does not dismiss the case, it should find the limitations on "political" activity in Section 501(c) (3) unconstitutional as a violation of the free exercise of religion protected by the First Amendment!]

Sharon Worthing makes a reappearance with a paper on de-conversion under court order, a description of a developing trend to obtain guardianship or conservatorship orders to legalize an activity known as "deprogramming" designed to reverse by duress religious conversions that are deemed undesirable by the de-programmers. Efforts have been made in several states to amend existing state laws to facilitate this process, whereby a court gives custody of the person of an adult convert to petitioning relatives seeking to "rescue" the convert from a "cult." Though the government is not the prime mover in such instances, its powers and authorities are lent to private purposes, often having the effect of reversing a religious conversion. Although she was already writing another paper for the conference, Miss Worthing was pressed into service by the Planning Committee to cover this subject.

The last paper, which summarizes much of the argument of the whole Conference, is entitled, "When Is Governmental Intervention Legitimate?" and is written jointly by two authors. One is Marvin Braiterman, Professor of Law and Public Policy at New England College in Henniker, New Hampshire, and Arundel, Sussex, England, who for many years served in Washington D.C., as director of the Religious Action Center of the Union of American Hebrew Congregations and as general counsel to the Commission on Social Action of Reform Judaism. He wrote the *amicus* brief submitted by the Synagogue Council of America in the *Walz* case, which championed the claim that churches and synagogues have an immunity from property taxation that is based in the First Amendment.

His collaborator was the organizer of the Conference and editor of this compilation, Dean M. Kelley, Director of Religious Liberty at the National Council of Churches since 1960. He is a Methodist minister with thirteen years of parish experience before coming to his present specialized responsibility. He organized the National Study Conference on Church and State for the National Council of Churches in 1964 and a Consultation on Churches and Tax Law in 1975. He is author of *Why Conservative Churches Are Growing*, 1972, 1977, and *Why Churches Should Not Pay Taxes*, 1977, both published by Harper & Row. He edited the November, 1979, issue of *The Annals of the American Academy of Political and Social Science* on "The Uneasy Boundary: Church and State." He is co-director with Father Charles Whelan, S.J., of the Project on Church, State and Taxation at the National Conference of Christians and Jews, financed by a grant from the Eli Lilly Endowment, which has been a major factor in underwriting the Conference and this volume.

Their paper is designed to correct the impression that there are *no* circumstances in which government should regulate the activities of religious bodies, but they contend that the occasions and extent of legitimate regulation are very limited.

These papers are offered to the public by the sponsoring bodies of the Conference on Government Intervention in Religious Affairs with the understanding that the views expressed are those of the respective authors and do not necessarily represent the policies of the sponsoring bodies, which hope that they will nevertheless contribute to a better general comprehension of church-state issues today.

Opening Statement of the Chairperson

WILLIAM P. THOMPSON

I am William P. Thompson. It will be my pleasure to serve as Chairperson of our gathering for these days. It is my privilege to welcome you to this important conference on Government Intervention in Religious Affairs. It is "important" for several reasons:

1. It brings together representatives of more than ninety percent of the adherents of organized religion in the United States, making it possibly the most inclusive such gathering in American history!
2. It gathers up a constellation of concerns that have been increasingly troubling this wide range of religious groups during the past decade; and
3. It has elicited the leadership of some of the outstanding thinkers and actors in the arena of church-state and First Amendment law to help us analyze the problems we confront and seek solutions to them.

Let me recall how we have come this far. Several years ago, in 1977 to be exact, the Governing Board of the National Council of Churches authorized a study of increasing "governmental intervention in the internal affairs of churches."

The next year, 1978, the National Conference of Catholic Bishops formed a committee headed by Archbishop John L. May called, "The Bishops' Ad Hoc Committee on Church-Government Issues," for a similar purpose.

In the National Council of Churches the Committee on Religious Liberty in the Division of Church and Society began work on the study authorized by the Governing Board. Soon they began to see the need to alert a broader range of religious leadership to the problem, and they envisioned such a conference as this as the way to do it. They assigned a subcommittee to plan for such a meeting and invited other religious bodies to share in that undertaking.

The Lutheran Council in the U.S.A. had held three conferences on a similar theme, primarily for people related to their Washington office, in 1978 and 1979, which produced a document that was included in your preparatory materials, representing one denomination's approach to the question.

The Baptist Joint Committee on Public Affairs likewise held a conference on a similar theme in 1979, and a paper by its then director, James Wood, representing that denomination's approach to the same question, was included in your preparatory materials.

The U.S. Catholic Conference, the Lutheran Council and the Baptist bodies were very receptive to joining forces in this present effort, as were the Synagogue Council of America and the National Association of Evangelicals when we approached them.

Each of the sponsoring bodies is represented on the Planning Committee which formulated the program and process of this conference. These are the members of that committee:

> William P. Thompson, Chairperson
> John Baker, Baptist Joint Committee on Public Affairs
> Charles Bergstrom, Lutheran Council in the U.S.A.
> Wilfred Caron, U.S. Catholic Conference
> Robert Dugan, National Association of Evangelicals
> Dean Lewis, Chairperson, Religious Liberty Committee, National Council of Churches
> Robert Nixon, General Conference, Seventh-day Adventists
> Dan Polish, Synagogue Council of America
> Earl Trent, American Baptist Churches
> Charles Whelan, S.J., U.S. Catholic Conference
> Sharon Worthing, Religious Liberty Committee, National Council of Churches
> Elliot Wright, Coordinator of the Project on Church, State and Taxation
> Dean M. Kelley, NCC staff, Secretary

The Planning Committee agreed on these purposes for this gathering:

a. To review the data collected in the preceding years of study and to explore their implications for religious bodies;

b. To develop and utilize preparatory materials, conference papers and other resources suitable for use by religious bodies;

c. To analyze alternate modes of response by religious bodies in such situations; and

d. To acquaint regional and local leadership of religious bodies with the problems and their ramifications.

What are the problems that so exercised the sponsoring bodies? They were troubled about the following actions by state and federal governmental agencies:

1. Efforts to regulate fund-raising solicitations by religious bodies;

2. Efforts to require religious groups to register with and report to government officials if they engage in any efforts to influence legislation (so-called "lobbying disclosure" laws);

3. Efforts by the National Labor Relations Board to supervise elections for labor representation by lay teachers in Roman Catholic parochial schools (which have since been halted by the U.S. Supreme Court);

4. Internal Revenue Service's definition of "integrated auxiliaries" that tends to separate church-related colleges and hospitals from the churches that sponsor them;

5. State departments of education's attempts to regulate the curriculum content and teachers' qualifications in Christian schools (which have since been halted by state courts in Ohio, Vermont and Kentucky);

6. Attempts by federal and state departments of labor to collect unemployment compensation taxes from church-related agencies that hitherto were exempt, as churches are;

7. Imposition by the then Department of Health, Education and Welfare of requirements of coeducational sports, hygiene instruction, dormitory and off-campus residence facilities at church-related colleges (such as Brigham Young University) which had religious objections to mingling of the sexes in such ways;

8. Efforts by several federal agencies (Civil Rights Commission, Equal Employment Opportunities Commission, Department of Health and Human Services and Department of Education) to require church-related agencies and institutions, including theological seminaries, to report their employment and admissions statistics by race, sex and religion, even though they received no government funds, with threats to cut off such funds to students attending such schools unless they hired faculty, for instance, from other religious adherences;

9. Sampling surveys by the Bureau of the Census of churches and church agencies, requiring them to submit voluminous reports, though the Bureau admitted it had no authority to do so;

10. Grand jury interrogation of church workers about internal affairs of churches;

11. Use by intelligence agencies of clergy as informants;

12. Subpoenas of ecclesiastical records by plaintiffs and defendants in civil and criminal suits;

13. Placing of a church in receivership because of allegations of financial mismanagement made by dissident members;

14. Granting by courts of conservatorship orders to parents to obtain physical custody of (adult) children from unpopular religious movements for purposes of forcing them to abandon their adherence thereto;

15. Withdrawal of tax exemption from various religious groups for failure to comply with "public policy";

16. Determination by IRS of what is "religious ministry" by clergy to qualify for exclusion of cash housing allowance from taxable income (often in contradiction to the religious body's own definition of "ministry");

17. Redefinition by the courts of ecclesiastical polity, so that hierarchical bodies are in effect rendered congregational in polity, and dispersed "connectional" bodies are deemed to be hierarchical, contrary to their own self-definition.

No one of these developments, taken by itself, is sufficiently alarming to necessitate a convocation like this, and indeed some of them might be thought by some people to be justified. But the *pattern* that they form when viewed *together* is an alarming one, and that is why we are here. (I have catalogued seventeen examples because we will not be dealing with them one-by-one, and we need to see them at least once all in single file. Our authors will be dealing with them, not at this level of recitation, but at the next level of analysis, comparison and generalization.)

We are not called together in a spirit of panic or desperation. We do not propose that the way to deal with this problem is to launch a militant counter-attack against all government on every front.

Indeed, we do not see the situation as one of automatic confrontation at all. We do not discern a calculated conspiracy in governmental circles to stamp out religion or religious bodies. We are not sounding a mindless battle cry, "Leave us alone!" as though there were never grounds for justifiable governmental action. Our final paper, in fact, suggests that governmental intervention is sometimes legitimate.

Rather, what we hope to do is to analyze the situation, suggest various forces and factors at work, and hear proposals about various kinds of responses that have been or can be made, and the advantages and disadvantages of each. Then the sponsoring bodies can reach their own conclusions about the course they severally may wish to follow.

Government as Big Brother to Religious Bodies

WILLIAM BENTLEY BALL

What does government intervention in religious affairs look like at the grassroots level to people who find themselves in court cases, caught between God and the State, wishing to offend neither, and put to an ultimate test, not as to whether they will choose God against the State, but as to whether they will choose self—that is, personal security and well being—against God?

Power v. Piety

Some years ago I was asked to defend twenty-four Old Order Mennonite parents in Virginia who had, for religious reasons important to some Anabaptists, declined to enroll their children in high school. This was a criminal prosecution, and I felt some trepidation, as a Northern attorney, appearing in such a case in a county court deep in southern Virginia. I had had pointed intimations that my type might not be welcome. The courtroom presented a remarkable scene. Somewhat huddled on a long bench, but quite serene, were my twenty-four young parents—with all the natural beauty of Plain People. In sharp contrast was a multitude of state troopers, with broad-brimmed campaign hats, loaded with artillery and almost crackling with vigilance. And to climax the scene and make it truly bizarre, there came upon the bench His Honor—in a Madras sports jacket! Something about that scene suddenly triggered in me a wholly inordinate impulse to ingratiate myself unduly with the court. And so I opened, outrageously, as follows:

"Your Honor," I said, "As a Pennsylvania attorney, I appreciate being in your court. I assure you that I do not come here as a carpetbagger, but with great respect for Virginia. Indeed, my mother-in-law is from Roanoke, my father-in-law is a graduate of the Medical College of Virginia. I was married at Norfolk, and the name of my only daughter is Virginia."

His Honor proved more than my equal in the pursuit of that kind of dialogue, and he promptly replied that he was honored to have a

Pennsylvania lawyer in his humble court; that Pennsylvania lawyers were known to be among the best lawyers to be found in all the fifty states in this noble land of ours; that in a court of that great sovereignty, the Commonwealth of Virginia, I would soon discover that Justice, Equity and the Constitution were indeed revered!

Vastly reassured, I proceeded with the hearing and at its end congratulated myself on how effective I had been and on how easily I had won over His Honor. I was surprised but even happier when His Honor announced that he would not reserve decision but would rule from the bench then and there. And then and there he found all my twenty-four clients guilty, dismissed as ludicrous our constitutional defenses, and announced the most savage sentences allowable to him under the law.

Weeks later we secured a new trial, got a reversal, and the case had, happily, a happy ending. That interesting chronicler of Dublin, Dr. Oliver St. John Gogarty, once remarked that the thing the Irish most detested about the English was that when they weren't drunk, they were sober. And G. K. Chesterton observed that Satan fell due to the force of gravity. So we can and should delight to point out things that are amusing even on the solemn topic of "Government Intervention in Religious Affairs." But you were also seeing, of course, another side to that story. It illustrates, in its most acute form, the essential problem with which we have to deal. The "power and prestige of the state"—with police, prison and other penalties in its arsenal—is brought to bear against individuals who are pursuing the faithful observance of the dictates of their religion.

But not every confrontation between government and religion is of this kind. Sometimes government does lurch against religious liberty; sometimes it merely leans a bit. And sometimes no confrontation ought ever to have been drawn because the root of the matter was mistake, ignorance, suspicion or even hysteria—whether on the part of government or on the part of the religious interest.

The First Step Is Remonstrance

Governmental intrusion upon religion is not always—or even usually —due to a conspiratorial design to put down religion. Frequently, it is due merely to inadvertence. In 1978, for example, the Bureau of the Census sent churches, seminaries, and other religious institutions Form CB-82. This form required at least the total disclosure, for 1977, of the amount of the "operating receipts and/or total revenue (from both taxable and tax-exempt activities) . . . ; expenses and annual and first quarter payroll," including data on full- and part-time employees. What was most remarkable about the form was its heading: "1977 Census of Service Industries." CB-82 also recited that this "Economic Census Form" was sent under the authority of Section 131 of Title 13 of the U.S. Code. But Section 131 covers censuses of manufactures, mineral industries and other like businesses. As churches greeted this form with disbelief, and hesitated to file it, they received warning from the Assistant Director for Economic and Agriculture Censuses of the Bureau of the Census. Here is what both St. Agnes Roman Catholic Church, Westmoreland, Pennsylvania, and Tabernacle Christian School, Midway, Kentucky, found in the mail:

> As of the above date we have not received your completed report for the 1977 Economic Census (Distributive Trades, Service, Construction, Transportation, Manufactures, or Mineral Industries). This letter will serve as notice that failure to report makes you subject to penalties under title 13, United States Code.

The CB-82 matter never reached court. And it ought not have. It was a mistake—indeed a rather large mistake—and one which occasioned expense to religious bodies which foolishly complied and distress to those who did not. The episode, however, was essentially one of inadvertence —hasty overbreadth in regulating, not even a hazy idea of the significant religious rights it touched, and a routine pursuit of non-filers. Happily, the Bureau, upon being apprised of its mistake, gracefully dropped its pursuit of religious bodies for Form CB-82.

The incident brings home an important point. The Bureau, "upon being apprised" of its mistake, dropped the matter. The "apprisal" step is a too-often-neglected step in church-state controversies. On the one hand, we have witnessed the unfortunate spectacle of major religious bodies, out of a totally false concept of public responsibility, or of justice, sometimes abandoning constitutional liberties as though to insist upon them were almost shameful. We sometimes hear them say that there are times or situations in which religious liberty must yield to the common good. Let a statute be enacted which is stated to be for a particular social justice end, and there are those who will say that its adverse impact upon a particular religious liberty must be endured. But that is most misleading. Religious liberty is *part* of the common good. The true common good and true religious liberty can never be in conflict. Or sometimes the quick concession to governmental demands appears based upon a mentality —peace-loving or truckling, as you may choose to call it—which despises "making waves." And out of this are born compromises, special concessions, corrupt political bargains—often fragile because based only on an administrator's say-so—but which do in fact rot the fabric of religious liberty for all others.

Why Government Infringes on Religious Liberty

We also must note that governmental intrusion is frequently due merely to such a thing as the failure of particular public servants to have mastered the elements of English language as children. Our legislators and administrators have not been immune to the general national decline in literacy, and that fact becomes explosive when government demands compliance with words which form bundles of unintelligibility. Here is Section 115-256 of the North Carolina Education Law:

> . . . instruction in [the nonpublic] schools . . . shall have courses of study for each grade conducted substantially the same as those given in the public schools . . .

Ponder that. And that is complicated by the fact that, throughout the North Carolina education statues, the terms "courses of study," "curriculum" and "branches of education" are used interchangeably, yet each being given different meanings. Yet, based in part upon the alleged nonconformity of a group of religious schools to Section 115-256, the State of North Carolina sought to put those schools out of business.

Unhappily, North Carolina does not provide a unique example of bad drafting. Most First Amendment cases arise, not out of bad intentions well expressed, but out of good intentions badly expressed. And this, in the face of the Supreme Court's insistence that, in statutes and regulations touching our most precious freedoms, "government may regulate . . . only with narrow specificity."[1] Guesswork as to meanings not only should not be needed; it ought not be possible. And let it not be said, when counsel questions language of dubious meaning, that "lawyers are always seeking loopholes." The loophole seeks the lawyer—cries out for correction—where it affects fundamental liberties. And where a regulation, with this, that, or some other meaning, may affect those liberties, counsel should never, in the interest of not "making waves," tell his religious client to conform to one "probable" meaning of the language. That does not serve the common good, and it may debase the currency of everyone's liberties. Precious church funds ought never to have to be diverted to legal struggles whose origin is in defective expression by public servants who are funded, staffed and mandated to speak with reasonable precision.

While we may speak of governmental inadvertence and (in a moment) of what really amounts to deliberate governmental aggression against religious liberty, we must also take note of that mentality which holds that government is inherently an alien body in our midst. It is "they," inevitably pitted against "us." It is "out to get" religious liberty. There have been court cases in the past three years which have been staged more with the atmosphere of revivalism than with respect for the Anglo-Saxon traditions of law. The case comes into court on a tidal wave of pious emotion, and the judge is sought more to be religiously coerced than legally persuaded. While these flamboyant tactics can only result in *losses* of religious liberty in the courts, and thus in the leading of credulous religionists into bitter disappointments, they also create an atmosphere quite inimical to the common good.

"The government," in the American system, is ourselves, "We, the people." Government agents frequently forget this, but let religious people not fail to remember it. Christ, Himself, commanded that we "render unto Caesar." Happily, in our country, the things that are Caesar's are simply things that are ours. In the incident of the Census Bureau, the proper action was neither to capitulate (as at least one major religious body did) nor to sue the Bureau. The proper first step was to apprise the Bureau—*our* Bureau—of the reasons why its action was illegal. When the confrontation between governmental action and religious liberty occurs, the first resort of each must be to do its homework (getting straight on facts and law); the second, in most cases, to dialogue in Christian spirit. Haste (and this is an admonition particularly applicable to government) should be avoided: almost always the governmental demand arises out of no real public crisis. In the dialogue, principle must never be negotiated away, but often it will turn out that a painstaking exploration of the facts and the law will cause the assumed controversy to vanish.

When the State Insists on Regulating

But there are still controversies which don't vanish, situations in which a grossly improper governmental intrusion upon religious liberty has been attempted and persisted in despite all efforts to negotiate. These situations include the imposing of governmental "quality" standards, or state licensing, upon religious ministries; cases of attempted governmental regulation of religion in the name of specific social programs, and cases of attempted uses of the civil courts for religious ends.

Consider first the licensing question, and good examples are to be found in the Fundamentalist School Cases[2] and in the efforts of the State of Texas to bring Brother Lester Roloff to heel. These cases are fascinating from many points of view. In substance, states, under a variety of terms—"accreditation," "approval," "certification," for example—have sought the licensing of a religious enterprise—an enterprise which is pervasively religious, an integral and mandated part of the religious mission of a church, which enterprise would not exist but for that fact—and which, by Biblical principle, will accept no tax-supported aid.

The church theologically believes that the existence of this form of its religious witness may not be made to depend upon the keeping or lifting of the prior restraint of governmental permission. Further, even though the license itself were not involved, the state's attempt to laminate a comprehensive overlay of regulations upon this ministry is unacceptable. The church, by Scriptural conviction,[3] must "render unto Caesar," but it rejects the notion that, in its schools, for example, a teaching apostolate may be state-defined, curriculum (except for a narrow area of "basics") state-mandated, or that, in its child-caring centers, certain secular modes for the regeneration of the drug-afflicted child are inherently superior and may be imposed.

What, typically, is the state's case? Whether we are in Green County Court, Wisconsin, Franklin Circuit Court, Kentucky, or the federal district court at Los Angeles, the government's case is always the same. Invariably it opens by solemnly pronouncing the great commonplace from the Latter-day Saints case, *Reynolds* v. *United States*, that "[l]aws are made for the government of actions, and while they cannot interfere with mere religious beliefs . . . , they may with practices".[4] Having said this (that is, having said nothing of any significance at all), government then absolves itself of any intent to offend religion. What goes on inside people's heads, the government wholeheartedly concedes, is something it must let be. But when people *do* things as a result of what goes on inside their heads, government must be vigilant.

Counsel then routinely proceeds to recite all manner of horrors that will surely ensue if the regulatory scheme is not clamped on tight. The prosecution in the Amish case foresaw the doom of public education if Amish teenagers were not mustered into high schools. I am always fascinated by the fact that this is invariably a mere recitation, with never a witness called who will supply any *proof*. Proof of the horrors, or of a compelling public interest in enforcing the regulations, is never offered. Apparently the reason the state does not feel obliged to offer proof is its assumption that the state has already regulated, and all state regulations are, by their very existence, of supreme importance.

The government proceeds to attack the religious claim raised by the church people in two ways: first, by acknowledging it to be *sincere*; second, by asserting that it is *misplaced*. The prosecution seeks so to exploit the sincerity as to suggest fanaticism. Rather often one hears: "Jim Jones was sincere, too!" But the prosecution is also prone to try its hand at theologizing and demands to know "just what *tenet*" of the defendant's religion is violated by the regulation. If the witness can't come up with a "tenet" (such as the dogma of transubstantiation) and then show that the government wants specifically to eradicate the observance of that tenet (*e.g.*, "It is hereby decreed that no act of transubstantiation shall be performed"), his religious liberty claim is said to lack substance. Under the "tenet" test, the Wisconsin Amish would probably still be in jail, because the heart of their resistance to Wisconsin consisted of such spacious and unparticularized concepts as a "community of faith" and "separation from the world."

The state's case, in these litigations, has also included very interesting notions respecting what is "secular" and what is "religious." And the state seems always to *know* which is which and who owns what in those domains. In the school cases, it has insisted that, since the schools teach English, mathematics, etc., state standards may be imposed, these being "secular" subjects. In the *NLRB* cases, the Labor Board, indeed, held religious schools subject to broad federal regulation on the ground that their teaching of so-called "secular" subjects rendered them "only partly religious." This religious judgment by government had fascinating results when recently employed by U.S. Labor Secretary Marshall in the unemployment compensation case involving Grace Brethren Church[5] in the federal district court at Los Angeles. Dutifully following Marshall's directives, state agents undertook on-site examinations of religious schools in order to estimate how "secular" or "religious" they might be. The affidavit of one of the school principals tells of the visit by one such agent:

> The fact that the school was controlled by the church apparently made little difference to [the agent]. His response was that the guidelines were to distinguish between the secular and the religious school. He began to look over our curriculum. He made two column headings on a paper, one of them being secular, the other religious. In looking over the brochure he saw the worship center and put that under religious instruction without qualification . . .
>
> He then inquired about a project where the children made cocoons with caterpillars in them. A few days later they were butterflies. This transformation was to symbolize the resurrection of Jesus Christ and our resurrection. The caterpillar had been transformed by the power of God. Thus the teaching of the resurrection became implanted in the young lives. God even teaches the resurrection in his creation. After giving him this explanation I asked . . . whether this was religious or secular. He ended by putting it in both columns.

Presenting Religion's Defense

Now to turn to the religionist's case. It is, of course, of the essence that the religious claim be clear and, upon trial, shown to be central and material. A difficulty not infrequently encountered by the religious witness is the fact that prior conduct of his may have been inconsistent with the claim he now makes. In the *Bible Presbyterian Church* case,[6] an intensively religious college was resisting state licensing on religious grounds. The State pointed out that this same college had earlier actually sought licensing. How sincere, then, could the present claim be? The court held it completely sincere, because it recognized that beliefs sometimes must emerge, that the theological implications of conformity may not be initially apparent, and that, when apparent, countervailing considerations of obedience to law, or of peaceableness, or of personal security, may act as heavy weights upon the impulse of conscience to resist. Finally, the religious claimant may never have been apprised of constitutional rights which are his, and which he ought enjoy. But liberty ought never to be denied merely because it was not always and consistently sought.

The religious claimant often faces another problem—one which, at first glance, appears not as a curse but as a blessing, not as trouble but as relief from trouble. It is the situation wherein a statute gives a government agency plenary regulatory power over a class of institutions which indiscriminately includes religious institutions. The government agency, however, asserts that it will "go easy" on enforcement against a religious institution depending upon whether the institution shows a proper "intent" by making a "good faith effort to comply" with the regulations. Precisely that situation arose in the *Rudasill* case. Top Commonwealth officials under cross-examination, though unable to explain the meaning of numerous mandated state "standards" that would have to be met in order that an institution might win "approval,"[7] did state that the Commonwealth would be lenient towards an institution making a "good faith effort" to get in line. But the religious claimants wanted no "favors" or "leniency." They repeatedly testified that they believed in obedience to valid law, as contrasted with obedience to the accordion-like personal will of administrators.

In *Rudasill* the Commonwealth indeed appeared in both Jekyll and Hyde roles. On the witness stand the state officials were anxious to show themselves benign—merely anxious to help raise up private religious institutions from a posture of an assumed inferiority to the level of the assumed superiority of state institutions. Then why were we all in court? The very reason we were all in court was the State's having announced and scheduled the mass criminal prosecution of all parents who insisted on good, non-licensed Christian schools for their children.

Regulation allowing for operation of the "accordion-like personal will of administrators" poses difficulty for the religious defendants[8] in other respects also. In the *Whisner* case, certain religious institutions, as the price of their existence, were commanded to comply with provisions contained in a volume bearing the Aesopian title, "Minimum Standards." The book was 125 pages in length and contained some 600 "minimum standards." Upon trial, our questioning of State officials necessarily proceeded along two lines. The first, of course, was to inquire what was really meant by a "standard" and how important the State believed these standards to be. The State witnesses were emphatic: the standards were a body of law; they were designed to insure high quality; they were supremely important. The second line of inquiry asked whether, in order to have State approval (and thus be able to exist), an institution must comply with 100 percent of the standards. Might not some be less significant than others? The State Benign promptly emerged: the State was no petty tyrant; of course it would not press 100 percent compliance. It would insist merely on "reasonable," or "substantial" compliance.

Then came a question of naturally enormous practical consequence to the administrators of the religious institutions involved: "What percent compliance would therefore constitute a passing grade?" Here the State waffled and wasn't perfectly sure. But what that meant was that the State servants were provided *unlimited latitude* in life-or-death decisions relating to religious institutions. A 1979 IRS Proposed Revenue Procedure went further, in this respect, by employing, in paragraph after paragraph, terms whereby individual public employees would judge whether the lifeline of a religious institution's tax exemption would be severed or not. For example, solely in an IRS official's judgment would rest the determination of the question whether a religious school's minority recruitment program had been "active and vigorous." (And how, constitutionally, may an Amish school be made to "recruit" on the basis of race and not of religion? But if any sectarian school were compelled to recruit on the basis of religion, would not that governmentally compelled evangelizing offend the Establishment Clause?) Bad enough that the Proposed Revenue Procedure was without the authority of Congress (and was thus nothing but homemade law); worse was its essential *lawlessness* —casting religious institutions upon the mercies, the subjectiveness, the varying abilities, the fairness or lack of it, the industry or the laziness—of administrators.

Litigation is costly to religious bodies in many ways. The financial cost is but one. Another may be the loss of supporters—as we are now seeing in the wake of the *Bible Presbyterian Church* case, where a completely religious college has been enjoined from issuing degrees unless it will become licensed, submit to 100 percent state control, and indeed become part of what the statute calls *"the state system* of higher education." As you can guess, this little college is dying due to decline in enrollments. A particularly expensive burden may be the insistence of government that a non-conforming religious party go through administrative proceedings —no matter how protracted, useless or costly these may be—before it can have access to a court of law. Lawyers term this the requirement of "exhaustion of administrative remedies." It would better sometimes be called the requirement of exhaustion of church resources. Two federal courts have recently held that where the National Labor Relations Board threatened the First Amendment liberties of a church, the church might have direct access to court and could not be forced into agency proceedings (and disobedience of the agency's ultimate determination) as conditions precedent to getting into a court of law. I especially commend to you, on this point, the superb opinion of Judge R. Dixon Herman (of "Harrisburg Seven" fame) in the case of *McCormick* v. *Hirsch*.[9]

Can Religious Bodies Ever Discriminate?

Anti-discrimination legislation appears to be another broad avenue for government trespass upon the free exercise of religion. The provisions of the Ohio Civil Rights Act, for example, bar any employer, "because of the . . . religion or sex . . . of any person, to refuse to hire or otherwise discriminate against that person with respect to . . . conditions of employment, or any matter directly or indirectly related to employment."[10] Under this overly broad language,

—St. John's Lutheran Church could not, solely on account of the applicant's religion, refuse to hire as pastor an individual of some other religious faith.

—Yeshiva Academy (a Jewish day school) could not, solely on the ground that an applicant for a teaching job was a Roman Catholic, refuse to hire that applicant for its Hebrew Department.

—Good Shepherd Convent (an Episcopal novitiate for nuns) could not, either on the ground that the applicant was male, or that he was Unitarian, refuse to hire that applicant.

The statute includes a remarkable "bona fide occupational qualification" exception which gives *the State* 100 percent latitude to determine whether a religiously imposed qualification for employment is bona fide! This is not mere entanglement; it is envelopment.

In rightly condemning unfair treatment of women, churches must nevertheless remember that religious liberty may embrace the use of differentiation on account of sex. If in obedience to its understanding of Scripture, a religious body refuses to classify the sexes as identical, any effort of the state to erase that differentiation raises grave constitutional questions. Unhappily some courts have recently shown gross insensitivity to religious liberty in Title VII cases. While Title VII of the Civil Rights Act of 1965 is inadequately worded for the protection of religious liberty, decisions such as that of the U.S. District Court for the Northern District of Iowa in *Dolter* v. *Wahlert High School*[11] have compounded that weakness by ignoring Free Exercise claims and holding in effect that a religious body's doctrinal teaching, as expressed in a rule of discipline for its employees, must always be set aside by the courts where that teaching and rule would call for discrimination between the sexes.

First Experiments: Possibility, Power and Precedent

The title of this paper refers to "Big Brother"—Orwell's ubiquitous, omniscient and omnipotent "Big Brother." In 1981 we are certainly not (yet) into 1984 or penned in an animal farm, and we ought not have hostility cocked and at the ready toward our mostly amiable and competent local, state and federal American public servants. But always we must remember the great inherent weight of governmental action and the relative fragility of religious liberty. This should result, in all questionable cases, in *government's* being put upon its proof, in *government's* being restrained from all looseness in defining the reach of the public interest, and from all carelessness where religious interests are involved. And in similar spirit, lawyers and lobbyists for religious bodies ought always to reflect the religious interest to the legislature and the agencies instead of reflecting the political desires of the latter back to their clients.

Finally, a word about government *power*. The Supreme Court of North Carolina once well stated in a religious case:

> "The statute's validity must be judged, *not by what has been done under it, but by what is possible under it.*"[12]

That but echoes two historic statements on unimplemented government power. Chief Justice Marshall, in 1827, said:

> "Questions of power do not depend upon the degree to which it may be exercised. If it may be exercised at all, it must be exercised at the will of those in whose hands it is placed."[13]

And Madison, in the great *Memorial and Remonstrance*, said:

> ". . . [I]t is proper to take alarm at the first experiment on our liberties. . . . The freemen of America did not wait till usurped *power* had strengthened itself by exercise, and entangled the question in precedents. They saw all the consequences in the *principle*, and they avoided the consequences by denying the principle."[14]

The Conference for which these papers were prepared might well have been given a subtitle, "A Conference on First Experiments." The congratulations of the nation should go to its sponsors.

Church and State in the Constitution

LAURENCE H. TRIBE

With these majestic words the Bill of Rights begins:

> Congress shall make no law respecting an establishment of religion, or prohibiting the free exercise thereof.

Thus liberty of conscience comes first, before even the freedoms of speech, press, petition, and assembly. Indeed, even in the main body of the Constitution, adopted before the Bill of Rights, only two spheres of personal liberty are consecrated. One is the ban on state laws impairing the obligations of contract (Art. I, Sec. 10); the other bars the requirement of any religious test as a qualification for any office or public trust under the United States (Art. VI, Para. 3). Religion and contract, the sacred and the profane—these are the only two substantive rights enshrined in the original Constitution. I am reminded of the cartoon showing two Pilgrims on the Mayflower gazing at the horizon, one saying to the other: "Religious freedom is my immediate goal . . . but my long-range objective is to go into real estate." For better or worse, much of our country's history is encapsulated in that brief exchange.

Notwithstanding the recent resurrection of rights of property and contract in the United States Supreme Court, the religion clauses have proven, if anything, more enduring. John Locke would undoubtedly spin in his grave to see what has become of the rights of property and contract in America. But the church-state compromise so carefully struck by the followers of Thomas Jefferson, Roger Williams, and James Madison —each with a different vision of the relationship of church to state—has not yet come unglued.

One reason for the endurance of that compromise—a reason not very often appreciated—may be the unique treatment afforded religion under the Constitution. As to other substantive rights, the Constitution establishes what is essentially a benchmark, a boundary, a line that government may not cross. But with respect to religion, the Constitution fixes no such single dividing line. Thus it is particularly unfortunate that we have become accustomed to thinking in terms of the "wall" separating church and state. For if any such metaphor is truly apt, we should speak rather of a "floor" and a "ceiling" in connection with the Constitution's guarantees of religious freedom—the "floor" set by the free exercise clause, defining an area of individual liberty on which government may not encroach; and the "ceiling" set by the establishment clause, announcing a social structure in which civil and religious authority are to co-exist without interpenetration.

The two religion clauses at times reinforce each other, and at times work at cross purposes—a familiar source of puzzlement for constitutional scholars. It is seldom appreciated, however, that the point at which the two clauses most powerfully reinforce each other is the very point at which the conflict between them is most profound. That is the point —"ground-zero," if you will—at which religious passion and expression, religious conviction and conduct, emerge from the crucible of faith as theological community: the congregational or hierarchical collectivity that interposes itself as an autonomous group between the individual and the state. It is at this point that all of the tensions between the religion clauses, all of their paradoxes, dramatically come to focus.

These tensions and paradoxes seem inescapable if one takes a "top-down" view of legitimate power, positing that such power flows *from* the state and derives its legitimacy from the democratic character of the state itself. On such a view, any step government takes to protect the autonomy and integrity of a religious body, whether congregational or hierarchical, may appear to be a bald delegation of state power to a politically unaccountable collectivity, empowering those who control it to subjugate the individuals within their reach—simultaneously violating the establishment clause by conferring state power on the church and the free exercise clause by facilitating the subordination of those within it. When legitimate power is seen to come down from the state, through religious bodies, to the people, such is the spectacle that emerges.

But if instead one takes a "bottom-up" view, this spectacle may be dismissed as an illusion. If one believes, as the Framers believed, that legitimate power is delegated *to* the state by individuals and groups, and that certain groups under our constitutional scheme have never relinquished their private authority and autonomy as centers of deeply shared experience and faith, then religious institutions emerge not as repositories of unaccountable, delegated state power, but as irreducible components of our social order, secure against all but the most limited and most compellingly justified forms of government intervention. When viewed this way—from the other end of the telescope, as it were—what otherwise appears to be a violation of both religion clauses turns out to be a vindication of free exercise and anti-establishment alike.

I believe that it is crucial to conceive the matter "bottom-up" because much religious experience is unavoidably communal and associational rather than solitary in character. Worship and practice both are commonly mediated through structures of social interaction; each would wither if such structures could be easily ruptured by government in the name of protecting individuals from what the majority conceives to be illegitimate activity by the religious group. So it follows that the autonomy of religious entities, both congregational and hierarchical, is not simply one of several doctrines supporting the religion clauses of the Constitution. It follows that such autonomy lies at the very core of religion's place in the Constitution's scheme.

But although such autonomy lies at that core, it is also in constant jeopardy. Witness, for example, how the "public trust" doctrine was used in the Worldwide Church of God case to throw an undeniably genuine and viable church into receivership in California in early 1979. As that case illustrated, church autonomy is under constant pressure because of continuing suspicion, often quite unfounded, that fraud or force is being invisibly and stealthily deployed behind the shield of group immunity—a suspicion leading Justices Rehnquist and Stevens, for instance, to warn that "arbitrary lawlessness" may result from excessive judicial deference to church authorities. (See *Serbian Eastern Orthodox Diocese* v. *Milivojevich*, 426 U.S. 696, 727 [1976] [dissenting opinion].)

This kind of suspicion—that, behind the shield of immunity, wrong-doing is being perpetrated—may at times be entirely healthy; at no point, after all, have the religion clauses meant that violent harm may be done to unconsenting persons behind a cloak of law. At no point have the religion clauses conferred an absolute shield against any and all inquiry. What I think problematic is not occasional suspicion but the escalation of suspicion into paranoia. And the catalyst for such escalation is envy, the feeling—seeming to express a hunger for retaliation—that religious groups are so uniquely privileged in our legal order—that the immunity they enjoy is so peculiar, so out-of-joint—that it is appropriate as a *quid pro quo* for society to clamp down upon them.

There are several ways of answering such an argument, but I know of none more effective than to observe that it is totally false. Specifically, the feeling of uniqueness in this sense is genuinely unfounded. Although the "ceiling"-to-"floor" treatment of religion under our Constitution may be unique, religion and religious bodies enjoy rights that are in truth far less extraordinary and singular than is often thought. Simply consider four other kinds of groups that have "unique" status in law: (1) the press, expressly mentioned in the Constitution; (2) Indian tribes, explicitly identified; (3) families, not once referred to; and (4) political parties, never mentioned. All four of these groups—two of them built into the text of the Constitution, and two of them long held to be implicit in the constitutional order of things—enjoy what amounts to a "sovereign immunity" closely analogous to that of religious bodies in American constitutional law. It is an unlikely juxtaposition of groups, but it is important to note the parallels.

The sovereignty I have in mind takes distinct forms depending upon the nature and aims of the group in question. In one case, it is a virtually unreviewable control over child-rearing, a control almost untouchable by the state. In another, it is immunity from state intrusion into such processes as internal organization, selection of members, and the choice of who is to represent such members in electoral processes; thus, for example, in *Cousins* v. *Wigoda*, 419 U.S. 477 (1975), the Supreme Court held that a state cannot interfere with the delegate-selection processes of a political party at a national convention. In a third case, sovereignty takes the form of authority over physical territory: the Indian tribes co-exist as virtual co-sovereigns with the states and the federal government in a number of important respects. Finally, in the case of the press, sovereignty consists of virtually unreviewable editorial discretion, a power of life and death over what material ultimately appears.

The analogue for religious groups—the corresponding form of sovereignty—is autonomous control over doctrine, governance, and practice, including the allocation of a religious group's physical resources. It is uncommon, to be sure, to compare these five forms of sovereignty, but I do so here in order to expose the fallacy of the charge that religious autonomy is genuinely unique. I hope by exposing that fallacy to help resist the mounting pressure to pierce the religious veil and thereby invade the sacred precincts of ecclesiastical community.

In the secular foursome I have listed, my reference to the press may suggest another kind of favoritism—raising another sort of issue, and posing a delicate problem for advocates of religious liberty. I am thinking now of special privileges *vis-a-vis* third parties—outsiders, the world at large—not special power with respect to internal affairs. These privileges are as unique to religion as the nearly absolute power to publish free from government censorship is to the press. I am not thinking here of anything like tax-exempt status, which a religious body enjoys not as a peculiarly privileged body but only as one among many closely analogous non-profit entities. I am thinking rather of privileges that in some sense *are* uniquely accorded to religion: the ability to invoke conscientious objector status in a military context, the ability to win a Sabbath exemption from work requirements—opportunities that come to religion but do not have precise counterparts elsewhere.

In the long run, one must recognize that, unless one is very careful about them, such special exemptions can come at a very high price—the price of resentment and ultimately the exaction of tribute and of ransom for that favored status. The usual form of the argument is that with special privileges there go special duties. Thus the medium of the electromagnetic spectrum—television—found itself on the not-very-happy end of that argument when the Supreme Court proceeded in a number of cases to treat television as basically different from the print media because of its privileged access to supposedly scarce airwaves, subjecting television's use of the electromagnetic spectrum to tighter control as a *quid pro quo*.

Interestingly enough, the Supreme Court has rejected the notion of special rights for the press as an institution—special rights *vis-a-vis* the outside world, as opposed to internal autonomy. But in a number of cases, most importantly in *Richmond Newspapers, Inc.* v. *Virginia*, 100 S.Ct.

2819 (1980), the Supreme Court has begun to accept a principle that carries useful lessons, by analogy, for the area of religion: the Court has begun to accept special rights, *not for the press as an institution, but for "newsgathering" as a process.* The crucial difference here is that special protection for an *activity* in which all may engage does not so quickly invite or provoke the retaliatory impulse, the resentment, the desire for exaction and *quid pro quo*, that one almost invariably encounters when one seeks special protection for a narrowly identified *class of individuals* or a specifically identified *institution.*

Among the advantages of proceeding in this way—of defining at a more generic level the activity to be specially protected—is the possibility of showing that what may look at first like special or unequal treatment in fact represents treatment that is indeed *equal with respect to the activity involved.* Justice Stewart made the point recently in his concurring opinion in *Houchins* v. *KQED,* 438 U.S. 1, 16 (1978). Access, he reasoned, is not equal simply because it is identical. The terms of access must accommodate the practical needs of journalism. To put it bluntly, television cameras occupy space, and a merely formal equality—"you get your little cubicle"—may not take that reality into account. You might remember how Anatole France described the majestic equality of French law: it forbids rich and poor alike to beg in the streets and to sleep under the bridges of Paris. That facade of equality, one may reasonably argue, is an illusion. Genuine equality may require what, on the surface, appears to be disparate treatment. And if one carefully identifies the activity which is to be protected, and then seeks to attain *equality with respect to the needs of that activity,* one has a powerful response to the claim that one is asking for some special, privileged treatment. Thus, it would be my suggestion that practical equality, as opposed to formal equality, as often as possible be made the constitutional banner under which religious claims are advanced.

For example, telling the Sabbatarian and the Sunday-worshipper that both will lose employment compensation if they refuse to work on Saturday may look like "equal" treatment, but it puts the Sabbatarian under a pressure to which it does not expose the Sunday-worshipper. It puts the Sabbatarian, but not her Sunday counterpart, to a cruel choice between spiritual salvation and economic security, so that, although exempting the Sabbatarian may at first *look* like unequal treatment, and perhaps even like an establishment of religion, it may be defended as "equal" with respect to a value that the First Amendment itself identifies as special. That the Supreme Court in religion cases has sometimes appeared to undervalue the norm of even-handedness without discernible warrant, and in a way that has generated needless resentment and difficulty, may in fact be traceable to the unwillingness of those who advocate the cause of religious freedom to take greater care to claim no more than practical equality when no more is genuinely needed to support the position being taken.

Consider, for example, a case like *Wisconsin v. Yoder*, 406 U.S. 205 (1972), where the Supreme Court upheld the right of the Old Order Amish to withdraw their children from public school—or indeed from any kind of organized schooling—after the eighth grade. The Court, in an opinion by Chief Justice Burger, said, in effect, that since children do not learn very much after the eighth grade anyway, the state has no compelling interest in requiring further schooling of the Old Order Amish, whom the Court plainly considered an exemplary group (the Court observed that they don't believe in welfare and have a low crime rate), and who have an old, established religion going for them. Now that kind of position seems insensitive to the need to show that what is really at stake is a genuine equality, appearing instead to go out of its way to single out a particular group for perhaps patronizing praise. It seems to say: "This group is fine; they meet our standard; they deserve this Court's Good Housekeeping Seal of Approval." When the Court takes such a position, it does little to advance the cause of religious freedom for all.

The same Court did a great deal better five years later in the case of *Wooley v. Maynard*, 430 U.S. 705 (1977). The Court there held that no one could be prosecuted for refusing to put a "Live Free or Die" slogan on her license plate. The State of New Hampshire, evidently oblivious to the irony of its law, threatened to jail the owner of any car not bearing the slogan, "Live Free or Die." The Supreme Court held that no one could be required to bear the slogan—and it didn't matter whether the particular group making the objection was a recognized religious group. It didn't matter *what* the group's motives were.

It seems, paradoxically, that the values of the religion clauses are preserved best when they are invoked least—that is, when one can prevail in a religion case at a higher level of generality by claiming that it doesn't matter that one's particular motives happen to be religious, since the challenged imposition involves something the government cannot do to anyone in any event. This is the way the Supreme Court approached the matter some years ago in the famous flag-salute decision, *West Virginia Board of Education v. Barnette*, 319 U.S. 634 (1943), when, writing for the Court, Justice Jackson found it unnecessary to inquire whether non-conformist beliefs will exempt one from the duty to salute if "we do not first find power to make the salute a legal duty." If the state does not have the power to compel something *at all*, it isn't the state's business whether your reason for objecting is political or religious, secular or sacred.

Of course, this broader approach is not always available. It *is* available when one can make a persuasive argument that the state lacks the power in the first place to command an action it has decreed. It is *not* available when the most you can persuasively claim is that, although the state *has* such power as a general matter, it must exempt people who are exercising certain kinds of First Amendment rights. There are times when that is the most that can plausibly be argued. For instance, there may be no winning constitutional argument against military conscription as such, but there may well be a winning constitutional argument in favor of some form of exemption for conscientious objectors. Thus there are some situations where the state may impose certain duties as a general matter but where the imposition of such duties on a universal basis may not be so compellingly justified that the state can insist on allowing no exemptions. It is in such contexts that one *must* rely on an exemption argument, and it is in such contexts that the best one can do is to couch the claim for exemption in terms of the most broadly defined activity possible, so as to avoid—as far as one can—claims of special privilege and risks of governmental selectivity among "acceptable" and "unacceptable" religious beliefs, practices, or groups.

Sensitive to these very dangers, the Supreme Court most recently extended *Sherbert* v. *Verner*, 374 U.S. 398 (1963), and *Wisconsin* v. *Yoder*, 406 U.S. 205 (1972), to strike down a state's denial of unemployment compensation benefits to a Jehovah's Witness who, for religious reasons, had quit his foundry job when he was involuntarily transferred to a department making tank turrets. In *Thomas* v. *Indiana Review Board*, No. 79–952, 49 U.S.L.W. 4341 (U.S. April 5, 1981), it mattered not, the Court reasoned in an 8–1 opinion by Chief Justice Burger, whether the worker's "religious beliefs seemed acceptable, logical, consistent, or comprehensible to others" (49 U.S.L.W. at 4343), or whether others of his faith did not share his interpretation of religious duty, so long as he acted from "an honest conviction that such work was forbidden by his religion" (*id.* at 4343).

To be sure, the Court's caveat about insincerely "bizarre" religious claims is a potential source of majoritarian intolerance and inquisition. But the very need to limit exemption to genuinely "religious" objectors in *Thomas* entailed setting *some* sort of boundary other than one defined and controlled by the objector himself. And in *Thomas*, unlike *Sherbert*, it could not be said that the exemption sought by the worker was one that in some sense merely "equalized" an exemption already made available by the state, but in a form that coincided with the religious needs or traditions of the majority while failing to coincide with those of the minority. Since unwillingness to work on Sundays, regardless of motive, did not render one ineligible for unemployment compensation, the extension of such exemption in *Sherbert* to "Saturday objectors" —without any second-guessing whatever as to whether their objections were "truly religious"—could be viewed as purely serving interests of evenhandedness and nondiscrimination. In *Thomas*, by contrast, although the Court spoke of *true* "neutrality" at times requiring departure from a facially "neutral" rule, there was no doubt that *only* genuinely religious claimants could be entitled to the exemption decreed by the Court.

Especially when religious exemptions as such *must* be sought, there is a recurring tendency to pay homage to the old slogan that "beliefs" are absolutely protected, while "actions" are, "of course," subject to governmental regulation as long as such regulation is "reasonable"—and it is not hard to find virtually *anything* "reasonable." The slogan is invoked, typically, as a way of defeating claims for exemption. But the slogan is empty; it is meaningless, embracing an essentially useless dichotomy, since—apart from direct "brainwashing" by government—it is not *belief* that government *ever* deals with but *action, behavior, conduct.* The question in virtually every case of any importance is whether the government can do something affecting one's conduct or other interests *because* of one's beliefs, or *despite* one's beliefs.

By way of example, in a California case some time ago, a state appellate court upheld a city's discharge of a school bus driver who believed in the ritual religious sacrifice of school children. *Hollon* v. *Pierce*, 257 Cal. App. 2d 808 (Ct. App. 1967). Is that a case which we are to characterize as involving government's interference with religious *belief*, and therefore as setting a precedent for more pernicious policies? Or is it simply a case of government's conditioning *access to jobs involving children* on a basis calculated to defend an important secular value—the lives of such children? I would say the latter. The relevant distinction is not between belief and conduct. The relevant distinction is between (a) government regulation predicated upon distaste for or disapproval of one's beliefs as such, either overtly or covertly; and (b) government regulation that is indifferent to one's beliefs as such but that might nonetheless result in restrictions upon one's opportunity for free exercise or for religiously motivated conduct. In the first case, when the government takes aim at the content of a belief, the religion clauses interpose an absolute barrier. It is in the second case—when government, ostensibly indifferent to the content of a belief, acts in such a way as to restrict the opportunities for people to act on their religious beliefs—that the standard is somewhat more lenient but still requires a real showing of necessity. In the case from California, it was not that the city government sought to ostracize people who *believed* as this fellow did. It was rather that government sought to *remove children from such people's reach.*

In dealing with regulations of the second kind—those that do not take aim at a particular belief as such, but nonetheless restrict opportunity for free exercise—it is worth observing that such regulations are often vulnerable on broader First Amendment grounds than those suggested by the religion clauses alone, so that, again, the need for asserting what looks like a special privilege on behalf of religion may evaporate. The classic case involved the Supreme Court's invalidation of a ban on leafleting in public streets and places, *Schneider* v. *New Jersey*, 308 U.S. 147 (1939), where the Court held that such a ban, even though it did not aim at any particular message or idea, was unconstitutional. The ban was unconstitutional because it left too little room for speech and press —particularly for communication by the very poor, who have access to literally no channel of communication other than that of speech in such open public forums.

But what about the garbage that will be left behind? What about the burden on the taxpayers of having to clean it up? Must the government foot the bill? The Court's answer was "yes." The Constitution, although it is largely a negative document, in effect imposed upon the polity as a whole the *affirmative duty* of bearing the expense of liberty—of absorbing the costs of those activities without which First Amendment freedoms will have inadequate breathing space. Now, if that is true of speech and press, surely it is no less true of religion. So when people are told that the unemployed Sabbatarian and the person who is jobless because the only work available involves building tanks in violation of his religion, each imposes a burden on the public fisc, the answer surely is that the public has a duty to accept the burden of leaving enough room for the exercise of First Amendment rights. What makes the case of the unemployed foundry worker in *Thomas* problematic is *not* that the Court there compelled government to go out of its way, and taxpayers to pay a price, so that First Amendment liberties might thrive, but that the particular path government was there required to travel in order that freedom survive potentially involves a treacherous inquiry into who really believes what, and an even more troublesome exploration of which beliefs count as truly "religious."

At this point, a fundamental choice is posed; and it is being posed in cases around the country with increasing frequency. It is a choice between, on the one hand, abstract and absolute neutrality— a "religion-blind" Constitution, which we could embrace only at severe cost to practical equality and free exercise—and, on the other hand, "realistic" freedom and equality, giving maximum play to free exercise of religion, but at the risk of entanglement of government with religion, at the risk of what some would regard as an establishment of religion, and indeed at the risk, in the long run, of the erosion of free exercise itself. It is not an easy dilemma to resolve. And even though the present Court, in cases like *Yoder* and *Thomas*, has resolved it in favor of "realistic" freedom with dangers of entanglement, an equally powerful trend in recent years has been that of formalistic anti-establishment and dis-entanglement—in cases involving school prayer and parochial school aid, to name just two examples.

It is said that those who live by the crystal ball eventually learn to eat ground glass, so I hesitate to predict whether *Sherbert* will ever be overruled. But if the tide of constitutional history does indeed flow in that direction, there is at least one second line of response, one back-up position, which can offer *some* protection for practical equality and free exercise even in the face of an insistence on neutrality, disentanglement, and anti-establishment. That response involves looking more closely at whether the laws from which religious exemptions are sought in the first place may *themselves* violate some norm of neutrality and evenhanded-ness as among religions or as between religion and non-religion.

For example, the unemployment compensation law at issue in *Sherbert* covered people who refused to work on Sunday—with no questions asked. No one assumed that such people were lazy simply because they didn't seek out the unusual job that happened to provide work on Sunday. But the law did not cover people who, for ostensibly religious reasons, refused Saturday work. Now, if a required exemption for some such people is to be criticized on the ground that it's not sufficiently neutral unless it is no less available to Saturday sports fans than to Saturday worshippers, I submit that the unemployment compensation law itself is vulnerable to attack on the ground that *it* is not truly neutral. Even if the Sunday-closing laws continue to be upheld because they are a reasonable means to the secular end of a shared day off from work for everybody, the corresponding value in the unemployment compensation context—the value of enforced Sunday togetherness among the unemployed—is rather hard to fathom.

Notice that such an argument might work for the Sabbatarian, but could hardly be of service for the objector to weapons manufacturing. In *Thomas*, therefore, the sole alternatives to a religion-only exemption are either vindicating an abstract neutrality at the cost of practical freedom, or asserting a substantive rule that due process forbids forcing anyone to choose between receiving needed public benefits and building weapons to kill other people. Or, to take an even more radical example, suppose a court is reluctant on neutrality grounds to exempt from a state's drug laws religious users of a mild hallucinogenic sacrament. Such a court might be urged to focus on the drug laws themselves, and to question the "neutrality" of the state's decision to permit the use of caffeine and nicotine but to ban other substances not demonstrably harmful—except perhaps in their tendency to undermine the work ethic, to interfere with assembly-line modes of social and economic organization, or to unleash visions that challenge the established order.

At this point, however, I am surely getting years, if not decades, ahead of today's Supreme Court. Perhaps that's a sign that I ought to stop, before I start forecasting the dawning of a new age of Aquarian tolerance and enlightenment in our nation's judiciary. It may indeed be more "realistic" simply to conclude by reminding ourselves of one of the sturdiest definitions of optimism and pessimism—a definition that may be all too apt in the religion context today: an optimist is someone who believes that this is the best of all possible worlds; a pessimist is someone who fears that the optimist may be right.

Responsible Government, Not Religion, Is the Endangered Species

WILLIAM LEE MILLER

One

The United States has a president whose campaign message was: get the government off our backs. He replaced a president who had presented himself as an outsider, untainted by the evil-doing of government bureaucrats in Washington. That president, in turn, followed a pair of presidents who had made clear that they didn't believe in government either, even while they stood at the head of it.

Of course, any gathering of oil men, manufacturers, bankers, or storekeepers, deplores the activities of "government." So it has been since Herbert Hoover rode glumly down Pennsylvania Avenue, speaking not a word to his smiling companion.

Now almost half a century later university administrators, intellectuals, and men in the street have joined in the recurrent American anti-governmental refrain. At the top of the best-seller list where one ought to find some peace-of-soul book by a kindly rabbi, preacher, or priest, one finds instead a book by an economist, explaining that the great name of Liberty equals opposition to government. In intellectual life, neo-conservatives dominate the magazines, editorial pages, and bookstores, complaining all the while about the domination by liberals. The message? Government (alas!) won't work, because of the unintended consequences.

The anti-governmental theme does not come from the conservative wing of society alone. It was also heard and seen in the new left of the late '60's. The young protestors of the counter-culture included as a central part of the "Establishment" they attacked: the Government. That period produced from the left a spice of rebellion, anarchism, and libertarianism that still flavors our politics. At times left and right seemed to collaborate in a pincer movement against the broad center, the not-so-vital center.

41

The effects of that curious Right/Left collaboration reverberate still. Inflation and other troubles give it a new credibility.

And so in this moment of another triumph for the ancient American anti-governmental chorus, one comes round to the world of religion, with its view of the human scene from another aspect, the aspect of eternity. What does one hear? Let Justice roll down like waters, and righteousness as a mighty stream? We are members one of another? Come let us reason together? Where everybody thinks alike nobody thinks very much (Soren Kierkergaard)? Where there is no vision the people perish? Do justice, love mercy, and walk humbly with thy God? Blessed are the poor? No man is an island? What I hear at the gathering that generated the papers in this book, somewhat to my dismay, is: get the government off *our* back, too.

Two

You had thought, I suppose, that the big issue right now about religion and government had to do with the Moral Majority's effort to inject the former into the latter. Wrong. According to the conference from which this book comes, the problem is the other way around. The very title of the gathering, rising above mere evenhandedness, told the story right away: "Government Intervention in Religious Affairs," or G.I.R.A. for short. By defining the topic in that unambiguously defensive way, the convenors were able to bring together, according to chairperson William Thompson, "representatives of more than 90 percent of the adherents of organized religion in the United States." That made the assemblage—to continue quoting Mr. Thompson, who as readers of this volume know is stated clerk of the United Presbyterian Church—"possibly the most inclusive such gathering in American history."

The conference certainly did spread a wide net. There were not only the Methodists, Presbyterians, Baptists, Episcopalians, Disciples, and—as the name used to be—Congregationalists that I remember from the conferences of my youth, and the Roman Catholics and Jews who joined the roster in the late fifties, but also Unitarians and Ukrainian Orthodox and Missouri Synod Lutherans and *Southern* Baptists and Christian Scientists and Mormons and Seventh-Day Adventists and Mennonites, who were not present in my old conference-going days, and the Moonies and Scientologists and World Vision Internationalists and The Wayists and First Freedomers and World Wide Church of Godists, whose religious groups, unless I am mistaken, had not back then as yet much manifested themselves in the material world. My constricted religious upbringing featured beardless Presbyterians; Episcopalians in well-cut vests; clean-shaven Methodists with dark suits, white shirts, and dark ties. This meeting, by contrast, was crowded with beards, turbans, sideburns, colorful robes, moustaches, elaborate head gear, neck chains, odd-shaped clerical collars, shaved heads, pure white costumes, pony tails, and natural fiber togas. The clean-shaven men in dark three-piece suits at *this* conference turned out to be lawyers.

In fact the omnipresence of lawyers—of advocates—told the story. A remarkable inclusiveness was attained by treating "religion" as an interest group, like the Cattlemen's Association, and by focusing the shared interest on a common enemy, Government. This was the ecumenism of self-interest.

Three

But, you may ask, what's wrong with that? There *are* religious "interests," and they need to be protected. If religious groups don't do it, who will?

And, you may say, just because many other people are complaining about government intrusions does not mean that the religious groups are wrong. In fact, it argues the opposite: all of these citizens, religious folk included, may be complaining because there is something to complain *about*.

Some may say: since so many in this society see government to be a threat, it is not surprising that religious groups see it to be a threat to them, too.

Others, who don't hold a laissez-faire or "minimalist" position about the state in general, nevertheless may distinguish the distinct realm of *religion*: it is fragile, ultimate, "spiritual," different. In that sensitive realm there is a menace in governmental intrusion not apparent in OSHA,* and EPA,† or the Pure Food and Drug Act.

And so the *factual* question arises: is there indeed now a menacing pattern of governmental intervention in religious affairs? My tentative answer is no.

As readers of this volume will have learned, Mr. Thompson read at the start of the conference a list of seventeen governmental threats—alleged threats—to religion which were supposed to add up to a trend. This long train of abuses included efforts to regulate fund-raising solicitations; to require lobbies to register; to obtain census data; to supervise election for lay teachers in parochial schools; to deny tax exemption to church-related but not very churchy activities; to use clergy as informants; to obtain information about matters internal to religious groups, including reports by race, sex, and religion (I was reminded of the administrator who when asked to list his staff "broken down by sex" replied that he didn't know how many were broken down by sex but he knew of several broken down by alcohol). I must say that Mr. Thompson's series did not induce in me what it was supposed to induce: fear and trembling at the heavy hand of

---

*Occupational Safety and Health Act.
†Environmental Protection Administration.

Big Brother government. Almost every one of the items in the list seemed to me to be arguable or explainable.

In the case of the withdrawal of tax exemption from Bob Jones University, for example, the conflict is not simply with a failure to comply with "public policy" in the ordinary sense—that's the way it was put in the stated clerk's list—but rather with a public policy reflecting the constitutional principle of equal protection of the laws. It would seem to be legitimate, and indeed necessary, for the courts and appropriate governmental agencies to examine the racial practices of Bob Jones University—and of other religious entities.

At the very least there is in such cases a clash between two constitutional principles: equal protection of the laws regardless of race, and free exercise of religion.

In one case on Mr. Thompson's list—the use of clergy as informants for intelligence operations—I did agree that there is a clear-cut danger.

But in many other cases I was inclined to feel that the government agency in question was just doing its duty . . . perhaps overdoing it, sometimes.

In other cases, I felt, the action of government—usually the courts —was thrust upon it out of necessity. The courts must intervene when they are appealed to to decide who owns a church building, for example, and that isn't easy to do.

Moreover, if our democratic society is to grant "religion" a special status with particular rights, then it will be necessary for the society to make the attempt, clumsy though it may be, to define what "religion" is.

If religious groups are to be granted tax exemption on their property, then it will be necessary for a governmental agency to have some criteria about what is and what is not a religion in order to decide who does and who doesn't receive it. And there will be court cases, like the *Fellowship of Humanity* case, in which the border between religion and non-religion will be explored.

Surely you can't solve the complicated issues of Jonestown, mail-order ministries, and coercive and fraudulent cults just by one absolute pro-"religion" principle.

In general, I felt that the list of 17 points testified less to a power-hungry government than to the complexity of modern life.

Four

More than we may now realize, religious liberty is an essential part of the underpinning of this country. In the realm from which belief and value come, as far as possible, we say with Jefferson: "Almighty God hath created the mind free." With respect to belief, Americans are not to be coerced. The state and the social order are, instead, to respond to the systems of meaning and value arising from the free decision of the people. That is a principle of our democratic morality, and an explicit claim—the first one in the Bill of Rights—in the written Constitution of this nation.

Nevertheless, it cannot be an *absolute* principle—any more than freedom of speech or freedom of the press can be absolute. There are in all these fields of fundamental freedom borderline problems of definition —what is and what is not speech, press, assembly, religion. There are conflicts with other deep and serious claims—of the very security and fabric of the nation. There is the possibility of terrible harm to persons other than those who exercise their freedom. And there are conflicts among the freedoms themselves.

Freedom of the press is one of this country's fundamental moral and constitutional principles, but claimed instances of it may have to give way to the right to a fair trial—another fundamental—or in a wartime instance (not the *Pentagon Papers*) to national security. It may not extend to the *National Enquirer* inventing gossipy stories about Carol Burnett. Freedom of speech is another such principle, also part of the underpinning of this society, but it may not extend to "fighting words" that are the equivalent of a blow, or incitements to assassinate a president, or sadistic sex shows that claim to be "freedom of expression." All these are controverted instances. I do not mean to decide them here, but only to generalize that the freedoms cannot be *absolute* in the sense that anyone who claims the right in any instance must have it honored. Life is too complex for that. So also, then, with freedom of religion. The society has to decide, and to keep on deciding, just which instances are analogous to shouting fire (falsely) in a crowded theater. There will be genuine exercises of liberty that because of a collision with some other good regrettably cannot be honored. And because these fundamental freedoms are such heavy claims upon society, there will also be attempts to make use of them to protect activities that really do not belong under the label or that do not represent its core.

When an ABC vice-president invokes the ancient valiant fight against censorship and book-burning in his defense of "Charlie's Angels" and "Starsky and Hutch" against what he calls "pressure groups," we need not regard his invocation of "freedom" as ranking with Milton's *Areopagitica*. When the owner of a cocktail bar insists that his requirement that the waitresses wear skimpy costumes represents his "freedom of expression," we need not rank that claim with Elijah Lovejoy's dying for freedom of the press. The attempt by Fundamentalist day-care centers to exempt themselves from state licensing requirements with respect to corporal punishment and child safety is not the same kind of a claim of religious liberty as was Roger Williams'. And if there are disputes about tax money for bus rides to parochial schools or about sectarians' button-holing people in airports, the stake—the pun is free if you want it—is not the same as for Joan of Arc.

I do not mean to make light of real and difficult current controversies; I mean only to say that their moral and political shape (in the free societies, I mean) may be very different from those controversies long ago in which the principles now invoked were originally articulated. And invoking those principles without noticing enormous alterations in power, opinion, law, and society may serve to discredit the principles where they really do still apply, to misunderstand the goods and evils of our own very different situation, and to allow or commit new misdeeds. In Poland now there is a fundamental struggle for Liberty in something like its classic form; but in the United States, which has its own problems as well as its accomplishments, the situation is not the same.

A related point—I hope the reader will see that it is related: Camels do not always follow their noses. Absolute-principle people regularly invoke the metaphor of the camel, the nose, and the tent. In the Religious Liberty field they regularly invoke the ringing sentence from James Madison's *Memorial and Remonstrance*: Not three pence! (of tax money to support religious establishments). Well, three pence does not necessarily grow to three billion, nor does the whole camel necessarily follow the nose. Organized society continually says, in effect, so far and no further. It must. The rhetorical device that compares one small action with the most extreme extension of some aspect of it (usually, in late 20th century polemics, Hitler, Stalin, or George Orwell's *1984*) is undiscriminating. If you would invoke a *principle*—as indeed in certain moments we must —be sure you have the right moment.

And "liberty" in this field will, as it does in others, turn into power: coercing others. The exercisers of liberty characteristically do not notice when and where this happens. But it is difficult to give a definition of liberty that is not very close to a definition also of power (the ability to do what you will), and that definitional problem reflects a social reality.

"Negative" liberty (being left alone), in the well-known distinction made by Isaiah Berlin and others, is not so sharply distinguished in the real world from "positive" liberty (empowerment) as it may be analytically. Moreover, the one tends to turn into the other: negative liberty tends to turn into positive liberty, or into power. In the actual buzzing, moving world of live human beings, in other words, "liberty" is dynamic. It is "exercised" (to use the First Amendment's verb as it applies to religion), and when exercised, it often grows: the "exercise" of freedom by some expands theirs, perhaps at the expense of others' freedom. The reason for this is not hard to discover: human beings are woven into a web of shared life. Do not send to know for whom the bell tolls; it tolls for thee. We are more interdependent, and have more of an effect upon each other, than 17th or 18th century individualistic philosophies, to which we are indebted for the charter of our liberty, allow for. Our interwoven-ness is particularly important in group life and in the new patterns created by modern technology.

A simple libertarianism implies solitary human beings in a limitless continent of possibility. Therefore, that libertarianism, false to our real situation, is a poor philosophy with which to defend freedom. Even in that primitive situation when "all the world was America" human beings did not live in that kind of isolation. Certainly they do not do so in the age of the television evangelists, the MX missile, and the Los Angeles freeways.

When individuals exercise freedom of enterprise, before long, if they are successful, they will dominate a market; perhaps they make arrangements with the competition to hold up prices, or to get a legislature to enact "fair prices," or a Congress to support prices at "parity." Or they turn into an oligopoly or a monopoly. Thereby through their exercise of freedom they restrict the freedom of others. The logic of the freedom of the press combined with modern technology and with modern commerce has been one town, one newspaper. That means others can exercise effective freedom of the press in a major metropolis if they have—what? —ten million dollars to lose in the first year? A rough balance of power is the realistic foundation of genuine freedom.

Ah, Liberty! what crimes are committed in thy name! (And so also in the name of equality, democracy, and the other words that represent a powerful social good). As I have already implied, these great values can be invoked ideologically—this is, as rationalizations for power and self-interest, for protection of "crimes." If religious liberty is made into an absolute barrier, protecting an untouchable extraterritoriality of "religion" against all social intrusion, then there will collect behind that barrier all manner of anti-social activities: racially segregated all-white academies; drug cults; Jonestowns; schools with pre-scientific curricula; abusive day-care centers; the Duke and Dauphin "missionaryin' around" for money.

In our American role as one of the prime bearers among the nations of the precious human heritage of civil liberty—of the liberties of the First Amendment—we don't want to do that wrongly or naively or ineffectively. Freedom is a deep and serious principle of the kind of society that we want—and it cannot be an absolute.

Five

I know these matters have an elaborate vocabulary in the law, but let me borrow from another, closely linked field, moral philosophy. Freedom of religion and these other freedoms seem to me to be principles of a democratic society in the way the English philosopher, W.D. Ross, framed the principles of duty for individual moral agents. Utilitarians and other opponents of "absolute" moral principles, of which Kant's Categorical Imperative is the prototype, argued against the outrageous results of unbending application of such principles. Kant himself, for example, stood firm on the duty to tell the truth, even to a murderer who appears at your door and asks whether the potential victim you've hidden in the house is hiding there. Tell the truth, he said, and the result is in the hand of God. Most people, including me, find that answer quite unsatisfactory, and would regard that as a situation where a white lie would be not only permissable but desirable, because another heavy moral claim—in this case overriding—is in conflict with telling the truth.

But then the utilitarian tradition (broadly speaking) tended to go too far in the opposite direction, washing out any distinct intrinsic claim in principles like telling the truth, or keeping promises, or paying debts, *if* on a simple calculation of the goods and bads those claims lost out. They said: Do the greater good, overall, whatever it is. W.D. Ross then went back to rescue the ethics of principle by saying of these intrinsic moral claims that they are *prima facie* duties—conditional duties. The presumption is that they are to be obeyed. Any disobeying of the duty to tell the truth, or to keep a promise, has the burden of proof. It is the rare instance only where that principle clashes with something deeper or equally deep that it may, or must be, violated. Justice Oliver Wendell Holmes is often quoted as having said, "It's not the man of principle I admire but the man of principles"—plural. He's the one who has a problem.

I suggest that these fundamental freedoms are *prima facie* duties of the social order: they are intrinsic principles with a heavy presumption in their favor, although they cannot be absolute.

Lawyers sometimes speak of a "balancing" of conflicting claims. And it is true that we must put one claim alongside or against another. But this "balancing" should not be reduced to a simple utilitarian or cost-benefit calculation. I am fairly sure that the "greatest happiness of the greatest number" is *not* served by allowing swarms of Jehovah's Witnesses to go door-to-door on Sunday morning awakening Catholic working men to try to sell them *The Watchtower* and to explain to them that their church is the whore of Babylon. Nevertheless we have protected the right to do that because there is a social principle at stake, and the Supreme Court found it to be grounded in the Constitution. The counter-claim would have to be heavier than the desire of the workingman to sleep later or of the town to protect itself against a nuisance in order for this free exercise of religion to be curtailed.

Six

There will continue to be border skirmishes—perhaps increasing —about the definition of the territory protected by the fundamental principle of religious liberty. But the main outlines nevertheless are clear. Religious liberty in this country is for the most part an accomplished fact. If you will remember the sad history of torment and torture, of battles and burnings—of the bloody tenet of persecution for cause of conscience —then you will agree that our religious liberty represents a considerable accomplishment.

And it has been expanding. In the nineteenth century the largely Protestant nation was loaded with explicit and implicit intolerance. Anti-Catholic novels were best sellers. The public schools had a Protestant flavor. The Know-Nothing Party (anti-Catholic, nativist) had real national power. The ugliest of all prejudices and persecutions in Western Civilization, anti-semitism, was by no means missing from this country. I do not want to present an unduly rosy picture of the present, but it does seem clear that religious toleration has significantly increased over what it was in the 19th century, let alone in 17th century Massachusetts Bay.

In most of the recent court controversies the claimants of religious liberty won. In a well-known case in Wisconsin, the Amish did not want to send their children to public high schools, where the girls would have to go bare-legged to gym class, and where the flavor of the classes and social life went against Amish upbringing and belief. In the highest court the Amish won. In one of our more remarkable cases in the middle of the passions of World War II, the Supreme Court reversed itself and upheld the claim of the Jehovah's Witnesses not to be compelled to join in a flag salute. The Jehovah's Witnesses, fiercely unpopular though they were, won case after case in the courts. A Seventh-Day Adventist was granted unemployment benefits after rejecting a job that would have required her to work on Saturday. Some Native Americans are allowed to use peyote, although it is illegal for others, because it has long been part of their religious ritual.

In the difficult area of religiously based conscientious objection, not only the courts but also Congress have done what they could. Although the law does not regard conscientious objection to war as a right—it is a "privilege" granted by the "grace" of Congress—it is nevertheless a privilege that has in fact been granted through the wars of this century, and to some degree expanded. During the Vietnam period, although selective conscientious objection—objection to one war but not to all war—was not allowed, the high court made remarkable interpretations of religious rights in order to allow folk who would ordinarily be regarded as non-believers to exercise the same right as religious believers. It devised the so-called parallel-belief test: that interesting invention of the society to keep from discriminating against non-believers. If you have a fundamental belief that "occupies the same place" in your life as a traditional religious belief is supposed to do with a believer, then you can make an appeal to that—in Paul Tillich's terms—"ultimate concern" on behalf of your conscientious objection.

This country has not adopted the point of view expressed by Felix Frankfurter in the flag salute cases: that "sectarian" belief could not make any claim of "immunity" to legitimate legislative acts. Instead we have gone out of our way as a society to allow many distinct exemptions and intrusions on the basis of religious conscience. Taken as a whole the story—especially under the provocations of the contemporary religious scene—has been one of rather remarkable social self-restraint. In fact this might even be a field in which one could obey the presidential injunction to Speak Up for America.

Seven

Nevertheless in this field as in others, eternal vigilance is the price of liberty. So it is helpful to pay attention to what is happening, in the way that the papers in this volume have done, even though the picture of a systematic menace is not convincing.

There may indeed be a recent change in the atmosphere. It may be that people in public life—editors, school superintendents, IRS examiners —now feel less of a need to defer to "religion"—to tiptoe around it, in the way that most used to do, some of them while complaining privately about the need to. Why? I suggest that this diminished deference is one result of the development of a society at the same time more secular and more diversely believing. Some of the celestial shine has worn off the claims of religion, partly because of the large number of people who don't believe in any part of it, and partly because out of the rich soil of liberty more and more unusual religious plants have grown. That some of these are repellent gives further cause to those who would pull up flowers with the weeds.

But even while paying the price of vigilance to protect religious liberty, I suggest that it is inappropriate for religious groups to present themselves *primarily* as a special interest among other special interests, joined together like the wool-growers to protect the price of wool. We live too much in a special-interest society, its common threads stretched by the pull of myriad groups and interests, protecting and pushing their own, making the claim on the society given classic expression by the early labor leader Samuel Gompers when asked what labor wants: "More."

Religious groups, with their acquaintance with justice and the common good, should not encourage the philosophies that justify a straight-out push-pull interest-group politics. It isn't easy in a world of interest groups contending for turf, each trying to get more for itself, for there to be deliberation about and commitment to the larger picture.

Of course there are legitimate "interests" that religious groups want to protect.

To be sure, members of one religious group may have a better appreciation of the legitimate claims of other believers than does the large unbelieving mass of the population, and one set of believers *can* be more sensitive to the legitimate claims of another (that's by no means the way it usually works, though, as the history of religious struggles tells us).

But the many religious communities that make up this extraordinary nation should not come into the political arena simply as another group seeking its own advantage.

The notion of the special-interest state sometimes implies analogy to the classic picture of the free market: every interest group pushes for its own thing, and the outcome somehow serves all. The particular groups and citizens who are part of those groups do not themselves need to worry about the common good or about justice to others. It is explicitly assumed that these great goods will be taken care of by the process itself—by an invisible hand—and need no conscious attention by reason and conscience of the citizenry.

Surely that's a bad mistake, and one that the religious communities in particular ought not to encourage. This modern American democracy is not well supplied with sources of an unembarrassed defense of a common good and of social justice.

Adherents of the biblical religions have helped to shape the working features of this civilization, with a vision that reaches to a ground of meaning beyond special interest, beyond the atmosphere of the moment, and beyond our nation's own limited understanding of itself. Many writers out of the tradition of the biblical religions have linked that tradition to the foundation of democracy: personalism, universalism, freedom, equality, grounded in Jewish and Christian beliefs. Moreover, democracy requires the capacity for a self-limitation, an acceptance of values and interests different from one's own. It requires an awareness that there are serious claims that go beyond self-interest. Democracy requires a difficult combination of an initial relativism in which my claims—whether of an interest or of a value—are not regarded as final—which at the same time does not fall over into a thoroughgoing relativism in which all moral meaning is washed out.

There are many modern sources for the view of human society as an amoral jungle. Religious groups should not imply by their action that they view it that way, too. Neither should they provide an absolutistic and fanatical crusading and moralistic politics wrapped around some single issue regarded as uncompromisable. Instead they can and should help to nurture the difficult genius of democracy. That genius rejects a thoroughgoing relativism on the one hand and a clash of absolutists on the other. It combines an initial relativism, a self-critical and self-limiting view, with a link to claims of the good and the just that are not simply functions of group interest. Religious groups should be equipped to provide that difficult combination.

Special-interest politics—so-called pluralism—speaks, as a political scientist has observed, with an upper-class accent. It's hard for people on the periphery, in neglected pockets and the lower rim of society, to get into the pluralistic contest for the spoils. And special-interest politics neglects the common good. The religious communities have been truest to their own nature when they have helped the society to see a social good or a claim of justice that was neglected.

Eight

"Government," not religion, is the endangered species in the United States—and American religion helped make it so.

This American society has at its foundation a series of movements of thought and belief that are more individualistic—more anti-social and anti-governmental—than the cultures from which we sprang or than most other societies in the world.

The United States has an unusually anti-governmental tradition, and an unusually anti-governmental contemporary climate of opinion.

This nation was built, not on Aristotle and Saint Thomas, but on John Locke and the flat land. The movements that created it were disinclined to believe that man is a social animal. We were founded by the movements in Europe that freed the individual from the restraints of the feudal and Catholic order. This was a nation—as Louis Hartz wrote—in which liberalism was on the ground floor. Here there was no feudal past to act as a restraint and an enemy. The middle-class movement that in Europe had to win its way against an entrenched class system here had a virgin land upon which to build the society implied in its principles. Here the ideas of the free individual antecedent to society, making society by a contract, had free rein. The idea that the state's role is strictly limited was played out to the fullest.

This was also a new land with classical capitalism on the ground floor. One points out always to students the neatness of the date of publication of *Wealth of Nations* in 1776. Here the logic of the link between the Protestant ethic and the spirit of capitalism could realize itself more fully than in a culture where other themes preceded it. When Max Weber wrote about that link, he turned to an American for an example: to Ben Franklin, in his autobiography. The maxims of Poor Richard about a penny saved and early to bed and God helping those who help themselves and working and using every minute and avoiding idleness, frivolity, and debt—the Calvinist virtues shifted over into the Yankee virtues—were prime examples of the link between Protestant individualism and capitalist success. The core idea was: Time is money. Here the free market and the idea of the "success" could work out their logic.

I said that religion had helped to make the anti-governmental warp in American culture. This was the land with Protestantism on the ground floor, and Protestantism of the left. It is the land of constructive Protestantism, in H. Richard Niebuhr's term. Here the individualizing impulses that led to the Puritan revolution in England had a chance to realize their constructive vision. If the United States, looked at politically, is John Locke writ large, it is also, looked at religiously, John Calvin writ large, and John Wesley also. The Puritan revolution, aborted in England, realized itself in the United States. The wing of the Protestant reformation that came to this land is that of Calvinism and of the sects, not of Luther or of the Church of England. It is, in other words, that part of the Reformation that keeps breaking up the collective past to make an individualist future. As with political liberalism, so with left-wing Protestantism: an antagonism to the state is implied. These are all movements of protest more than of constructiveness.

These movements in politics, economics, and religion reinforce each other and make a people whose best known slogan about government is the less of it the better.

> "That government is best which governs least;" and I should like to see it acted up to more rapidly and systematically. Carried out it finally amounts to this, which also I believe: "That government is best which governs not at all . . ."
> . . . this government never of itself furthered any enterprise but by the alacrity with which it got out of its way. It does not keep the country free. It does not settle the West. It does not educate. The character inherent in the American people has done all that has been accomplished, and it would have done somewhat more if the government had not sometimes got in its way."

That quotation comes, not from some right-wing polemicist attacking the New Deal, but from Henry David Thoreau.

With the coming of the modern industrial era, the older warp in the outlook of the American nation was accentuated by powerful new interests. The growth of the giant industrial organizations after the Civil War brought an argument about the degree to which the public through government should restrain their activities. In the populist and progressive movements and then in the New Deal and its successors, the reform tradition came to use Hamiltonian means to Jeffersonian ends: it endorsed a strong central government in behalf of egalitarian and reformist politics. As that social idealistic heritage gained votes to triumph, especially in the New Deal, the conservative opposition, now dominated by the business community, came to do something like the reverse: it endorsed a Jeffersonian view of government in service to Hamiltonian ends.

Meanwhile there arrived on the scene the unsettling forces of modernity: bureaucracy, advanced technology, complexity. E.B. White wrote in a story in the late thirties: "I predict a bright future for complexity." In the United States (not elsewhere in the world) the discontents of that complexity have been blamed primarily on government.

One result of all this is that the United States has very little respect for public service. The "private sector," in the modern lingo, is regarded as somehow automatically superior to the "public sector." "Government," "politician," and especially now "bureaucrat," are terms of abuse. There are negative stereotypes of government as a demon, and of "bureaucrats" as peculiarly evil folk.

Much popular political thinking deals of course in such stereotypes, and especially in stereotyped villains. The worst episodes occur when this impulse fastens onto a racial or religious group. But "prejudice" against groups is not its only form. Institutions can be made to bear the responsibility for the evils and faults of society. In the current climate "government," "bureaucrats" and "politicians" are very close to that slot, as "oil companies" are in another way, and as the "trusts" were in the old populist days—and so on.

With clear-cut villains and clear-cut heroes, one's political outlook is conveniently simplified. In Orwell's *Animal Farm* the animals learn to say two legs, bad; four legs, good.

These oversimplifications and slogans not only falsify the situation factually and intellectually; they falsify it morally and emotionally.

The reason for our doing that is not only that it's hard to think about a huge complicated social order; it's also that we want the emotional satisfaction of clarity and the personal exculpation of having somebody to blame.

One of the analyses of the way this works presents the picture of people on a streetcar—this goes back to the days when there were streetcars —complaining about the service. One passenger says we should get together and visit the transit company and talk about the defects of their service. Somebody else says the problem is all the foreigners who've moved to the city. The latter is a much more emotionally satisfying answer. It serves the scapegoat function—the emotional need to have some visible group, person, or entity, graspable by the mind and hateable by the spleen.

With a little honest self-examination, we can all discover in ourselves this emotional push to make personal or to make easy and concrete the characters we praise and blame in politics—especially those we blame. Most of what passes for political discussion consists simply in trading the bubble-gum cards of these stereotypes and prejudices.

"Government" has long been a scapegoat of this sort, to some extent to people everywhere, but to a distinct degree and in a distinctively individualist way in the United States.

The word "politician," and its cognates, has long been a pejorative in the American lexicon; "bureaucrats" have now joined "politicians" in the American doghouse of the popular imagination. When one hears a gathering of religious folk piling up further denunciations of "bureaucrats," one wonders whether they are doing something that really needs to be done right now.

Under *contemporary* American conditions, would you think federal bureaucrats rated very high? In popular esteem, I mean. Is their *hybris* given encouragement? Not at all. They have a hard time even admitting what it is they do when they sit by a stranger on an airplane. The beleaguered bureaucrats are now mostly in danger of being fired, and are always in danger of a Congressional investigation or a press exposé, and regularly subject to presidential denunciations. They do tasks, some of them actually useful, but all of them now not only thankless but disdained. I suggest to you that by income, power, and especially popular attitudes, "bureaucrats" are not remotely as powerful as doctors, lawyers, the programmers of a television network, the modern preachers of the electronic church, the leaders of conservative political groups, top corporation folk or, for that matter, almost anybody you could name. They have become whipping-persons.

Moreover there's a confusion in that. "Bureaucracy" is a phenomenon whose defects are not at all confined to government. We all have tales to tell about mysterious errors in payroll divisions, about computers being "down," about useless paper work and red tape, about underlings who tell us our problem is not their department, in giant organizations that have nothing to do with government. Yet the whole force of our reaction to this widespread disease of modernity is lodged, in this country, against government.

Where anything is not much respected, it is not done very well. Where the principle of government is not well understood, then the practice will not be what it should be. To mention only one effect, the selection of people will have a bias in it. Able and ambitious people who might in another culture aspire to public service and governmental leadership are discouraged from doing so here. This is not the place to try to sort out these huge historical and philosophical issues. I wish to say just that, compared, for example, to the Japanese or to most of the nations of Western Europe out of which our heritage is come, we have a warp in our understanding. On a spectrum of the history of humankind, our outlook is skewed.

We do have something important to contribute in thinking through the way big modern industrial societies govern themselves, preserving the values of the human person, including civil and religious liberty. We haven't done what we could do with that because of our anti-intellectualism and sloganeering. You can't build a responsible democratic government if you don't believe in it.

Government is at once a danger and a necessity in human societies. The state may indeed be a menace and do evil things; often in human history it has. In the century that has seen Nazi Germany and Stalinist Russia, not to mention all the other examples, we do not need to be reminded how evil a central government, captured by an evil ideology, can be. But nevertheless—to make this point in the language of a mainstream of our religious traditions—the state is not rooted in "sin." It is instead rooted in creation: that is, in the way human beings are originally and naturally before a "fall." It is rooted in our social nature: in the fact that human beings were made to live with each other and are not fully human if they live from birth as wolf children or Robinson Crusoes. Government is not only the restraining force which human society requires but also the instrument of common purpose that it can use. It is defined not only by its having a monopoly of legitimate violence—its being legitimately coercive—but also by its being so in the interests of the shared desire for pattern and direction in society.

In part just because of the modern totalitarian perversions, we need to show how ordered liberty—government in a free society—can work, under modern conditions.

We respond much more favorably to the word "law" than to the word "government." A great accomplishment of the societies that have shaped us is to bring these two words together, with liberty. The democracies have grounded the sovereign decision about law in the people.

The role of high religion, Reinhold Niebuhr said, is to contribute depth to human life. The American political argument needs it.

I put it to you that the religious community in the contemporary United States should not add to the superficial anti-governmental theme that surrounds us everywhere.

Who Owns the Churches?

CHARLES M. WHELAN, S.J.

The title question has been in the headlines because of the actions taken by the Attorney General of California against the Worldwide Church of God. The question, indeed, is perfect for headlines: it is brief, uses only familiar words, and raises a very interesting point.

Unfortunately, all the correct answers to this admirably short and brisk question are lengthy, complex, tedious, and dull.

I say, "all the correct answers," because there are more than one. Both "ownership" and "church" have several meanings, and the correct answers to the question, "Who owns the churches?," depend on which meaning of "ownership" or "church" the questioner has in mind.

For example, one meaning of "church" is the body of religious believers who make up the church membership. Under this meaning, the only possible answer to the question of ownership is "No one."

Again, one meaning of the word "ownership" is the right of enjoyment and disposition, including the right to convert the property to any lawful use that the owner desires. Under this meaning, the only possible answer to the question of the ownership of churches is, again, "No one." The property has been dedicated to religious uses, and no one—not even the State—has the right to convert it to any other use.

In all probability, however, the headline writer used the word "churches" to mean "church property," and the word "owns" to mean "the right, especially in cases of disputes within the church membership, to make the ultimate decision about the proper use of that property."

Moreover, the headline writer was using the word "owns" in the sense of American civil law rules governing property, not in the sense of the internal ecclesiastical laws of the various American churches. But since the civil law is made by fifty states and the federal government, the writer should at least have recognized the possibility that there might be fifty-one different answers.

What made it possible for the writer to compress such an intricate question into four short words? It was the assertion by the Attorney General of California that "the public owns the churches"—a five-word answer to a four-word question. Brevity is the soul of wit, but not the salt of common sense. The Attorney General's statement was all the more

outrageous because, in addition to distorting fundamental legal principles, it was a calculated, striking affront to common sense.

In fairness to the Attorney General, I must note immediately that his
statement about public ownership of the churches has some support in
some very respectable legal treatises. I have not yet found a treatise that
puts the matter quite as flatly as the Attorney General did, but even a
quick perusal of Scott's *Abridgment of the Law of Trusts* (1960) or Bogert's
Law of Trusts (1973) will provide some legal authority for a chain of
reasoning like the following:

1. Churches, whether organized as charitable trusts or as charitable
   corporations, hold their property in trust for religious uses.
2. The essence of a trust is the division of ownership into two parts, the
   right of management and the right of enjoyment. The right of
   management (legal title) is in the trustee; the right of enjoyment
   (equitable title) is in the beneficiary. Thus, both the trustee and the
   beneficiary own the trust: the trustee, legally, and the beneficiary,
   equitably.
3. Religious trusts are one species of charitable trusts. Churches are one
   subspecies of religious trusts.
4. The beneficiary of all charitable trusts is the public.
5. Therefore, the public owns the churches (equitably).
6. Furthermore, the Attorney General, as the representative of the
   public (both at common law and by statutory designation in all fifty
   states), has the right to vindicate the public's interest in the proper
   administration of all charitable trusts (including churches).

This chain of reasoning would be unassailable were it not for a number
of Supreme Court decisions which clearly demonstrate that the religion
clauses of the First Amendment do not permit the states or the federal
government to treat churches simply as one variety of charitable trusts (or
charitable corporations), subject to the same rules as schools, hospitals,
museums and symphony orchestras.

Before discussing these Supreme Court decisions, I wish to emphasize
that most American churches *are* charitable trusts or charitable corporations (or a combination of both). Church lawyers have nothing to gain by
trying to prove the opposite—which, in any event, I do not think they
could possibly do. For hundreds of years, American churches have
claimed to be, and have been treated as, charitable trusts or charitable
corporations.

Indeed, the law of charitable trusts and the law of charitable corporations have been extremely important safeguards for the free exercise of
religion. These laws have provided a stable framework within which
churches could carry on their ministries and acquire the property
indispensable for those ministries.

Moreover, churches should not flinch at the consequence that the

Attorney General has *some* type of enforcement power over them. The status of charitable trust or charitable corporation disposes of far more plaintiffs than it provides. *Only* the Attorney General, the trustees or the corporate directors can sue to enforce a charitable trust or the purposes of a charitable corporation. If the American churches were private trusts or private corporations, every one of their members would have the right to sue (either as beneficiaries of the private trusts, or as the equivalent of stockholders in the corporation).

Until the Worldwide Church of God case came along, American churches were comfortable with the law of charitable trusts and charitable corporations. Now that the churches have seen that this law can be sword as well as shield, they are understandably concerned. But what went wrong in the Worldwide Church of God case was not the law of charitable trusts or charitable corporations. What went wrong was the grievous inattention of the California Attorney General and the California courts to a series of Supreme Court decisions which clearly show that the Constitution imposes special rules on the government when it comes to the enforcement of religious trusts and the supervision of religious corporations.

There is, of course, no Supreme Court decision directly in point that says that it is unconstitutional for the Attorney General and the state courts to do what was done in California. If such a decision existed, the Worldwide Church of God would have been able to vindicate its rights quickly. But the Supreme Court decisions that we do have clearly show that government is not allowed to treat churches exactly the same way it treats other charitable trusts and charitable corporations, either in the settlement of property disputes or in the areas of supervision and regulation.

1. Church Property Law

In the preface to the 1917 edition of his *American Civil Church Law*, Carl Zollmann wrote:

> It was at first intended to include in the book all questions of charitable trusts, so far as they affect the various denominations. This plan has proved to be impracticable. Just as charity covers a multitude of sins, so questions of charitable trusts are concerned with a veritable throng of diverse institutions. The questions thus arising cannot, in a legal discussion, be disentangled one from the other and those relating to churches put to one side. An attempt to discuss them in this volume could not but result either in an insufficient treatment of them or in a discourse that would go far beyond the proper scope of the book. While the subject has of necessity been occasionally referred to, its complete elucidation, in its religious as well as eleemosynary, educational, and purely public aspects, has therefore been reserved for a separate volume [*American Law of Charities*].

In the 1933 revision of Zollman's treatise, retitled *American Church Law*, Chapter 7 deals with "implied trusts," Chapter 8 with "schisms," and Chapter 9 with "church decisions." Chapters 3, 4 and 5 deal with church "corporations." Any one who doubts the applicability of the law of charitable trusts and charitable corporations to churches should read these chapters thoroughly. Nevertheless, the chapters are seriously outdated, not so much because of changes in state law, but because of a series of later rulings by the United States Supreme Court on the impact of the First Amendment religion clauses on state laws regulating the settlement of church property disputes.

Much of Zollman's Chapter 9 ("Church Decisions") is an attack on the 1871 decision of the Supreme Court in *Watson* v. *Jones*.[1] This decision rejected the "implied trust" approach to the settlement of church property disputes that arise within a church divided by schism. Under the "implied trust" approach, civil courts decide which faction within the church holds the "true faith" of that church. The Supreme Court held that this approach was improper because it involved the civil courts in settling difficult points of church doctrine and because it interfered with the autonomy of the churches. The Court held that the proper approach was for the civil court to determine which body within the church had the right to settle the dispute, and then to determine what decision that church body had made. The civil court should then enforce the church body's decision.

The Supreme Court did not base the *Watson* decision on the religion clauses of the First Amendment. The Court could not do so because in 1871 the Court did not yet realize that the Fourteenth Amendment (enacted three years earlier in 1868) had "incorporated" the First Amendment and forbade the States to do what the First Amendment forbade the Federal Government to do. The Supreme Court did not become aware of this "incorporation" until 1925. In the last 55 years however, the Court has discovered that the Fourteenth Amendment "incorporates" (that is, protects against state action) almost all of the freedoms that the Bill of Rights protects against federal action. In particular, the Supreme Court discovered in 1940 that the Fourteenth Amendment incorporated the free exercise clause of the First Amendment,[2] and in 1947 that the Fourteenth Amendment incorporated the no-establishment clause of the First Amendment.[3]

Accordingly, it is no surprise that the Supreme Court "constitutionalized" the *Watson* rule (rejecting the "implied trust" approach to the settlement of church property disputes arising out of schism) in 1969 in *Presbyterian Church in the United States* v. *Mary Elizabeth Blue Hull Memorial Presbyterian Church*.[4] In this case, the Court held flatly that the religion clauses of the First Amendment forbid American civil courts to use the "departure-from-doctrine rule" (another name for the "implied trust" approach) in the resolution of church property disputes. Civil courts must resolve such disputes "without resolving underlying controversies over religious doctrine."[5] Civil courts must not engage "in the forbidden process of interpreting and weighing church doctrine."[6]

Seven years later, the Court went considerably further in limiting the powers of civil courts to settle religious disputes within a church. In *Serbian Orthodox Diocese* v. *Milivojevich*,[7] the Supreme Court reviewed and reversed a judgment of the Supreme Court of Illinois that had itself reviewed and reversed a decision of the highest authority of the Serbian Eastern Orthodox Church to defrock one of its bishops and to reorganize the structure of the Church in the United States. The Illinois Supreme Court held that the highest church authorities had acted arbitrarily and "in clear and palpable excess" of their jurisdiction. The United States Supreme Court held that the religion clauses of the First Amendment forbade such a decision by the Illinois Supreme Court. Church organization, church procedure and church discipline are territory just as forbidden to the civil courts as church doctrine.

Must, then, the civil courts defer to the decisions of the competent church bodies when the civil courts are called upon to resolve church property disputes that arise from a schism? The answer to this question lies in the most recent Supreme Court decision about church property disputes, *Jones* v. *Wolf* (1979).[8]

In this case the Supreme Court held (5–4) that the States are free to follow "neutral principles of law" in adjudicating church property disputes *unless* the dispute involves an "issue of doctrinal controversy."[9] The First Amendment requires civil courts to "defer to the resolution of issues of religious doctrine or polity by the highest court of a hierarchical church organization."[10] As long as civil courts stay out of "doctrinal matters, whether the ritual and liturgy of worship or the tenets of faith," the courts may adopt *any* approach for settling church property disputes.[11] Moreover, the civil courts are not bound by the decision of the competent church authority if that decision was the product of fraud or collusion.[12]

The "neutral principles" approach that the Supreme Court held constitutional in *Jones* v. *Wolf* examines the deeds to the property, the corporate charter of the local church, the state statutes dealing with implied trusts, and the constitution of the parent church. If none of these documents clearly shows that the property of the local congregation is held in trust for the parent church, the state courts may award the property to the local congregation even if it has seceded from the parent church (and the parent church has decided that the property belongs to the parent church or some local representative of the parent church).

In some ways, *Jones* v. *Wolf* is a very puzzling decision. It seems to say that the States are free to adopt either "neutral principles" or the "deference principle." But it also seems to say that the First Amendment mandates the "deference principle" if the church property dispute turns on the resolution of some question touching church tenets, discipline, procedure or organization. As a professor of law, I have become adept at inventing hypotheticals, but I find it difficult to conjure up a probable situation in which a local church would secede from the parent church when there was no dispute about doctrine, discipline, organization or procedure.

To my rescue, fortunately, comes *Lawrence Parent et al., Trustees of the Frabrique du Paroisse de Notre Dame de Mont Carmel* v. *Roman Catholic Bishop of Portland et al.* from the State of Maine.[13] According to the brief of the appellants in this case, the Roman Catholic Bishop of Portland has violated the rights of the Catholic inhabitants of the Village of Lille by disposing of the property that they and their ancestors gave the Bishop so that he would provide them with religious services. "He repudiated his promise to provide religious services," the brief argues, "and therefore should not be allowed to keep [or sell] the property we gave him for the purpose of providing religious services."

There is no dispute between the Catholic parishioners of Lille and the Bishop of Portland over any aspect of Roman Catholic belief, discipline, procedure or organization. The parishioners concede that it was within the bishop's authority to decide to discontinue providing religious services within their church in the Village of Lille. But they argue that, under "neutral principles" of Maine law, the church that they and their ancestors "gave of themselves, their property, their monies and their labors" is impressed with a constructive trust, and that the bishop has no right to sell the property and use the proceeds for other religious purposes.[14]

How the Supreme Judicial Court of Maine will resolve the Village of Lille case remains to be seen. Of more immediate interest to us is how the United States Supreme Court probably would have decided *Worldwide Church of God, Inc.* v. *State of California*, if the Supreme Court had ever gotten to the merits of the case.

2. 'Public Trust' Supervision

In his admirable Petition to the United States Supreme Court for a Writ of Certiorari in the Worldwide Church of God case, Prof. Laurence H. Tribe set forth the many reasons why the Supreme Court should decide to review and reverse the actions of the California courts in that case. Among those reasons the following are particularly pertinent to the question of how much supervisory authority the Attorney General has over churches because of their status as charitable trusts or charitable corporations:

—It is unconstitutional for the State to assert supervisory authority over the churches on the ground that they are charitable entities and therefore owned by the public, because the ownership assertion "is comprehensible *only* on the State's own explicit premise that a charitable organization such as 'the Worldwide Church of God derives its position, its existence, from the State of California'," and because acceptance of the ownership assertion would "sanction a naked confiscation of private property without just compensation."[15]

—The State's avowed purposes in exercising the supervisory authority are unconstitutional because they aim impermissibly at:
a. supervising spending choices by church officials;
b. superimposing external standards on internal church relationships; and at
c. altering church policy and leadership.[16]

It is impossible for me to improve upon Professor Tribe. In the course of his argument, he relies on the decisions about church property disputes that I have summarized in this presentation and on many other Supreme Court decisions, including the series of "aid to parochial school" cases that the Court decided during the 1970's and which clearly establish that the religion clauses of the First Amendment forbid "excessive entanglement" between Church and State—including specifically, excessive entanglement in each other's financial affairs.[17]

For reasons known only to itself, the United States Supreme Court decided not to review the Worldwide Church of God case. Perhaps the Supreme Court wanted to wait until the case had moved further along in the California courts. In any event, now that the Attorney General of California has dropped the proceedings against the Church, it is unlikely that this case will provide the vehicle for a final ruling by the Supreme Court on the issue of "public ownership" of the churches.

Nevertheless, I think it clear that the Supreme Court would have rejected the Attorney General's assertion out of hand. Certainly, the Court would have rejected the Attorney General's assertion that he has the same supervisory authority over the administration and expenditure of church funds that he has over the administration and expenditure of the funds of other types of charitable trusts and charitable corporations. The Attorney General's fundamental mistake—a mistake shared by the lower courts in California—was that the status of a church *as a charitable trust or corporation* gave him special powers over church finances. The truth is that the special status of a charitable trust or corporation *as Church* severely limits and curtails those powers.

Without doubt, the Attorneys General have *some* supervisory authority over the administration and expenditure of church funds. Otherwise, there is no protection for church members against gross financial abuses by church leaders. But the supervisory power must be exercised with at least as much caution and restraint, and with at least as many procedural safeguards, as in the case of business corporations, labor unions, or nonreligious charitable trusts and corporations. How much *more* protection the First Amendment gives churches, the Supreme Court will have to tell us on another day.

Frontier Issues of Tax Exemption for Religious Organizations

STANLEY S. WEITHORN

MARK D. TURKEL

This paper is designed to address the general issue of how "bureaucratic tyranny," if not unconstitutional infringements of First Amendment religious guarantees, may result from the exercise by the Internal Revenue Service of its excessively broad and undirected power to define and, thereby, in effect to shape religious institutions. Two areas of bureaucratic intervention in the existence and operation of religious organizations will be discussed: first, the right of the Internal Revenue Service to recognize the tax-exempt status of, or to deny such recognition to, the various forms of "new" religions (whatever their shape or size) and, second, the right of the Internal Revenue Service to revoke the tax-exempt status of religious organizations which do not satisfy the "public policy" test.[1]

Denial or Loss of Exemption Due to Nonexempt Activities or Private Inurement

To be exempt from income taxation under Section 501(a) of the Internal Revenue Code of 1954 as an organization described in Section 501(c)(3), a religious organization must meet three statutory requirements:

1. it must be organized and operated exclusively for religious purposes;
2. no part of its net earnings may inure to the benefit of any private shareholder or individual; and
3. it must not engage in substantial lobbying activities or intervene in any political campaigns.

The regulations under Section 501(c)(3) do not shed much light on the requirements for a religious organization to obtain recognition of its tax-exempt status. They state generally that "an organization will be regarded as 'operated exclusively' for one or more exempt purposes only if it engages primarily in activities which accomplish one or more of such exempt purposes specified in Section 501(c)(3)" and further provide that "an organization will not be so regarded if more than an insubstantial part of its activities is not in furtherance of an exempt purpose."[2]

However, the regulations do not provide any specific definition of "religious" (in contrast to the regulatory definitions of, for example, "charitable," "educational"[3] and "scientific"). Thus, the Internal Revenue Service, in fulfilling its obligation to determine whether a religious organization should be accorded tax-exempt status, is afforded little, if any, statutory or regulatory guidance. Instead, it is required to utilize imprecise, and possibly inappropriate, guidelines in attempting to resolve the fundamental problem which it faces in distinguishing between those new religious organizations which, although unconventional, nevertheless are *bona fide* and those new religious organizations which are fraudulent.

Sorting Out "Mail-Order Ministries"

Recently, the Tax Court has considered a number of cases involving organizations espousing "new" religious doctrines, and in all of those cases the Service's denial of tax-exempt status was upheld by the courts.[4]

The facts of the various cases are substantially similar and illustrate the problems faced by the Internal Revenue Service in its struggle to determine whether to grant recognition of exempt status to "new" religions. Characteristic is the case of *Basic Bible Church* v. *Commissioner*. Basic Bible Church is an unincorporated association which was organized in October, 1976, in Washington State. Its charter was granted by the Basic Bible Church of America in Minneapolis, Minnesota. Under that charter it is identified as a subsidiary or auxiliary church of the Basic Bible Church of America, established to further the religious doctrine and principles of its purported "parent" organization, which had previously been recognized by the Service as a tax-exempt organization described in Section 501(c)(3).

The local "church's" charter was signed by an officer of the Basic Bible Church of America and by Francis Duval, his wife Janice Duval and their daughter Misty. Although an officer of the Basic Bible Church of America signed the charter, it had no control over the finances of the local auxiliary. Its bylaws provided, among other things, that Francis was its head officer and, as such, the sole authority in doctrinal disputes and disbursements of the church's assets, including disbursements to himself. In addition, the bylaws provided that Francis held title to all the church's property in his own name.

Further, Francis, as the head of the local church, took a vow of poverty, which asserted that Francis and his wife were making an irrevocable gift to the church of all their income and their property. However, the gift was conditioned on the church's receiving recognition of tax-exempt status so that, if such status was not achieved, the gifts were to revert to the donors. From May, 1977, to January, 1978, the church received gross contributions of approximately $33,000, the bulk of which was contributed by the Duvals. During this same period, its expenses totaled $32,000, $24,000 of which was its ministers' subsistence allowance (its two ministers being Francis and Janice Duval) and $8,000 was expended for the "promotion of the church and its doctrine," including travel expenses of $4,000 (presumably for travel by the Duvals) and $3,700 for "parsonage" expenses, including utility payments and miscellaneous upkeep (all for the Duval home).

The Tax Court focused on whether the church satisfied the operational test in the regulation which had been cited as the basis for the Internal Revenue Service's denial of the church's application.[5] The Court noted that the operational test requires that an organization's activities be primarily those which accomplish one or more exempt purposes specified in Section 501(c)(3), and not, except in an insubstantial part, those which do not further an exempt purpose. Moreover, the Court stated, an organization is not operated exclusively for exempt purposes unless it serves a public rather than a private interest.

Applying these tests to the facts in the case at issue, the Tax Court concluded that the "church" served the private interests of its founder, Francis, and his family, and the presence of this substantial non-exempt purpose prevented the "church" from qualifying as a Section 501(c)(3) organization. While the Court acknowledged that the church served certain religious and charitable purposes, it noted that less than one percent of Petitioner's contributions were disbursed directly for church-related purposes and that, to "a great extent," the church existed "to serve the private benefit of the Duvals." In addition, the Court stated enigmatically that "since Petitioner's financial decisions are controlled by Francis, there exists the opportunity for abuse . . ."[6]

Similarly, in the very recent case of *Church of the Transfiguring Spirit, Inc.* v. *Commissioner*, the Tax Court held that a religious organization controlled by two of its ministers, whose contributions provided virtually all its income and who received virtually all such contributions back as housing allowance distributions, is not exempt under Section 501(c)(3). The Court noted that the "petitioner and its members are sincere in their convictions" . . . but that "petitioner . . . [did not comply] with the statutory requirements for exemption."[7]

The *dicta* of the Tax Court in these decisions appears to reveal the difficulty, philosophical rather than legal, which the courts are experiencing in attempting to determine whether a religious organization satisfies the requirements of Section 501(c)(3). On the one hand, the Court, as in the *Transfiguring Spirit* case, recognizes the sincerity of the religious beliefs of the various petitioners but implies that it is constrained by the requirements of Section 501(c)(3), as interpreted by the Service, to deny tax-exempt status. On the other hand, the Court, as in the *Basic Bible*

Church case, has intimated that it is the potential for fraudulent abuse—that perhaps the *raison d'etre* of the "church" was tax evasion —which provides the basis for sustaining the Service's denial of that particular church's claim for tax exemption.

The statutory and regulatory framework by which the Service, initially, and the courts, ultimately, determine whether a religious organization is exempt as a Section 501(c)(3) organization appears inadequate to serve the twin goals of granting recognition of tax exemption to new or unconventional religions while, at the same time, excluding patently fraudulent arrangements—so-called "mail-order ministries"—that serve personal pecuniary goals. The "private inurement" sword, particularly as wielded by the Internal Revenue Service, may not be the most appropriate mechanism for achieving the desired result because it may operate to exclude a genuine organization.

A Religious Commune: "Walden III"

Consider an actual case currently pending before the Internal Revenue Service. (At the request of the parties involved, names and other confidential material is omitted.) The organization is a Christian communitarian entity which will be referred to as "Walden III."

The beliefs of the members of Walden III are based on the concept of communal Christian living which they find described in the New Testament. Their religious needs are not satisfied by the conventional pattern of denominational worship. Instead, they seek to live in a totally Christian environment 24 hours a day, seven days a week. Accordingly, they have chosen to live in an isolated community which they created in a rugged and remote region of this country. They have constructed several buildings, including a meeting hall and dwelling units for the members of the church, as well as a number of modest structures related to their agricultural and logging activities. Walden III is not involved in any commercial activity but, rather, all its agricultural, farming, lumbering and similar activities are performed solely for the maintenance and subsistence of the members of the church and for the advancement of their missionary work.

Because it is the credo of its members that they should live together as a Christian community, Walden III supplies them with food and shelter, and they provide financial support to the church to the extent that their respective charitable motivations dictate; no tithe is imposed on them. Further, Walden III is not concerned with the assets or income of individual members. Because the church leadership has not established any membership requirements with respect to the taking of a vow of poverty or the transfer of assets to the church, many members hold substantial assets outside its control. In addition, Walden III receives significant charitable support from individuals not directly connected with it and not resident in its community. Finally, and perhaps most importantly, there is no *quid pro quo* between the contributions made by a member and the value of support received by that member.

The Internal Revenue Service denied recognition of tax-exempt status to Walden III, basing its denial on the two closely related issues of (i) the organization's serving a private rather than a public interest (i.e., not being operated exclusively for exempt purposes) and (ii) private inurement. With respect to the first issue, the letter from the Service stated that Walden III was not operated "exclusively" for religious purposes because "your major function appears to be supplying room and board to your members in exchange for the donations." However, the Service's conclusion ignores the fact that there is in fact no exchange on a *quid pro quo* basis. Further, and of far greater importance, because the furnishing of food and shelter to its members is inextricably intertwined with Walden III's fundamental religious beliefs in a communal Christian way of life, for the Service to state that such function is a substantial nonexempt activity is to question the basic tenets of the religion.

The courts have consistently held that the government may not assess the merits or fallacies of a religion without violating the guarantees provided by the First Amendment.[8] Further, in the case of *Golden Rule Church Association*, the Tax Court held that simply because most religious organizations do not carry on their activities in the manner of the Golden Rule Church, it would not be a "proper justification for our refusal to recognize that *this* religious organization did engage in its activities for exclusively religious purposes."[9] Citing the case of *Unity School of Christianity*, the Tax Court stated that "in considering whether a corporation is religious . . . we must always be guided by the character of the organization and its activities. Religion is not confined to a sect or a ritual. The symbols of religion to one are anathema to another. . . ."[10]

Thus, the Service's contention that private rather than public interests are served by Walden III's religious practices of providing food and shelter to its members appears to violate the proscription against the government's scrutinizing the doctrines and tenets of a religion to determine whether the organization is "religious" within the meaning of Section 501(c)(3).

The Service also suggests in its letter that Walden III violates the proscription against private inurement. However, as stated in the Tax Court case of *A.A. Allen Revivals*,[11] "the usual and normal expenses of a religious organization do not constitute any part of its 'net' earnings." Thus, the Service might focus on whether the provision of food and shelter to Walden III's members is a "usual and normal expense" of a religious organization. However, such an inquiry leads inevitably to questions of the *bona fides* of the practices and beliefs of the religious organization, an inquiry which, as already stated, raises a serious constitutional issue.

No final determination has been made as yet in the Walden III case, but it may be expected that a decision adverse to the organization will result in litigation seeking judicial review of the Service's failure to grant recognition of tax-exempt status to the organization. However, judicial review of this case is likely to present its own difficulties for the organization. In the recent case of *Beth-El Ministries, Inc.* v. *United States*,[12] the District Court for the District of Columbia upheld, on facts not too dissimilar from those of Walden III, the Service's denial of the organization's application for recognition of tax-exempt status.[13] The courts are bound by the same imprecise statutory and regulatory guidelines as is the Internal Revenue Service. In an era in which certain organizations and individuals are promoting the use of mail-order ministries as methods of tax avoidance, the Service, understandably, is compelled to focus closely on the *bona fides* of any new religious organization. Thus, it is imperative that Congress, acting in concert with the religious community, establish more precise statutory guidelines for determining whether organizations claiming to be religious are in fact religious rather than merely devices to avoid taxes.

To achieve this goal, and to recognize the sensitive issue with respect to the intrusion of government in the affairs of religious organizations, Congress could provide that the prohibition against the inurement of net earnings to the benefit of any private shareholder or individual would not apply to the provision of room and board (and other similar necessities) to members of a religious group if (i) such provision is necessary to fulfill the religious purpose of the organization and (ii) it is able to demonstrate that its members who are being so provided for have made substantial sacrifices with respect to the material aspects of their lifestyles, and are not availing themselves of the provision of room and board by the religious organization for personal benefit but to be able more fully to participate in the religious practices of the organization.

Under such definition of "inurement of net earnings," the mail-order ministries described in *Basic Bible Church* and *Church of the Transfiguring Spirit* would continue to fail the private inurement requirement because their members are not making any sacrificial changes with respect to their lifestyles but are maintaining their previous physical existences—residing in the same homes and driving the same cars —under the guise of their "new" religions.

In contrast, the members of Walden III—who clearly are sacrificing most if not all of the creature comforts to which they had become accustomed for the sake of living in a communal Christian environment as required by their religion—would not run afoul of the private inurement requirement of Section 501(c)(3). Exchanging a life filled with the typical amenities of our society for one in which there is a lack of many modern conveniences represents a substantial sacrifice that testifies to the devotion of the believer, and evidences that the provision by a religious organization of basic (not luxurious or even comfortable) room and board and other similar necessities does not constitute private inurement.

Walden III and other similarly situated organizations would then be entitled to be classified as religious organizations within the meaning of Section 501(c)(3).

[Editor's Note: The Internal Revenue Service has since conceded that "Walden III" is an organization exempt under Section 501(c)(3).]

Denial or Loss of Tax Exemption Due to Violations of Public Policy

In 1958 in the case of *Tank Truck Rentals* v. *Commissioner*,[14] the Supreme Court superimposed a "public policy doctrine" on the Internal Revenue Code by ruling that business expenses could not be deducted for tax purposes where the allowance of these deductions would "frustrate sharply defined national or state policies proscribing particular types of conduct"[15] (in *Tank Truck*, at issue were fines paid for violation of maximum truck weight laws). This case and its progeny dealt typically with the application of the public-policy doctrine to *business deductions.*

Congress, in the Tax Reform Act of 1969 codified the public policy doctrine with respect to business expense deductions and explained that it had not included other types of deductions because "[p]ublic policy, in other circumstances, generally is not sufficiently clearly defined to justify the disallowance of deductions."[16]

In 1971, in the case of *Green* v. *Connally*,[17] the public-policy doctrine was engrafted onto the area of the Internal Revenue Code dealing with the granting of tax-exempt status. In *Green*, the Supreme Court affirmed an order of the Federal District Court for the District of Columbia which required the Internal Revenue Service to deny recognition of tax-exempt status to segregated private schools in Mississippi and precluded the Internal Revenue Service from granting recognition of tax-exempt status to racially discriminatory private schools in the future. The District Court invoked the federal public policy against a declared Federal public policy against racial discrimination in education, citing the Thirteenth Amendment to the United States Constitution, various landmark civil rights decisions of the Supreme Court, and the Civil Rights Act of 1964 and concluded that "the Internal Revenue Code provisions on charitable exemptions and deductions must be construed to avoid frustrations of federal policy."[18]

In response to the *Green* case, the Internal Revenue Service ruled[19] that racially discriminatory private schools, whether or not state-supported, are not entitled to tax-exempt status under the Code and that, to qualify for tax exemption, private schools must adopt a racially nondiscriminatory admissions policy. In 1972, the Service established guidelines for publication by private schools of their racially nondiscriminatory policies, and in 1975 it strengthened those guidelines.[20]

The Court in *Green* v. *Connally* noted that it was not being called upon to "consider the hypothetical inquiry as to whether tax exemption or tax deduction status may be available to a religious school that practices acts of racial restriction because of the requirements of the religion."[21] In addition, the ruling issued by the Service in 1971 did not deal specifically with religious private schools, but in the 1975 ruling, the Service announced that those policies applied to church-affiliated and church-operated schools.[22]

Further, the issue which the Court did not consider in the *Green* case was decided by a federal District Court in *Goldsboro Christian Schools, Inc.* v. *United States.*[23] It applied the "public policy" doctrine as enunciated in *Green* v. *Connally* to an educational organization which, in accordance with its religious beliefs, maintained a racially discriminatory admissions policy. In response to the school's constitutional objections to the denial of recognition of tax-exempt status, the Court in *Goldsboro* stated simply that "incidental distinctions in government treatment of religions which indirectly arise from the valid exercise of legitimate governmental interest are not prohibited by either the establishment or the free exercise clauses of the First Amendment.[24] However, the Court did not face squarely the issue of whether a religious organization *per se* could be denied recognition of tax-exempt status because the tenets or basic principles of the religion conflicted with "public policy."

The Bob Jones University Case

In a recent decision of the Fourth Circuit, *Bob Jones University* v. *United States*,[25] the application of the public-policy doctrine to a religious organization was considered more specifically. Bob Jones University is an organization which is dedicated to the teaching and propagation of fundamentalist religious beliefs, among which is its belief that the Bible forbids miscegenation.

The University's controversy with the government began in 1970, when the Internal Revenue Service announced publicly in two press releases that it could no longer find legal justification for allowing the continued tax-exempt status under Section 501(1)(3) of private schools with racially discriminatory admissions policies. In September 1971, the University filed suit to enjoin the Internal Revenue Service from revoking its tax-exempt status. In the culmination of that suit, the Supreme Court held that injunctive relief was precluded by the anti-injunctive statute (Section 7421 of the Internal Revenue Code).[26]

On January 19, 1976, the Internal Revenue Service revoked the tax-exempt status of Bob Jones University retroactively as of December 1, 1970. In response, the University filed Federal Unemployment Tax Act returns for the period from December 1, 1970, through December 31, 1975. Thereafter, the University filed a claim for refund of the tax paid with those returns, and the claim was rejected by the Internal Revenue

Service, which gave rise to litigation between the parties, a trial in the Federal District court for South Carolina, and a decision rendered in 1978.[27]

The nature of the discrimination practiced by Bob Jones University changed substantially during the period in question. Prior to 1971, Bob Jones University had excluded blacks completely. From 1971 to May, 1975, the University accepted no applications from unmarried black students with the exception, since 1973 of staff members who had been at the University four years or longer. After May 29, 1975, unmarried blacks were permitted to enroll, but a disciplinary rule was added to prevent interracial dating and marriage.

In the 1978 *Bob Jones University* case, the District Court determined that the University's primary purpose is religious and that its principal activities relate to instruction in and advancement and propagation of its religious beliefs. Therefore, it is most properly categorized for purposes of Section 501(c)(3) as a religious organization.[28] The Court concluded that the Service's revocation of Bob Jones University's tax-exempt status was improper since the "public policy" limitation on tax-exempt status enunciated by the Internal Revenue Service is applicable only to educational organizations. The Court acknowledged that while "there is substantial authority to support a finding that there exists a federal public policy which condemns racial discrimination in educational institutions," it concluded that ". . . there is no corresponding clearly declared federal public policy against the practice of racial discrimination by religious organizations such as plaintiff."[29]

Further, the Service's revocation of Bob Jones University's tax exemption because of policies based on the organization's religious beliefs unconstitutionally infringed upon the University's right to the free exercise of religion. The Court stated that "to condition the availability of benefits upon plaintiff's willingness to violate a cardinal principle of its religious faith effectively penalizes the free exercise of its constitutional liberties."[30]

Finally, the Court raised the fundamental issues and the dangers inherent in the Service's revoking tax exemptions of religious institutions for violations of federal public policy.

> Federal public policy is constantly changing. When can something be said to become federal public policy? Who decides? With a change of federal public policy, the law would change without congressional action—a dilemma of constitutional proportions. Citizens could no longer rely on the law of Section 501(c)(3) as it is written, but would then rely on the IRS to tell them what it had decided the law to be for that particular day. Our laws would change at the whim of some nonelected IRS personnel, producing bureaucratic tyranny.[31]

Without addressing itself to any of these fundamental policy problems raised by the District Court, the Fourth Circuit, on December 30, 1980, reversed the decision of the District Court and upheld the Service's revocation of the tax-exempt status of Bob Jones University.[32]

The Fourth Circuit appears to have focused on Bob Jones University primarily as an educational institution rather than a religious organization. Specifically, the Court stated:

> Bob Jones University is subject to the revenue procedures prohibiting racial discrimination in private schools. The University is an educational institution as well as a religious one . . . and the rulings and procedures promulgated by the Service apply to all private religious schools. We decline to create an exception for religion-based schools where the Service has made none.[33]

Thus, the Court of Appeals avoided deciding the difficult question of whether a religious organization *per se* is subject to the public-policy limitation imposed on other tax-exempt organizations. It is significant that in its brief on appeal, the government stated that "churches and similar religious organizations are concededly not subject to the non-discrimination condition on federal charitable tax benefits."[34] But the Fourth Circuit appears to have made no such "concession" in its opinion, but seemed to imply that a religious organization *per se* would be subject to the public-policy limitation.

Indeed, the Fourth Circuit rejected the limited purview of the doctrine evolving out of the *Tank Truck* line of cases, stating that "unlike Section 162, Section 501(c)(3) is rooted in public policy considerations wholly apart from the broad basic policy of taxing 'net, not * * * gross, income.' The public policy limitation, therefore, need not be so narrowly applied."[35] Accordingly, it appears that the Fourth Circuit is giving considerable support to the application of the public policy doctrine to all tax-exempt organizations, including churches and other purely religious organizations.

The dissenting Fourth Circuit opinion of Judge Widener in *Bob Jones* insisted that, because the District Court's findings of fact were not determined to be clearly erroneous, the Court of Appeals was bound to accept as correct the finding that Bob Jones University is a religious organization. Accordingly, Judge Widener stated that the case at bar was not one dealing with the right of the government to interfere with the internal affairs of a school operated by a church but rather with the internal affairs of the church itself, and he maintained that the Internal Revenue Service could not revoke the exemption granted to a religious organization on the grounds that it was not operating in accordance with public policy.

Judge Widener's dissent explained that, in making public-policy evaluations, the courts must consider the Constitution, laws and judicial decisions of the United States and "primarily the Acts of Congress."[36] In actuality, Congress has been emitting certain signals with respect to religious schools which conflicted with those cited by the majority opinion in its definition of public policy, namely, certain provisions of the Civil Rights Act of 1964 which excepted from its purview certain religious organizations, and the Ashbrook Amendment to an appropriation act which was designed to prohibit the use of funds by the Internal Revenue Service to revoke the tax-exemption of religious-oriented schools.

"Bureaucratic Tyranny"

The differing perceptions of public policy offered by the majority and dissenting opinions in the Fourth Circuit's decision in *Bob Jones* illustrate dramatically the problems envisioned by the District Court if the Internal Revenue Service is made the arbiter of what constitutes public policy. If such revocations are based on whether an organization's policies fail to satisfy a particular revenue agent's perception of what the public policy of the nation is at a particular point in time, "bureaucratic tyranny"—if not infringement on the constitutional rights of religious institutions—could indeed result.

The *Bob Jones* case contains another important lesson. No matter how repugnant the doctrines of a particular institution may seem to many (in the case of *Bob Jones University*, its doctrine of racial discrimination), it must be remembered that what is at stake is the constitutional guarantee of free exercise. So long as the institution in question is classifiable as "religious," its right to function within the framework of its own religious doctrines without governmental interference should generally be defended.[37] However, it must be emphasized that the religious doctrines in question must predate the development of a Federal public policy in a particular area. Thus, only pre-existing doctrines of religious organizations which because of subsequent development in the definition of what constitutes Federal public policy should be "grandfathered" to protect such organizations from loss of tax exemption. In addition, a new religious organization claiming to have a doctrine which violates a sharply defined Federal policy proscribing particular types of conduct should not be allowed to obtain tax exemption.

Perhaps the key issue is the role of the Internal Revenue Service as the arbiter of what the national public policy is and the decision-maker of whether a particular organization contravenes that policy. Without clear signals from Congress, such determinations will be made on a highly subjective basis.

In view of the trend of the cases, as evidenced by the Fourth Circuit's decision in the *Bob Jones University* case, Congress should delineate more clearly the parameters for the application of the public-policy doctrine to religious organizations. Particularly in the highly sensitive area of possible infringement of First Amendment rights, if the tax exemption of religious institutions is to be conditioned on adherence to public policy, then that public policy should be articulated clearly by

Congress, amending the statutory scheme under Section 501(c)(3) if necessary.

To minimize the infringement of the public-policy doctrine on the First Amendment rights of religious organizations, Congress could except specifically such organizations from the purview of that doctrine.[38] Thus, an organization which was primarily religious in its organization and operation would not be faced with the threat of the revocation of its tax-exempt status if it seemed to contravene public policy. Although the determination of whether an organization was *primarily* religious would be made initially by the Internal Revenue Service and ultimately by the courts, it would appear that such determination would constitute but a slight infringement on the constitutional rights of such organization.

However, while this proposal may lessen the potential constitutional infringements of an "overreaching" public-policy doctrine on religious organizations, it does not address the more fundamental question of defining "public policy." Clear, precise guidelines should be drafted (akin to those enacted by Congress in the Tax Reform Act of 1969 with respect to codifying the public-policy limitation on business deductions) in order to achieve an objective statutory basis upon which the public-policy doctrine is to be applied to tax-exempt organizations—if at all.

Thus, for example, Congress might amend the Code to provide that all Section 501(c)(3) organizations must comport with "public policy"—as defined by a new section of the Code, which might be titled Section 501(k). That section could stipulate that any organization which discriminates on the basis of race, religion or sex, where such discrimination bears no compelling relationship to the purposes of the organization, should not be accorded the benefits of tax exemption or, if it already is exempt, its exemption should be revoked, with the proviso, however, that this limitation would not apply to an organization which is primarily religious in its structure and operation—so long as its discriminatory doctrines, if any, predated the development of a sharply defined Federal policy in that area.

This hypothetical definition of "public policy," while providing some uniform statutory guidelines for the application of the public-policy limitation to tax-exempt organizations, raises as many questions as it answers (e.g., what is a "compelling" relationship?). Thus it is clear that fashioning such a statutory framework must be the subject of intensive congressional debate. It is the responsibility of the entire tax-exempt community—and perhaps most particularly the religious sector of that community—to focus congressional attention on this pressing and sensitive issue.

The IRS Cracks Down on Coalitions

JOHN E. STUMBO

On April 27, 1977, the Board of Church and Society of the United Methodist Church was notified by the District Director of the Maryland District that the Internal Revenue Service was auditing the Board in regard to its relationship with the National Coalition to Ban Handguns and the Coalition for a New Foreign and Military Policy. Neither of the coalitions involved had applied for or received tax-exempt status for the separate coalition entity prior to the audit. After several months of working through the audits with the Service, the Board decided to terminate its administrative relationships with the coalitions and to cease permitting them to operate under the aegis of the Board's exemption. Though the Board continued as a very active member of both coalitions, they were encouraged to seek their own independent status as tax-exempt organizations forthwith.

The purpose of this paper is to recount and examine the basis for the Board's decision and the resultant position of the Service in the audits. The Board, through several of its staff members, had been instrumental in organizing those coalitions. The staff had served in officer and leadership roles in both coalitions. Though the coalitions were formed as separate jural entities, they were made up of member organizations which either had their own separate Section 501(c)(3) status or could trace their connectional relationship to a parent organization's Section 501(c)(3) status. The coming together of separate Section 501(c)(3) organizations or connected agencies for a common purpose, employing the coalitional structure, frames the unique issue of this paper. The result of the audit would imply that the whole is not always equal to the sum of its parts.

Coalitional enterprise has become an increasingly attractive format for various religious bodies to join forces for common programmatic purposes. Acting independently, they often find themselves with inadequate funds to work effectively in a particular area of social concern. By joining forces, they are able to broaden their effective program and to intensify their impact in many diverse areas of concern. The collective mind and conscience represented in the coalition provide technical expertise that each member might not be able to afford by itself. In fact, the effectiveness of the two coalitions which were the indirect subjects of the audit in question perhaps prompted opposition forces to complain to the Service, asking questions of tax status and the deductibility of contributions made to support them.

Frequently, audits of the exemption status of charitable organizations are triggered by effective work done on issues of social concern when the opposing interests do not have tax-exempt status or their contributors cannot deduct contributions. In addition, sometimes the "opposing force" may be the same government which also regulates the tax status of the charity. As will be indicated later in this paper, the original impetus for the present limitations on "lobbying" emanated from such differential tax treatment.

From their beginning, the coalitions expected to operate under the tax exemption of one of their member organizations, and the Board was the one chosen. The Board expected that the use of its tax status would be allowed only if it had significant connection with the coalitions. For this reason and others, the Board was well represented on the governing bodies of each of the coalitions from their inception. Their financial affairs were managed by the Board. In addition, the staff of the coalitions were classified as employees of the Board. (The importance of "control" by the Board will be discussed later in this paper.)

The coalitions were not unbiased on the issues, nor did they ever intend to be. The names chosen for them typify their position. The nature of their work was to educate the general public on the facts and to engender action by the populace in support of the philosophies which they espoused. An examination of the literature and activities used, particularly on banning handguns, did not show much evidence of direct lobbying (contact with Congress by staff) and a minimum of so-called "grass roots lobbying" (encouraging voters to contact Congress in support of or opposition to particular legislation). The Service made some early assumptions that the activities of the coalitions were "lobbying" activities proscribed by the Internal Revenue Code. As will be discussed, these assumptions may have been incorrect.

In examining the legal issues involved, we must begin with a brief review of Section 501(c)(3), its original rationale and its later development. Section 501(c)(3) in its current form describes certain organizations that are exempted from taxation by Section 501(a) as follows:

> . . . Corporations . . . organized and operated exclusively for religious, charitable . . . purposes . . . no part of the net earnings of which inures to the benefit of any private stockholder or individual, no substantial part of the activities of which is carrying on propaganda, or otherwise attempting, to influence legislation, (except as otherwise provided in subsection (h)), and which does not participate in, or intervene in (including the publishing or distributing of statements), any political campaign on behalf of any candidate for public office. . . .

The second important aspect of Section 501(c)(3) status is that it permits contributors to such entities to deduct their contributions from their taxable income according to Section 170.

The basis for the granting of tax-exempt status has a long history, a detailed analysis of which is beyond the scope of this paper. However, a key conceptual element is *public benefit*. The "charitable" organizations, including organizations established exclusively for religious purposes, enhance the public good, relieve poverty, foster good public morality, help maintain values which perpetuate society, etc. The revenue code does not define "charitable" or "religious." The "public benefit" criteria goes back to the Statutes of Elizabeth in the England of 1601.

In determining whether an organization satisfies the statutory requirements for Section 501(c)(3) status, two broad tests are randomly applied. The "means" test considers whether the means of the organization are "charitable" in nature.[1] A second test more directly on point is the non-inurement of private benefit or individual purpose. It has its roots in the public benefit rationale. The statute itself prohibits inurement of benefit to private concerns.[2]

The noninurement test and rationale prompted Congress to amend the tax exemption code provision in 1934 to add the limitations on lobbying and political activity. A group of private businesses had established the National Economic League as a tax-exempt organization to engage in lobbying activities. It is important to recall that at that time such expenses were *not* deductible by private business whereas their contributions to the League were. It is clear that a major impetus for the passage of the limitation was in response to a concern by Congress and the Service that private business was being allowed a tax advantage by doing something indirectly they could not do directly.[3] Limited deductions for political activities have been subsequently allowed to private business. Therefore, the original rationale for the 1934 amendment has been obviated.[4] However, the limitation has remained and the Courts and Congress have simply developed a different rationale for the continued application and interpretation of the limitation.

Though it may seem academic to emphasize the legal rationale, the Internal Revenue Code, if left without definitions and employing "loose" language, gives license for broad and varied interpretations by Courts and regulatory bodies of Section 501(c)(3) and its attendant sections. Therefore, any thorough examination of a particular fact situation calls one back to the basic rationale.

Unlike most areas of tax concern, the area of Section 501(c)(3) religious activities is complicated by the balancing of Constitutional First Amendment mandates with the Internal Revenue Code. For example, if Congress, through Section 501 or the Service through regulations, attempts to define what is religious, such a definition, no matter how written, will result in some organizations which claim to be religious being determined not to be. Would not such a definition and the resulting application result in the "establishment" of some religions at the expense of others? Obviously, if such were to occur, then the guarantees of the First Amendment would be violated. This concern about "establishment" was the basis of the objection by many religious bodies to the possible inclusion of churches or church bodies in the lobbying ceiling amendment in 1976.[5] The concern was that I.R.C. Section 501(h) would result in more specific limitations on lobbying activities by churches, which would be an improper regulation of the free expression of religion. In addition, churches are not required to file informational returns, and Section 501(h) requires such returns from all electing organizations.

Courts have avoided defining "religious," as demonstrated in *United States* v. *Ballard*:

> Man's relation to his God was made no concern of the state. He was granted the right to worship as he pleased and to answer to no man for the verity of his religious views. The religious views espoused by respondents might seem incredible, if not preposterous, to most·people. But if those doctrines are subject to trial before a jury charged with finding their truth or falsity, then the same can be done with the religious beliefs of any sect. When the triers of fact undertake that task, they enter a forbidden domain.[6]

However, they have maintained that religious purpose and motive must be primary in "thought, word and deed" of a Section 501(c)(3) organization.[7] Therefore, against this background the issue narrows to examine specifically whether religious bodies may engage in political expression and social reform activities without "lobbying" in violation of the limitations of I.R.C. Section 501(c)(3).

One other factor employed by Courts in reviewing "lobbying" activities has been to interpret the word "substantial" in Section 501(c)(3). At least one court quantified the test, by saying that less than five percent of budget expenditures was *in*substantial.[8] However, rarely would "lobbying" activities exceed five percent of a religious body's budget, and the Courts have moved to more qualitative tests. A review of facts and circumstances weighed in the context of the objectives of the organization seems to be the most frequent judicial review process of late.[9] Treas. Reg. Section 1.501(c)(3)-1(c)(3)(i) & (ii) reads as follows:

> . . . For this purpose, an organization will be regarded as attempting to influence legislation if the organization
>   a. Contacts, or urges the public to contact, members of a legislative body for the purpose of proposing, supporting, or opposing legislation; or
>   b. Advocates the adoption or rejection of legislation.

This regulation, though appearing to be objective in its approach, really shows a qualitative test process. The subjective tests also include

suggestions that, just as courts should not determine what is religious, charitable entities should not intrude into politics. For example, the widely known and learned jurist, Judge Learned Hand, said in *Slee* v. *Commissioner*, "Political agitation as such is outside the statute, however innocent the aim."[10]

At times the Service or Courts will admit that the purpose of the organization is religious or charitable but will examine the activity for "lobbying" characteristics. This technique results in the balancing of attempts to influence legislation with overall purpose. This is the famous case involving Billie James Hargis and his radio ministry, in which the court upheld the revocation of Hargis' exemption for substantial lobbying activity.[11] Another case at about the same time by a different court further entrenches the same concepts and methodologies of interpretation.[12]

When the activity of a religious body is examined for "lobbying" activities, there is a serious question whether courts in recent times have attempted to decide whether the activity represents a carrying out of the fundamental doctrinal beliefs of the body. Historically, "speaking out" on political issues has at times been found to be authorized, the rationale being that the beliefs espoused were so fundamental and entrenched in the basic theology of the religious body that the purpose or motive was allowed to be carried out in the political forum. A case in point is *Girard Trust Co.* v. *Commissioner*, which concerned the efforts of the former Board of Temperance of the Methodist Church, an antecedent of the Board of Church and Society. The Court determined that temperance was fundamental to the theological doctrine of the Church and, therefore, advocating temperance was permitted.[13] Can opposition to handguns and the violence and harm to human beings they perpetuate or a foreign policy based on peace and self-development of peoples be any less fundamental to the theology of the religious bodies in the coalitions at issue?[14]

In a recent case, not involving a Section 501(c)(3) organization, the Supreme Court has affirmed the right of a corporation to spend funds to advertise for the defeat of a state referendum as a guaranteed right of free speech under the First Amendment. Though the case does not involve a religious body, it does include religious and charitable analysis and seriously threatens the validity of the rationale for the decision in the *Christian Echoes* case.[15] The basis of the decision and its importance to this discussion is Justice Powell's comment that the First Amendment should not allow the government to channel the expression of views. An analysis of the case simply reinforces the concern about the balancing of the rights under the First Amendment against the privileged tax status of religious and charitable entities.

It is hard to find a consistent rationale for decision-making in this area because loose statutory language is perpetuated, "religious" and "charitable" are not defined, the courts resist examining basic theological doctrine of religious bodies and, finally, there is a strong resistance to risking conflict with the First Amendment. The penalization of political expression by religious groups on political issues stems from the unwillingness of the Courts to confront the basic issues squarely and to fashion a consistent rationale and application.

For example, if the original rationale, not to allow private business a deduction for the costs of lobbying, is no longer valid, then either a solid new rationale ought to be developed or the law ought to be revised. How valid is the granting of preferential tax treatment in exchange for limitations on freedom of speech and the free exercise of religion?

When the religious bodies come together for the purpose of forming coalitions, a new jural entity comes into existence. This phenomenon creates a unique problem in application of the Section 501(c)(3) statute. The first impulse is to attempt to qualify the coalition as a Section 501(c)(3) organization individually and on its own merits. However, it was the experience of the Board during the audit process that several factors make the task very difficult, if not impossible.

In the audit in question, little evidence could be found that the Service was willing to examine the "doctrine" of the entity, but rather it wished summarily to assume that "lobbying" activities were the coalitions' primary purpose for being. Though the literature used by each was submitted, it seems unlikely that it was examined closely with a view to determining fundamental purpose or distinguishing between education of the public on the issues versus proposing legislative action or grass-roots lobbying. One of the distinctions between the members and the coalition is probably the easier ability of the members to demonstrate a theological statement or foundation of belief as a rationale for speaking out. Though coalitions are formed around issues which are seen as carrying out the members' theology, they very often have no distinct doctrine except as it is developed to frame their actions.

The other alternative to independent tax status for the coalition was that taken by the Board. In permitting the coalitions to use the tax exemption of the United Methodist Church, the Board had to demonstrate "control" over the coalitions. As already described, the Board had exercised effective *administrative* control, but it became obvious early in the audit that the Service was looking, not only for administrative control, but also programmatic and substantive control. Minutes of both the Board and the coalitions were requested. The expressed purpose for this review was to determine if the Board had framed and dictated policy to the coalitions.

The author would submit that the criteria of control which the Service used were not justified. There would appear to be two different sets of criteria for determining the necessary relationship between the Board and the coalitions in order to permit them to operate under the aegis of the tax-exempt status of the United Methodist Church. A parallelism could be drawn to the legal concept of parent-subsidiary relationships in corporate law, in which great programmatic latitude is given to the subsidiary to operate without daily supervision and decision-review by the parent. The second possibility would be the "integral agency" theory that is found elsewhere in the Internal Revenue Code. In considering the obligation of employers to withhold income tax and social security taxes on clergy, the Service has used language in various regulations which permit self-employed (non-withholding) treatment on several conditions, one of which is that the employer is an "integral agency" of the religious body. In this instance, as well as the first, "ownership" is shown by the selection of the governing body of the agency, not whether the parent body "controls" the daily decision-making.

It is doubtful whether a true coalition can tolerate the type of control that the Service seems to require to justify using a member's tax exemption. The nature of the coalitional effort is that several independent religious and charitable bodies come together for a purpose. Each of these members is autonomous and has its own reasons for participation in the coalition. They exist substantially in equal capacity and relationship, and to deviate from that in order to allow one of the members to control, in the full sense of the word, the functions and operations of the coalition would seriously jeopardize its continuation. It would no longer be a common enterprise of equal partners, but all of the partners would be obliged to subordinate themselves to one in order to use its tax exemption. The result would no longer be a coalition but a hegemony, to which the other partners could not accede without truncating their own nature and character.

If the control criterion cannot be satisfied, then the coalitions are left with the need to qualify themselves independently as Section 501(c)(3) organizations. In order to do this in the future, it is imperative that they test the criteria of the Service in granting the status. They must overcome the tendency of the Service unfairly to assume that their program is strictly political and constitutes "lobbying." If the tax exemption is to be retained, then the Service, and ultimately the Courts, must be willing to refrain from jumping to conclusions. Not all political expression is lobbying. Religious bodies do not enter the political arena for personal gain; they do so to carry out sincere religious views on the right course for the whole society.

What is the future in this area of the law for coalitional activities? It would seem that they are caught in the unfortunate position of having actions and operational style confused with motive by the Service, which precludes the analysis of the organization with reference to the basic rationale for the lobbying prohibition.

One other distinction which must be understood is that between advocacy and education. Even with the present statutory language, "lobbying" implies advocacy. There is also case precedent permitting education. Education about the danger of handguns is not "lobbying." It may be advocacy of a philosophy of peace and human welfare, but that "public benefit" fits squarely with the original rationale permitting tax-exempt status. Government through its courts and tax agencies has grown increasingly critical of those who question the continuation of the status quo.

The Service and, in turn, the Court need to face squarely the issue of the conflict between the guarantees assured by the First Amendment and the tax status recognized by Section 501(c)(3). For reasons previously stated in this paper, until that confrontation is satisfied, there will always be reasons and excuses to deny coalitions independent tax-exempt status. The Coalition to Ban Handguns was successful in obtaining Section 501(c)(4) status, which permits exemption from income taxation but denies them the ability to attract funding from tax-deductible contributions. In addition, (c)(4) status imposes restrictions on (c)(3) organizations' making contributions to the coalition.

What is the cost of privileged tax status to religious bodies and coalitions if it results in their inability through coalitional activity to carry out their ministry in the political and social fields? To deny religious bodies the freedom for a political and social ministry by the limitations on tax exemption creates the risk of the silencing of their social and political criticism. Such a result constitutes an unlawful prohibition of the right of the free exercise of religion and freedom of speech. Religious bodies need to continue to carry out their ministry where they find it. They have a justification for their presence in the political and social scene, and they will need to continue to work at designing new systems of operation.

Ultimately, if they are faithful to their task, they will always walk up to the line of risk and doubt. In doing so, they are going to have some setbacks and adverse decisions. The loss to a coalition of its tax-exempt status, or at least its inability to offer tax deductibility for contributions, should not prevent the existence of coalitions or their ministry in the political and social scene. And if it came to that, the increased cost of religious ministry as a result of taxation would not necessarily stifle the carrying on of the ministry. If individuals are committed to the ministry of the religious body, then whatever extra cost there is, they will be willing to pay. The tragedy of the problem is that the government would perpetuate the suggestion that political and social criticism by religious bodies in a free society must be eschewed in order for them to retain their privileged tax status.

Concordia College Challenges the IRS

PHILIP E. DRAHEIM

The Lutheran Church—Missouri Synod has been maneuvering for a battle with the Internal Revenue Service since January, 1977, over whether its colleges must file annual informational returns pursuant to the regulations adopted in that month defining the term "integrated auxiliary" as used in Section 6033 of the Internal Revenue Code. Section 6033 requires all organizations exempt from taxation under Section 501 to file Form 990 every year *except* "churches, their integrated auxiliaries, and conventions or associations of churches" (and a few other kinds of organizations).[1]

Form 990 is a long and detailed form requiring the organization to report its income and expenses, its activities, officers and major contributors each year. It calls for extensive information that many churches feel the government cannot constitutionally demand of them, presumably the reason that Congress excluded churches from the requirement to provide it. But the question remains as to which organizations themselves are "churches . . . conventions or associations of churches," and which are related to churches so closely as to share in that "mandatory exception." Filing the informational return is onerous, but that is not the reason for the church's objection. The Lutheran Church—Missouri Synod is more concerned about the principle involved: whether the government can declare a church college is *not* a part of the church when the church says it *is.*

Concordia College is one of twelve colleges which are among the 53 civil law corporations that together comprise the Synod, and it is preparing to act as a test case on behalf of all the rest. The Synod, as an international, multi-corporation church denomination, claims the mandatory exception given to churches and conventions or associations of churches in Section 6033 for all of its component corporations—without regard to the phrase "integrated auxiliaries." A brief description of the Synod's structure will clarify that claim.

The Synod

The Synod is a "union" of Lutheran congregations which is the second largest Lutheran church body in the United States. The Synod's 6,043 congregations, encompassing 2,720,000 individual members, profess the same religious beliefs and have joined together in order to achieve certain religious objectives which they could not achieve separately. (The term "Missouri" in the name of the Synod does not mean that its activities are limited to the State of Missouri, but merely recalls the fact that the Synod had its origin in Missouri more than 130 years ago.)

The Synod, as such a union of congregations, operates under a Constitution and Bylaws which govern the Synod in all its component parts. The Synod, almost from the time of its origin, established itself as a collectivity of component parts, which usually are civil law corporations. Among the first of these corporations were the districts (of which there are now thirty-five operating within the United States). The districts carry out the objects and purposes of the Synod within the state or states assigned to them by the Synod.

Also included in that collection of corporations since early in the Synod's history are the educational institutions which together comprise a system of education established by the Synod to train pastors, teaching ministers and other church workers. (There are other educational institutions to which the Synod is related which are not component parts of the Synod because they are not operating under and subject to the provisions of its constitution and bylaws.)

Others in the collection of corporations are the Synod's official archives, the Synod's arm for editing and disseminating Bibles and other religious literature, the Synod's organization for receiving and handling gifts and bequests, and the Synod's organization for aiding its member congregations in acquiring land and building churches, schools and related facilities.

This union of congregations operating under a constitution has been recognized as an exempt organization by the IRS, most recently confirmed on January 8, 1965.

The Synod's Educational System of Seminaries and Colleges

The educational institutions which are component parts of the Synod form a system of education extending from the high school level through the seminaries and colleges which produce the pastoral ministers, teaching ministers and other workers who serve in the congregations of the Synod. Each of the institutions in the system of education is linked to the other institutions and to other component parts of the Synod in carrying out the Synod's objectives, including finding and training full-time church workers. (Each of the institutions, of course, has students who do not anticipate becoming workers in the church or who ultimately decide that full-time church work is not the vocation to which they wish to devote their lives. However, on the average, approximately ninety percent of the students at all of these institutions are Lutheran, and approximately sixty-five percent continue their education in other institutions of the Synod, or, upon graduating, enter one form or another of full-time church work.)

The governance of all of the seminaries and colleges rests in boards of the Synod, established and governed by bylaws of the Synod's constitution, and elected by the Synod in convention. One of the Synod's bylaws provides: "The Synod administers each educational institution of the Synod through a Board of Control, which is to provide effective local administrative organization to facilitate the achievement of the purposes for which the Synod operates and maintains the respective institution, and to foster and safeguard its religious, academic and financial interests in it."

Two other bylaws of the Synod establish the number and qualifications for members of the Boards of Control of the seminaries and colleges. The president of each seminary or college, being the chief executive officer of the institution as a component part of the Synod, is selected by procedures established by the Synod and by "electors" of the Synod, not by the governing board of the educational institution.

Other provisions of the Synod's bylaws deal with the policies of the educational institutions, the selection of faculty members and other crucial matters in the governance of the institution.

The educational institutions are component parts of the Synod, both under the legal relationship in the structure and by reason of their role in carrying out certain of the functions of the Synod. Specifically those functions are set forth in the Synod's constitution, Article III, paragraphs 2, 3 and 6, as follows:

2. The joint extension of the Kingdom of God;
3. The training of ministers and teachers for service in the Evangelical Lutheran Church; and
6. The furtherance of Christian parochial schools and of a thorough instruction for Confirmation; . . . .

The educational system of the Synod exists in order to train individuals who can, individually and through the congregations, extend the Kingdom of God and provide for worship, education, service and a basis for life firmly established on the Christian faith and Lutheran doctrine. The Synod contends that without its educational institutions it would be unable effectively and efficiently to carry out these functions.

Legislative History of the "Integrated Auxiliary" Problem[2]

In order to understand Section 6033 and the Regulation, it is necessary to know their origin and purpose. Prior to 1969, the exception from filing Form 990 afforded by Section 6033 extended to each "religious organization described in Section 501(c)(3)." There were other exceptions for certain educational organizations, charitable organizations primarily supported by contributions from the general public, and organizations described in 501(c)(3) which were operated, supervised, or controlled by or in connection with a religious organization. None of these exceptions was limited to an organization which fell into only one of those categories; the exception clearly was available even if an organization would qualify under two or more of those categories.

In considering tax reform in 1969, the House of Representatives determined that the exceptions from filing information returns should be entirely repealed. When religious organizations suggested to the Senate that such repeal might raise First Amendment issues as to them, the Senate proposed that the exception be continued for "churches, conventions or associations of churches." Senator Wallace Bennett (R., Utah), a Mormon, insisted that the exception be available to "churches, *their auxiliaries*, conventions or associations of churches." The term "auxiliaries" has a distinct ecclesiastical meaning in the Mormon church, but it had no prior legal meaning whatsoever. The joint conference committee adopted the final wording of Section 6033 with the words proposed by Senator Bennett, except that at the behest of the Treasury it added the word "integrated" to modify "auxiliaries." The only indication in the legislative history of what this meant was the Senate Finance Committee's statement that the explanation of "integrated auxiliaries" was the same as that which had previously been given for "auxiliaries." (That explanation was that "among the auxiliary organizations to which this exemption applies are the mission societies and the church's religious schools, youth groups, and men's and women's organizations, and inter-church organizations of local units qualifying as local auxiliaries."[3])

The Writing of the Regulation

After struggling for eight years with the meaning of "integrated auxiliaries" in Section 6033, the Internal Revenue Service finally issued a regulation purporting to define it. The first attempt evoked such protests from religious bodies that a revision was made and promulgated in 1977.[4] The gist of the regulation is that in determining whether an organization is an "integrated auxiliary of a church, convention or association of churches" and thus exempt from filing informational returns, the Internal Revenue Service will (without consulting the church, convention or association of churches involved, as might seem the obvious course) determine for itself:

1. that the claimant organization is described in Section 501(c)(3); and
2. that its principal activity is exclusively religious, that is, if it were applying for its own exemption, it would be entitled to a *religious*, rather than a charitable, educational or other, exemption (among those listed in Section 501(c)(3)).

The problem with that Regulation, which has been widely expressed in the religious community, is that it seems to allow, perhaps even to require, the government to determine what is "religious." After all, it is urged, if the filing of an information return is to be predicated on whether the primary purpose of an organization is "exclusively religious," someone in the government (beginning with the IRS and finally the courts) must judge whether some or all of the activities of the particular organization are "religious." Treasury, of course, obviously believes that it is unnecessary under the Regulation even to address the question of whether an activity is religious; it would argue that it is sufficient merely to be able to show that the activity is, or also is, educational, charitable or motivated in any way other than "religious" that would qualify the organization as an exempt organization under Section 501(c)(3).

Though the Treasury might theoretically have the better of this argument, the Regulation, as a practical matter, is both offensive and unworkable. The offense which is given by the Regulation lies in the fact that many perceive the term "integrated auxiliaries," defined on the basis of whether certain activities are or are not "exclusively religious," to be, not a neutral concept, but a biased implication that those activities are not motivated by the sense of mission or ministry which is declared as *the* motivation of those engaged in them. Indeed, it can often be demonstrated that, but for this sense of mission or ministry, many organizations would not conduct or give the same degree of priority to certain activities, notwithstanding the educational, charitable or other value which they may have. It is this perceived "tilt" of the Regulation to which the Lutheran Council in the U.S.A. addressed itself when it said:

> . . . The heart of the issue is that the regulation relative to "integrated auxiliaries" seeks to impose on the churches a definition of "religious" and "church" which the churches cannot accept theologically, one which constitutes an unwarranted intrusion by the government into the affairs of the churches. The narrow definition introduces confusion within the churches and their agencies and institutions. Questions are raised in the agencies and their constituencies about whether these ministries are considered to be part of the churches' mission. . . . These agencies and institutions perform ministries which are essential to the churches' mission and must not be put in a different category from the strictly sacerdotal functions of the churches. (See "The Nature of the Church and its Relationship with Government," Lutheran Council in the U.S.A., 1979.)

The offense is deeply felt because the tax laws give signals that the integrated auxiliary definition represents a prying apart of a church from its agencies. To many people, those signals are stronger than the ones suggested by Alvin D. Lurie, then IRS Assistant Commissioner for Employee Plans and Exempt Organizations, in his address to the

Sixteenth Religious Liberty Conference.[5] Mr. Lurie talked about "unmistakable signals" from Congress of what was intended by use of the term "integrated auxiliaries." He said that:

> . . . the issue addressed in the Regulation is not which churches should file returns, but rather how to identify those organizations which, though corporately separated from a church, are so closely integrated with and auxiliary to the church *as to have been meant by Congress to enjoy the same constitutional immunity from public accountability reserved to the church itself.* (Emphasis added.)

The Concept of "Secular Counterparts"

Mr. Lurie then said that he would have been successful in his presentation if he had communicated that *an organization is not an integrated auxiliary if it has "secular counterparts."*[6] From this, one might conclude that, to the extent the secular community is or becomes involved in any activity, that involvement alone preempts a claim of protection under the free exercise clause of the First Amendment for that activity or at least denies the same degree of protection for that activity as carried out for reasons of religious faith or tenets as there would be if the activity did not have "secular counterparts." Thus, perhaps for the first time in history, the right to religious liberty without undue regulation by government as to any particular activity will depend on whether others choose to perform that same activity, but not in the name of religion. Think of the scope of that!

The Regulation is unworkable because, if the reason for the mandatory exception is to assure First Amendment protections, the definition of "integrated auxiliaries" cannot be consistently applied so as to achieve that result. The abstract illustrations in the Regulation do no more (and do not pretend to do more) than illustrate. To the extent they are advanced as rules, as has been done to the Synod's colleges, there is an improper application of the Regulation because proper application requires analysis of specific facts.

However, analysis of specific facts is also unacceptable. A case-by-case application would require in-depth evaluation by government of facts which could only lead to a subjective conclusion on motivation. For example, elementary and secondary education in church-operated schools is believed to be one of the very important, but not absolutely essential, functions of congregations of the Synod. Generally congregations of the Lutheran Church in America, on the other hand, do not view such schools as particularly important compared to other activities of mission and ministry. Certain other churches believe that such education is so essential that not providing it is a wrong by the church, and not utilizing it when provided is a sin by the parents. In which of these situations is operating a school an "exclusively religious" activity? Or are none of them "exclusively religious" (even though the people who have organized and supported them have done so as an exercise of their religious beliefs) because Treasury has surveyed the land and found that most or all of the functions in those programs of education are also being provided by public schools and private non-religious schools?

Finally, there is no substantial basis for believing that Congress ever contemplated an "exclusively religious" test in determining whether an organization is an "integrated auxiliary." Neither is there adequate showing that Congress intended that the term "integrated auxiliary" should be defined so as to require the kind of initial evaluation and continuing or periodic surveillance of the organization and ultimate subjective analysis of motivation required under the Regulation.

A spokesman for the Treasury sought to justify the definition on what seems to be an "end-justifies-the-means" argument. Charles Rumph, Special Assistant to the Commissioner for Exempt Organization Matters, is reported to have exhorted the churches testifying against the proposed Regulation to "let the sunshine in" by letting the government and the public know about their financial affairs. The great danger is that, although the end result (filing the return) may be neutral or even good, the means of achieving it can remove or significantly dilute the protection otherwise afforded by the free exercise clause of the First Amendment. Under current constitutional principles enunciated by the Supreme Court, the government must show that prohibiting or regulating a particular activity motivated by religion is necessary because of a compelling state interest. This regulation seems to relieve the government of the obligation to make that showing. In fact, it seems designed to subsume religiously motivated conduct into the category of similar activities carried on by "secular counterparts," and thus to deny it the protection to which it is entitled as the "free exercise" of religion.

The Synod Challenges the IRS on Two Grounds

The Synod claims that each of its educational institutions is exempt from filing Form 990 because of the mandatory exception from filing afforded by Section 6033(a)(2)(A)(i) to a church or convention or association of churches.

The Synod argues:

1. Applying the Regulations promulgated under Section 6033 so as to deny to the Synod's educational institutions the exception afforded to a church or convention or association of churches is in error, contrary to both fact and law.
2. But if the Regulation is construed to be properly applied to the educational institutions of the Synod, then the Regulation itself is invalid either because (a) it is inconsistent with the law or because (b) it violates the religion clauses of the First Amendment, or both.

1. Invalid Application of the Regulation.

The exception afforded under Section 6033 to "churches, their integrated auxiliaries, and conventions or associations of churches"[7] should not be confined to those church bodies formed as a single corporation but must also be extended to all of the corporations which comprise multi-corporation church bodies. Whether a certain corporation is a component part of a multi-corporation church body is a fact question. Whether the mandatory exception is to be afforded a certain corporation which is a component part of a church or convention or association of churches is a question of law.

As to the question of fact, the Synod believes that its own structure must be the only source for a determination of whether its educational institutions are part of the Synod or are merely "auxiliary" to it.

As to the question of law, despite the many instances of the use of the term in the Code and regulations, there is no meaningful legal definition of "church," and there has never been an adequate effort by Treasury or the IRS to define the phrase "convention or association of churches." However, there certainly seems to be no basis for interpreting the words, "churches, their integrated auxiliaries, and conventions or association of churches" (in Sections 508(c)(1)(A), 6033(a)(2)(A)(i) and 6043(b)(1)) by segmenting those words one from another. Rather they should be read and applied as a whole. As so read, the phrase would apply to single religious organizations, including units at the local level and also to bodies made up of numerous local units without regard to the existence or degree of "hierarchical" structural control. In this sense, the entire phrase would cover not only congregations, parishes, temples, synagogues, etc., but also what is often referred to as a church "denomination."

However, the intent of Congress is more crucial than Treasury's phrasing. The only helpful clue for dealing with the phrase "church . . . convention or association of churches" as it reflects the intent of Congress comes from the legislative history of Section 170 in the 1954 Code. An earlier version of the bill used the words "a church *or a religious order*." During hearings held by the Senate Finance Committee, the director of the legal department of the National Catholic Welfare Conference (now the United States Catholic Conference) testified as follows:

> To classify separately religious orders would indicate that they are not considered a part of or come within the meaning of the term 'church.' To do so ignores facts and pertinent church law resulting in a legislative determination of what is or is not a church. This the Congress has never done.[8]

In deleting the phrase "or a religious order" from Section 170, the Senate Finance Committee reported as follows:

> Your committee understands that 'church' to some denominations includes religious orders *as well as other organizations which, as*

> *integral parts of the church are engaged in carrying out the functions of the church whether as separate corporations or otherwise.* It is believed that the term 'church' should be all inclusive. To retain the phrase 'or a religious order' in this section of the bill will tend to limit the term and may lead to confusion in the interpretation of other provisions of the bill relating to a church, a convention or association of churches. Accordingly, your committee believes that this section of the bill will be clarified by this amendment.[9]

Incidentally, it should be observed that in this legislative history, as well as in other ways, the word "church" or the words "conventions or associations of churches" may be used alone, but with the obvious belief by the user that the words are interchangeable. In the exchange just noted, the spokesman for the Catholic Church used the word "church" because in that body that word covers all. If the spokesman had been from a Lutheran church body, he or she would probably have used the words "conventions or associations of churches," because those words within the phrase come closest to describing the Lutheran church bodies. In using the term with which they were most comfortable, neither would wish to use it to the exclusion of other church bodies.

More important, it would not be constitutionally permissible for such to be done, nor is there any indication that Congress has so intended. To the contrary, there is legislative history supporting the idea that the phrase is to be all-inclusive. In 1950, when the predecessor section to present Section 511 was being considered, the bill provided an exemption to "churches" from the tax on unrelated business taxable income. During the hearings conducted by the Senate Finance Committee on H.R. 8920, Mr. Culbertson, Vice President of the Baptist Foundation of Texas, sought an extension of the exemption accorded to churches. He pointed out:

> The exemption of a "church" does not protect these independent churches [Baptist churches and other churches having a similar structure] in their cooperative religious activities as it does the churches of other faiths integrated into an organic church, having overall ecclesiastical authority, and being itself autonomous.[10]

As a result of this testimony, the Senate amended Section 310(b)(1) of H.R. 8920 so that it used the words "church, convention or association of churches." The House agreed to this amendment in conference, and the amendment was ultimately incorporated into law.[11]

In a letter to the Commissioner of Internal Revenue dated March 17, 1976, Robert W. Barker, Washington counsel for the Mormon Church, argued persuasively that separate incorporation of an organization should not automatically suggest "auxiliary" status.

The Church of Jesus Christ of Latter-day Saints maintains that Congress did not intend for the IRS to scrutinize every molecular, internal, departmental function of large, regional or national churches in order to determine whether such functions or activities themselves might be required to file information returns. Rather, Congress intended to exempt all churches from filing of information returns; and it further intended that the term church be given its ordinary broad meaning. *In addition to the exemption granted churches,* Congress also intended to grant a *further exemption* to those separate entities closely affiliated with and complementary to churches which might meet the definition of "integrated auxiliaries of churches." (Emphasis added.)

It should be pointed out that there have been good reasons for denominations being formed with two or more corporations. For example, prior to 1968, non-profit organizations which operated in two or more states (which usually is the situation with respect to a church "denomination") were afforded property tax exemptions only if they were incorporated in the state in which the property existed. In 1968, however, the Supreme Court held unconstitutional a law which provided such an exemption only for domestic non-profit corporations.[12]

Church denominations should not be shoved from pillar to post by changes in the laws or by changed interpretations of the laws, unless there is (i) some meritorious substantive reason for that treatment, and (ii) no alternative method available. There is no meritorious substantive reason for providing an exception from filing Form 990 to a church denomination which consists of a single corporation but requiring the filing as to portions of that denomination when the denomination is made up of two or more corporations. However, to the extent that it is believed that there is some meritorious substantive reason for obtaining a Form 990 as to certain activities of a church or convention or association of churches, then it is certainly possible to enact a law requiring such without the degree of risk of constitutional violations inherent in the present Section 6033 and its Regulations.[13]

2. Invalidity of the Regulation Itself.

If the application of the regulation to church bodies would deny the exemption to some or all of the corporations of multi-corporation "denominations," then the regulation itself would be invalid, not only because it would be inconsistent with the Code, both in its plain meaning and as shown by legislative history to be the intent of Congress, but also because it would violate the religion clauses of the First Amendment.

(a) It has already been shown that the term "a church or a convention or association of churches" as used in Section 170 includes a "denomination," even one which is constituted of two or more corporations. There is no indication that Congress used the phrase in a different way in adopting Section 6033. And in adding a further term, "integrated auxiliaries,"

Congress clearly intended to make the exemption broader, not narrower. Therefore, the composite term should surely be applicable to the component parts of "denominations" which are made up of two or more corporations.

There is nothing in the phrase "integrated auxiliaries" as used in the Code or in the legislative history of the 1969 Tax Reform Act which would support the notion that it is to be applied according to a *functional or activities test*. The phrase itself is entirely one of *structural* relationship. Furthermore, there is nothing to support an activities or functional test in determining whether that structural relationship exists.

In the public hearing held after the regulations to Section 6033 were proposed, Meade Whitaker, Chief Counsel of the Internal Revenue Service, asked church spokesmen how they would reconcile the exemptions provided under clauses (i) and (iii)—"the religious activities of religious orders"—of Section 6033(a)(2)(A). He apparently felt that basic fairness and equality of treatment required the "religious activities" test of clause (iii) to be read into the exemption afforded by clause (i). The fact is that Congress did not see fit to write that "religious activities" test into the section exempting churches, their integrated auxiliaries, and conventions or associations of churches. Since Congress knew how to write such a test into the law if it wished, the necessary assumption must be that it did not intend to write such a test into clause (i), and therefore the regulation using that test is inconsistent with the statute and legislative intent behind the statute.

(b) Even if the regulation were consistent with the statute, it would be invalid because regulation and statute both would then be contrary to the religious clauses of the First Amendment.

(1) Determining whether the activities of an organization are "exclusively religious" would require the government to define what is "religious," thus potentially excluding activities which are nevertheless religious in violation of the free exercise clause.

(2) Use of this highly subjective standard would also violate the prohibition against an establishment of religion if it led the IRS to classify certain activities as non-religious or insufficiently religious to justify exempting the organization performing them from filing informational returns while at the same time exempting other (religious) organizations performing what IRS deemed to be sufficiently religious activities, thus "preferring one religion over another," contrary to the Supreme Court's test of "establishment" enunciated in *Everson* v. *Board of Education* and elsewhere.[14] In addition, merely obtaining the information necessary to make such a determination would itself pose a strong likelihood of creating "excessive entanglement" between government and religion, contrary to the Supreme Court's strictures in *Walz* v. *Tax Commission* and elsewhere.[15]

All of the foregoing strongly suggests that the Regulation exceeds the law, does not reflect legislative history and constitutes a vehicle by which the Internal Revenue Service can unevenly, without due process of law, and in violation of the Equal Protection Clause of the 14th Amendment, characterize church organizations as it wishes, and extract from them such information and impose upon them such restrictions as it sees fit. Therefore, the Lutheran Church—Missouri Synod is prepared to resist this undertaking by the government until it can be tested in the courts.

Appendix: A Closely Related Issue

There is a closely related struggle being carried on by the Synod (and other church bodies) with the Department of Labor over an exception from unemployment insurance coverage. The similarities in time and language cast light on the matter of "integrated auxiliaries." The Federal Unemployment Tax Act provides an exemption, and permits states to provide an exemption, from coverage for those in the employ of (i) a church or convention or association of churches or (ii) an organization which is operated primarily for religious purposes and which is operated, supervised, controlled or principally supported by a church or convention or association of churches (see Section 3309(b)(1) of the Code). Effective January 1, 1978, another provision of Section 3309, which had provided an exemption to those "in the employ of a school other than a state school which is not an institution of higher education" was repealed. In April of 1978, Labor Secretary Marshall announced, without hearings or notice, that the repeal of the latter exemption meant that employees engaged in "church-related" (his phrase) schools were covered. It quickly became apparent that the Secretary was going to apply that interpretation even to those elementary and secondary schools which are not separately in-corporated from congregations or parishes, even though all the employ-ees are engaged, directed and paid by the church itself.

The Synod has been at the forefront of efforts to challenge the Secretary of Labor's interpretation. Its congregations operate more elementary and secondary schools in the United States than any other Protestant denomi-nation.

Another Lutheran Synod (the Wisconsin Synod) suffered the only judicial loss in this issue (while at least nine other courts have rejected Marshall's interpretation) when the South Dakota Supreme Court upheld the Secretary of Labor's interpretation. The United States Supreme Court accepted the Wisconsin Synod's request that it review the case.[16]

Two quotes from the brief filed with the U.S. Supreme Court by the Department of Justice in the Wisconsin Synod case will demonstrate the importance of that case to the "integrated auxiliaries" issues and other future cases involving the meaning and extent of exceptions based on "church" or "religious":

    a) "Petitioners (the Wisconsin Synod and a member congregation) mistakenly contend that the 'church' exemption plainly extends to parochial school employees if the school is not separately incorporated from the church.

. . . [T]he Department of Labor has consistently followed its interpretation . . . that 'church' was used by Congress in the limited sense of *an individual house of worship* . . .

. . . [I]ndividuals employed in the operation of the house of worship are exempt . . ." [Emphasis and brackets supplied.]

b) "Congress clearly indicated that the . . . exemption for organizations 'operated primarily for religious purposes' is to be narrowly construed in the context of educational institutions . . . Only schools devoted primarily to preparing students for the ministry and schools *engaged exclusively* in religious instruction (such as Sunday Schools) are exempt . . ." [Emphasis supplied.]

It should be sufficient for purposes of this report to note that there is reason for genuine concern about both an interpretation of "church" which narrows it to a physical structure where worship services are held, not an organization, and an interpretation of "primarily for religious purposes," which is as narrow and unrealistic as Treasury's "principal activity is exclusively religious." If the Department of Labor is upheld on either point it will represent a severe contraction of many existing exemptions, especially in the tax laws.

A Baptist Seminary Resists the Equal Employment Opportunity Commission

JAMES E. WOOD, JR.

This essay is concerned with the efforts of the Equal Employment Opportunity Commission to establish jurisdiction over denominational theological seminaries, specifically Southwestern Baptist Theological Seminary.

Background of the Case

On May 24, 1977, the Equal Employment Opportunity Commission filed suit against Southwestern Baptist Theological Seminary in the federal district court for failing to submit to the Commission the Higher Education Staff Information Report, Form EEO-6. In taking this action, the EEOC requested a permanent injunction ordering the Seminary to file the reports, as required by the Civil Rights Act,[1] for the years 1975 and 1977 and for future years, and to reimburse the Commission for all costs and expenses incurred in bringing this action.

Form EEO-6 seeks to obtain data on the number and duties of seven categories of employees—their compensation, tenure, race, sex, and national origin. Under the regulations of the Commission, submission of Form EEO-6 is required of all institutions of higher learning, both public and private, with fifteen or more employees. Beginning in 1975, the Seminary refused to file the form on the grounds that the presumed jurisdiction of the EEOC over the Seminary violated the religion clauses of the First Amendment.

Meanwhile, Southeastern Baptist Theological Seminary in Wake Forest, North Carolina, seriously questioned the jurisdiction of the Commission over it. Subsequently, at a meeting of the presidents of the six theological seminaries of the Southern Baptist Convention, a decision was reached that none of the seminaries would file Form EEO-6 to the Commission, and that Southwestern Baptist Theological Seminary, as the largest of the Southern Baptist seminaries, should serve as the defendant in the litigation. Later, agreement was reached with the counsel of the EEOC that the outcome of this litigation would be determinative for the other seminaries. As a part of this agreement, the five remaining Southern Baptist seminaries were prevailed upon by the counsel of Southwestern Baptist Theological Seminary and the counsel of the EEOC to file Form EEO-6 "under protest" pending the outcome of the litigation. Both the EEOC and the Seminary publicly acknowledged that the case would be appealed all the way to the U.S. Supreme Court. The far-reaching implications of the case for U.S. church-state relations were readily acknowledged.

In a pre-trial brief, the EEOC sought an order from the court requiring Southwestern Baptist Theological Seminary to comply with the Commission's regulations which mandate that biennial reports of employee data be filed by institutions of higher learning. The Seminary argued that Title VII is not applicable to the Seminary in view of the protection granted religion by the First Amendment. No material facts between the litigants were in dispute. The Seminary, as a wholly religious entity or activity of the Southern Baptist Convention, refused to submit the Higher Education Report (EEO-6) on the basis that the jurisdiction presumed by the Commission over the Seminary was unconstitutional.

The Commission argued that the First Amendment does not make the agency's reporting regulations inapplicable to the Seminary. "It is well established," the Commission maintained, "that an organization affecting commerce may not escape the coverage of social legislation (such as Title VII) by showing that they were created for . . . religious purposes,"[2] adding that, while freedom to hold religious beliefs is absolute, freedom to act on those beliefs is not, and "is not totally immune from reasonable government regulation."[3] Enforcement of the application of the Act to non-minister employees of a religious employer, the EEOC argued, has been upheld on constitutional grounds.[4] The contention by the seminary that EEOC jurisdiction over it would result in unreasonable government involvement with religion or religious activities was declared by the Commission to be "without merit."[5]

Summary judgment was denied by Judge Eldon B. Mahon and trial was scheduled to ferret out what Judge Mahon termed rather substantial facts in the case.

The Government's Case

Basic to the EEOC's original action of filing a lawsuit against Southwestern Baptist Theological Seminary was the Commission's contention that its alleged right of jurisdiction stemmed from statutory authorization given the agency in Title VII of the Civil Rights Act of 1964, as amended. The statute requires that employers, both public and private, keep records and make biennial reports to EEOC.

> Every employer . . . subject to this subchapter shall (1) make and keep such records relevant to the determination of whether unlawful employment practices have been or are being committed, (2) preserve such records for such periods, and (3) make such reports therefrom, as the Commission shall prescribe by regulation or order, after public hearing, as reasonable, necessary, or appropriate for the enforcement of this subchapter or the regulations or orders thereunder.[6]

(Form EEO-6, or the Higher Education Staff Information Report, requires information only from educational institutions which employ more than fifteen persons. The Commission had noted that the term "employee" refers to any person on the payroll of an employer, and would, therefore, include both non-exempt and exempt employees.)

Judge Mahon asked the Commission attorneys if "we're going" in the direction of requiring "large churches . . . such as First United Methodist Church of Fort Worth" to file "employee information." Charles David Nelson, an attorney for the EEOC, stated that he would be surprised if churches had to file the employee information similar to that requested from the Seminary.[7] The Commission later responded to Judge Mahon's inquiry by stating that churches which employ more than one hundred persons are required to file Form EEO-1, the same form required of business, commercial, and industrial enterprises. Upon questioning by Judge Mahon as to the reason for requiring employee data from the Seminary, Nelson indicated that the information would be "stored" and used later if a sex or racial discrimination suit were filed against the Seminary.[8]

The Seminary admitted during the trial that it met all the jurisdictional requirements of Title VII. "We have admitted from the outset," the defendant declared, "that there are more than fifteen employees; that our activities are involved in Interstate Commerce; [and] that the Seminary does grant degrees, a college level education in the religious area."[9] But the Seminary maintained that since the Seminary's sole purpose is the training of Southern Baptist ministers, the Commission is precluded by the religion clauses of the First Amendment from bringing the Seminary under its jurisdiction.

The Commission categorically rejected the complaint of the Seminary that such jurisdiction would cause impermissible involvement of the agency in the operations and administration of the Seminary. "It is clear," the plaintiff stated, "that the Establishment Clause has no relevance to this claim."[10] The Commission's regulation pertaining to Form EEO-6 does not abridge religious belief, does not have the effect of establishing a religion, and does not have a negative impact on the administration or operation of the Seminary.

The Commission argued that the congressional mandate, as embodied in Title VII of the Civil Rights Act of 1964, reflects an interest of the "highest order." It is based on a compelling government interest to eliminate discrimination based on race, sex, color, religion, and national origin. Congress has given the EEOC its mandate for the administration, interpretation, and enforcement of Title VII, and Congress has accorded this social purpose the highest priority.

The Supreme Court has provided a three-pronged test for violation of the Establishment Clause. In *Lemon* v. *Kurtzman* (1971), the Court stated: "Every analysis in this area must be gleaned from our cases. First, the statute must have a secular purpose; its principal or primary effect must be one that neither advances nor inhibits religion; . . . finally, the statute must not foster 'an excessive entanglement with religion.' "[11]

According to the EEOC, application of these tests shows that (1) the statute does have a secular purpose—the elimination of all forms of discrimination in employment, (2) the primary effect of Title VII neither advances nor inhibits religion, and (3) the exemption of religious preference granted religious institutions by the statute avoids any excessive government entanglement with religion.[12]

The exemption for religious institutions which permits the exercise of religious preference, it was noted by the Commission, is not an issue in this case. However, the application of Title VII's ban on discrimination based on race, sex, or national origin to non-minister employees of a religious employer has been viewed by the courts as within the jurisdiction of the EEOC's regulations.[13] In *McClure* v. *Salvation Army*, the Fifth Circuit Court of Appeals declared: "The language and the legislative history of Section 702 compel the conclusion that Congress did not intend that a religious organization be exempt from liability for discriminating on the basis of race, color, sex or national origin with respect to their compensation, terms, conditions or privileges of employment."[14] In view of the U.S. Supreme Court's criteria and the opinions enunciated in the courts in similar cases involving religious institutions and organizations, the "defendant's constitutional defense to Section 709(c) and the regulations promulgated thereunder, is without foundation."[15]

The Commission summarily dismissed any applicability of the U.S. Supreme Court's decision of a few months earlier in *NLRB* v. *Catholic Bishop of Chicago*,[16] since there was no evidence of congressional intent to place religiously affiliated institutions within the purview of the Labor-Management Relations Act and thus under the jurisdiction of the National Labor Relations Board.

Finally, the Commission argued that the Seminary, as a recipient of federal funds through participation in the Veterans Administration programs, is subject to the Non-Discrimination Clause of Title VI of the Civil

Rights Act of 1964.[17] By participating in the Veterans Administration's program for student veterans and permitting annual on-site compliance surveys by the State of Texas, the Seminary has established itself as a "recipient" of federal funds. The Supreme Court, in *Bob Jones University* v. *Johnson*, stated: "A 'recipient' within the meaning of Title VI is not to be confused with the 'beneficiary' of Federal assistance. The 'recipient' is the intermediary entity whose nondiscriminatory participation in the federally assisted program is essential to the provisions of benefits to the identified class which the federal statute is designed to serve."[18]

Thus, according to the EEOC, the Seminary is a "recipient" of federal funds, and the student veterans who are subsidized by the federal educational benefits are the "beneficiaries." Since Title VI covers "recipients" and not "beneficiaries," the Seminary is also covered by Title VI, Section 601 (as well as Title VII) of the Civil Rights Act of 1964. This act expressly prohibits discrimination on the basis of race, color, or national origin in "any program or activity receiving Federal financial assistance."[19] Compliance of the Seminary with policies established by the Veterans Administration (Title VI) is a reasonable basis for concluding that compliance with the policy of the EEOC requiring the filing of Form EEO-6 (Title VII) "would not inhibit or impinge upon the defendant's First Amendment Constitutional rights."[20]

On the basis of these arguments, the counsel for the EEOC urged the Court to grant the relief requested.

The Seminary's Argument

Central to the defendant's case was the argument that Southwestern Baptist Theological Seminary is protected from the jurisdiction and regulations of the EEOC, including the filing of Education Staff Information Report (EEO-6), by the religion clauses of the First Amendment. It was this position that constituted the basis of the Seminary's deliberate failure to file Form EEO-6 for the years 1975 and 1977.

The Seminary is a wholly religious activity of the Southern Baptist Convention and its churches.[21] While it is an educational institution, the Seminary is an agency of the Southern Baptist Convention and integral to the mission and purpose of the Convention. The Seminary's sole purpose is to train men and women to serve the churches and the denomination, and it is owned, operated, and controlled and principally funded by the Southern Baptist Convention. Its faculty, all of whom are affiliated with the Southern Baptist Convention, are required to sign statements of Baptist doctrines and Articles of Faith. Administrative and support staff, along with the faculty, are required to maintain a life-style in keeping with the teachings of the denomination and to reflect a personal commitment to the mission of the Seminary.

Enrollment at the Seminary is not open to the public or to Baptists in general, but it is restricted to men and women who have evidenced a divine calling to a full-time Christian vocation of ministry and have been recommended for admission by their local church. No other students are permitted to enroll, even on a part-time basis. Only theological degrees are granted by the Seminary, with moral and spiritual considerations being made a part of the preparation and qualification for graduation. In the light of guidelines formulated in *Roemer* v. *Board of Public Works of Maryland*, the Seminary would clearly be classified as "pervasively sectarian" and religious in character.[22]

In view of the totally religious character of the Seminary and its integral relationship to the Southern Baptist Convention and its associated churches, any exercise of jurisdiction by the EEOC over the Seminary constitutes an "impermissible breach" of the religion clauses of the First Amendment. The issue was a jurisdictional one in view of the constitutional guarantees, as reaffirmed by the U.S. Supreme Court, in denying government the right to enact any law "respecting an establishment of religion or prohibiting the free exercise thereof." The Seminary noted that in *Walz* v. *Tax Commission of the City of New York*, Chief Justice Warren Burger "appropriately" said: "The general principle deducible from the First Amendment and all that has been said by the Court is this: that we will not tolerate either governmentally established religion or governmental interference with religion."[23] While "judicial paths may vary and at times be blurred," the Seminary argued, "each is clearly directed toward the common constitutional principle or mandate that prohibits governmental establishment of religion or governmental interference with religion."[24]

Contrary to the argument of the plaintiff, the Seminary contended that "Congress did not intend or contemplate that the Equal Employment Opportunity Act apply to religion or religious activities." Furthermore, the Commission's definition of "an institution of higher education," the details of the data requested, the extent and nature of record keeping, as well as employment guidelines, were all developed on the basis of regulations promulgated by the EEOC and were not provided by an Act of Congress.

In the foreword to *Legislative History of the Equal Employment Opportunity Act of 1972*, Senator Harrison A. Williams, Jr., Chairman of the Committee on Labor and Public Welfare, who directed the floor fight for the passage of the Act, wrote: "It is clearly in the law that, where the question is religion, this legislation does not apply."[25] "For good reason [i.e., First Amendment] . . . government should not be involved in religious activities. Therefore, where we are saying that nobody should be discriminated against in employment, we will not carry that into an area where we have a First Amendment situation, where we have religious activities."[26] Although the legislation did not explicitly exempt "religious bodies," the sponsors of the legislation had assurance that the EEOC would recognize and afford First Amendment protection. It was understood that this protection would be accorded church institutions or agencies whose primary function was the propagation of faith. With regard to this legislation, Senator Williams declared further, "I believe it is reasonable for Congress to permit an institution such as Catholic University to require its employees to be Catholic. The major function of that university is the propagation of its faith and we should not interfere with that program."[27] Clearly, the confidence of the Act's sponsors in the Commission's recognition and exercise of First Amendment protection "was misplaced." Any claim of EEOC jurisdiction over local churches, such as was set forth in the plaintiff's post-trial brief, would have "astounded" Senator Williams and most members of Congress who originally supported the Act.

Other governmental agencies have recognized their lack of jurisdiction over the Seminary. For example, the Internal Revenue Service's regulations, under Code Section 6033, spelling out exemptions for filing its information Form 990 for "integrated auxiliaries of a church," includes the Seminary, as distinguished from church-affiliated institutions such as hospitals and educational institutions serving the public. Or, again, the National Labor Relations Board, which also has a non-specific act which does not expressly exempt churches and religious activities, has, as a matter of policy, refused to exercise jurisdiction over "completely religious organizations."[28]

Recently, the U.S. Supreme Court, in *NLRB* v. *Catholic Bishop of Chicago*, denied jurisdiction of the National Labor Relations Board over parochial schools, recognizing that such jurisdiction represented a "significant risk" of infringement upon the First Amendment. "We see no escape," Chief Justice Burger declared, "from conflicts flowing from the Board's exercise of jurisdiction over teachers in church-operated schools and the consequent serious First Amendment questions that would follow." In its final judgment, however, the Court found that a decision on constitutional grounds was not required, since NLRB's claim of jurisdiction lacked both statutory authorization and any clear evidence of legislative intent on the part of Congress to grant such power to the NLRB.

Analogies between the case against the Seminary by the EEOC and *NLRB* v. *Catholic Bishop of Chicago* are fundamentally similar, both with regard to legislative intent and First Amendment considerations. In view of the Court's concern with "significant risk" of First Amendment infringement, however, as enunciated in *NLRB* v. *Catholic Bishop of Chicago*, the present case is of even greater substantive merit on constitutional grounds. As the counsel for the Seminary stated, "The risk and probability of impermissible entanglement is many times multiplied over that of the NLRA [National Labor Relations Act] because both the scope and coverage of EEOC and its regulations are far greater than the limited and specific scope of the NRLA and the strict and necessary spiritual criteria governing all employment relationships of the Seminary."[29]

Many cases arising out of intra-church disputes have shown that government jurisdiction over or intervention in church operations and governance is prohibited on constitutional grounds. In *Serbian Eastern Orthodox Church* v. *Milivojevich*,[30] the North American Diocese severed its relationship with the Serbian Orthodox Church of Yugoslavia. The U.S. Supreme Court denied the right of the Illinois Supreme Court to uphold the action of the new diocese to claim title to the Church's assets in North America and to appoint bishops for the new diocese. In effect, the U.S. Supreme Court denied the state's right of jurisdiction. Speaking for the majority of the Court, Justice William J. Brennan ruled that matters of governance, the appointment of bishops or hierarchy, and the internal organization were matters of church determination, and the courts were prohibited from passing judgment on such determination in the absence of fraud.

In *McClure* v. *Salvation Army*,[31] Ms. McClure argued that her civil rights as a minister were violated with respect to her employment, i.e., duties, salary, and assignment. The Court disallowed her contention, based upon First Amendment considerations. "*McClure's* basic premise," it was noted, "is that those engaged in a religious mission cannot be covered by the Act."

Finally, the counsel for the Seminary argued that the exercise of jurisdiction of the EEOC over the Seminary would foster an "impermissible degree of government entanglement with religion." By the Commission's monitoring, evaluating, and ruling on all personnel and by requiring information as to the Seminary's structure and organization— employment practices of hiring, firing, and promotion; the assignment of duties; the determination of salaries, promotions, and tenures; the nature and duration of employee contracts; and the various categories of employees as to race, sex, and national origin—government would be brought into virtually every employment and personnel decision within the Seminary. Excessive entanglement between government and a wholly religious activity of the Southern Baptist Convention would inevitably result.

Each witness from the Seminary, including the Seminary's chief administrators, chief faculty officer, and maintenance supervisor, all affirmed the necessity of the personal faith and spiritual commitment to the mission of the Seminary for its personnel. Each witness from his own individual perspective underscored that "whatever secular duties they [i.e., Seminary employees] may perform cannot be separated from their spiritual contribution to the spiritual atmosphere and fulfilling of the mission of the Seminary." All employees of the Seminary, faculty and non-faculty, are governed by the same religious and sectarian criteria, both upon initial employment and thereafter.

Monitoring and regulating the Seminary's policies and practices would clearly constitute excessive and impermissible entanglement of government in the basic operations and management of the Seminary in carrying out its religious mission. In the final analysis, "If the Religious Clauses say anything, they mandate freedom to the Seminary from such government entanglement . . . and freedom from civil inquiry and litigation relating to these spiritual decisions."

The Seminary vigorously denied that its acceptance of fees from the Veterans Administration (which, the Seminary declared, are "akin to a school charging for copies of a student's transcript") constitute "federal financial assistance." In years past, forms were sent by the Department of Health, Education and Welfare to the Seminary to be completed in order to earn eligibility for possible federal assistance programs. The forms were never returned and, as a result, the Seminary was listed as ineligible for federal aid or assistance programs. The Seminary also has no contracts to perform services or furnish materials to the federal government that would come under the jurisdiction of the Department of Labor. The Seminary acknowledged that the Veterans Administration paid "reporting fees" to reimburse the Seminary for the handling of VA checks to beneficiaries. However, even if these small recording fees were viewed as constituting federal aid, Section 601 (2000 d) of Title VI clearly grants jurisdiction only to agencies extending federal aid. Since the fees are from the Veterans Administration, how can the EEOC bring a case to bear against the Seminary based on its acceptance of fees from the VA? No jurisdiction, it was argued, can be extended to EEOC on the basis of fees received by the Seminary from another government agency.

The Commission's presumed jurisdiction over Southwestern Baptist Theological Seminary therefore lacks both statutory authorization and constitutional permissibility.[31b]

The Opinion of the U.S. District Court

On January 18, 1980, almost thirty-two months after the EEOC's initial filing of the lawsuit, Judge Mahon handed down the Court's opinion, denying the EEOC jurisdiction over the Seminary and, thereby, preventing the Commission from seeking data on employees from the Seminary.[32] He ruled that the EEOC cannot force the Seminary to provide records on the race, sex, national origin, or salaries of employees, nor can the Commission take action against the Seminary while enforcing federal laws on discrimination.

In the opinion of the Court, "The issues presented in this case cannot be resolved by balancing the compelling interests of the state against the sanctity of irreconcilable religious belief, as in *Cantwell* v. *Connecticut.*"[33] The Court noted that the Seminary denied the existence of any tenets of faith that would require or justify discrimination on the basis of race or national origin, but recognized that the Seminary may at some future time discriminate on the basis of sex. Even so, the Court concluded, the fact is that the Seminary regards all its employments "as divinely guided assessments of each employee's suitability" for a given position and thus seeks the right, which the Court upholds, to make these judgments without government entanglement or supervision.

While the Court conceded that it was not the legislative intent to exempt any religious organization, whether a church or a seminary, from liability for discriminating against their employees on the basis of race, sex, or national origin, the issue of excessive entanglement still remains whenever there is government intrusion into the employment policy or practice of an institution whose activity is wholly religious and whose mission comprises "the very heart of religious propagation." Judge Mahon wrote:

> The risk of unseemly governmental entanglement increases exponentially as the function of any institution becomes more fundamentally and pervasively religious. The originative power of any religion lies in the institution that schools its ministers, preserving and transmitting dogma in a pure form in the academic sense and endeavoring to animate sterile doctrine into communicable faith. A seminary's function within a particular religion is to replenish the core of [the] faithful who provide its structure, a role even more essential to its mission than that served by parochial elementary and secondary schools, e.g. *NLRB* v. *Catholic Bishop of Chicago*, [440] U.S. [490], 59 L.Ed.2d 533 (1979); *Lemon* v. *Kurtzman*, 403 U.S. 602 (1971); *Committee for Public Education and Religious Liberty* v. *Nyquist*, 413 U.S. 756, 767 (1973); *Brown* v. *Dade Christian Schools*, 556 F.2d 310 (5th Cir. 1977), and one qualitatively different than that of religiously affiliated colleges offering liberal arts or other secular courses of study to the public, *see* e.g., *Bob Jones University* v. *Johnson*, 396 F. Supp. 597 (D.S.C.1974) *affd per curiam* No. 74,2163 (4th Cir. 1975); *EEOC* v. *Mississippi College*, 451 F. Supp. 564 (S.D.Miss. 1978). The operation of a seminary is an ultimate religious activity entitled to the highest degree of first amendment protection.

In addition, the Court ruled, application of Title VII to any part of the employment policy or practice of the Seminary, by virtue of the requisite religious and spiritual qualifications, is also an infringement upon the Free Exercise Clause of the First Amendment.[34] Acknowledgment was made that the Seminary's employment practices are an essential part of a "virtually cloistral environment" which the Seminary has attempted to create and that its employment decisions are inseparable from its mission. To dissect seminary employment functions into religious and secular components will inevitably lead to excessive government entanglement with religion. Judge Mahon denied the argument of the Commission that the Seminary had waived any First Amendment objections to enforcement of Title VII by virtue of its seeking of approval of its course of study under the accreditation standards of the Veterans Administration. Surveillance of sectarian schools for the purpose of accreditation, the Court ruled, has never been viewed as amounting to entanglement of church and state. Nor has the Seminary risked any infringement of its free exercise of religion in permitting periodic investigations of its record-keeping requirements by the Texas Education Agency.

Compliance with Title VI as a condition of approval by the Veterans Administration for veterans to receive educational benefits, the Court concluded, is entirely independent of coverage under Title VII. Title VI forbids discrimination against the participants in the program and not the recipient's (i.e., the Seminary's) employment practices as to other employees. The regulations required under Title VI are not coextensive or parallel with those under Title VII. The Commission's argument that the Seminary cannot submit to government regulations to gain some benefits from one government agency and then object on religious grounds to similar regulations by another government agency is a specious argument and is not supported by the law. The power to issue regulations with respect to the awarding of federal assistance or subsidies is valid only "so long as those terms are themselves constitutional." Accordingly, the Court "declines to hold that acceptance of veterans receiving federal assistance constitutes a waiver of religious objections to the more comprehensive and intrusive enforcement possible under Title VII." In sum, the Seminary cannot be required to file Form EEO-6.

The Arguments on Appeal

An appeal of the district court's decision was promptly forthcoming from the EEOC.[35] The Commission acknowledged that the issue presented in the appeal was whether the Commission's biennial reporting for institutions of higher learning "impermissibly infringes upon the Free Exercise of religion when imposed upon a seminary."

In the Commission's appeal it was noted that the Seminary administration testified that race or national origin would never be a factor in employment and that no tenet of the Baptist faith requires discrimination in employment on the basis of sex, race, or national origin. Bound by the charter of Southern Baptist Convention and its own charter to abide by the requirements of state and federal laws, the Seminary maintains various contacts with government—e.g., the Internal Revenue Service, the Veterans Administration, and on-site inspection by Texas officials of compliance with fire and food-service regulations.

The Commission argued on appeal that the concern of the district court over entanglement which may result in the EEOC's jurisdiction over employment practices of a fundamentally religious nature is of no concern in this case, which is restricted solely to Title VII's reporting require-ment. Under Title VII, religious employers are granted the freedom to implement those employment practices which are deemed necessary for the accomplishment of their religious purpose. At some later time, should an employment discrimination suit be brought against the Seminary or a constitutional issue be raised, the district court could then consider the

First Amendment questions involved in carrying out Title VII's reporting requirements. The mere possibility that constitutional problems *may* arise is not a sufficient basis for an advisory opinion in this case.

The Commission maintained that Form EEO-6, filed biennially, is a reasonable requirement for carrying out the provisions of Title VII and does not violate the Free Exercise Clause of the First Amendment. The Seminary has not alleged that compliance with this requirement would be burdensome or in conflict with its beliefs. The biennial filing requirement is one which neither advances nor inhibits religion and would not result in excessive entanglement in the administration of the Seminary.

The district court's opinion was one which "ranged far beyond the question" of Title VII's reporting requirement—to an inquiry far more appropriate in any employment discrimination suit involving the enforcement of the Act's discrimination provisions. Federal courts, it was noted, are "without power to give advisory opinions . . . to decide abstract, hypothetical or contingent questions, . . . to decide any constitutional question in advance of the necessity for its decision, . . . or to decide any constitutional question except with reference to the particular facts to which it is to be applied. . . ."[36] "Given the contingent nature of any employment discrimination suit against Southwestern Baptist," the plaintiff charged, "the district court's inquiry was premature." Furthermore, the Seminary has never contended that filing Form EEO-6 would impose a burden on its free exercise of religion and has never filed for an exemption, as 709(c) expressly permits. Meanwhile, there is a legitimate government interest in the statistical data contained in Form EEO-6 "for innumerable public and private uses." For these reasons, the judgment of the district court should be reversed and the Seminary ordered to file Form EEO-6 for 1975, 1977, 1979, and biennially thereafter.

In its appellate brief, the Seminary reaffirmed that it did not constitute "an institution of higher learning" under Title VII and "in any event is protected from enforcement of Title VII by the religion clauses of the First Amendment to the Constitution of the United States."[37] As a wholly religious activity of the Southern Baptist Convention and its churches, the Seminary's sole purpose, as set forth earlier, is the training of "God-called church-endorsed individuals to the full-time ministries of the churches." Based on the history of the legislation, there was no affirmative intention on the part of Congress that the EEOC jurisdiction should be extended over the churches, unlike religiously affiliated institutions which serve the general public. EEOC surveillance and evaluation of Seminary employment practices, which are indissolubly linked with a divine calling and the mission of the Seminary, are "fraught with the sort of entanglement that the First Amendment forbids." The Commission's presumed jurisdiction over the Seminary is without congressional or constitutional basis. In view of these facts, the judgment of the district court should be sustained.

The primary emphasis of the Seminary's appellate brief was that the exercise of jurisdiction by the EEOC over the Seminary "constitutes an impermissible breach of the religious clauses of the First Amendment to the Constitution." Both the Establishment Clause and the Free Exercise Clause require protection, but both frequently overlap. The basic element in the Free Exercise Clause is one of interference with religion. In *Kedroff* v. *St. Nicholas Cathedral*, for example, the U.S. Supreme Court, in denying the constitutionality of government interference in church administration, ruled that "legislation that regulates church administration, the operation of the church [or] the appointment of clergy . . . prohibits the free exercise of religion."[38] Under the Establishment Clause the central impermissible element is state entanglement in religious activities and programs. Form EEO-6 seeks data from the Seminary as to its structure and organization, financing, and employment (promotion, salaries, tenure, evaluation, discharge, nature and duration of contracts, race, sex, and foreign nationals), and all such data furnished without any protection of confidentiality. "How could one dispute," the defendant concluded, "that the complete monitoring and determining of the validity of the Seminary's every employment decision, its good faith and motives, would ultimately constitute impermissible involvement, intrusion and entanglement of the government in the operations and management of the Seminary in carrying out its divine mission?"

The Ruling of the Court of Appeals

In July, 1981, the circuit court's three-judge panel affirmed in part and in part reversed and remanded the judgment of the lower court. The circuit court reaffirmed that the Seminary is a wholly religious institution and is, from a legal point of view, to be regarded as a church. "Since the Seminary is principally supported and wholly controlled by the [Southern Baptist] Convention for the avowed purpose of training ministers to serve the Baptist denomination," the court declared, "it . . . is entitled to the status of 'church.'" The court ruled, however, that only teaching members of the faculty or those who are connected with teaching or those who have supervision of teaching are to be considered *ministers* and to be beyond the jurisdiction of the EEOC.

Of special importance was the overturning of the lower court's ruling that those administrators and support persons who are not "ministers" are subject to EEOC jurisdiction. "Application of Title VII's reporting requirements to the Seminary's non-ministerial employees," the judges ruled, "does not violate the [E]stablishment [C]lause."[39] The real significance of the circuit court's ruling was perhaps best summed up by the chief counsel for the Seminary when he declared that, to his knowledge, "This is the first decision . . . that any court has made sanctioning a federal agency's invading the operation and administration of a church."[40]

The request by the Seminary for an *en banc* hearing was denied by the circuit court on September 16, 1981. Because of the far-reaching implications of this case to the denomination and its program of theological education, not to mention its eventual impact on the churches themselves, the circuit court's decision was appealed by the Seminary (with full support from the five other Southern Baptist seminaries) to the U.S. Supreme Court.[41]

The Potential in Recent Statutes for Government Surveillance of Religious Organizations

SHARON L. WORTHING

Is there a file on your church?

As we go through life, many of our actions are reflected by records of one sort or another—transcripts on our performance in school, medical records, dental records, motor vehicle records, a credit rating, records held by insurance companies, employment records. We willingly seek and establish some of these records—such as our right to a driver's license. We are neutral about others—dental records. And then there are records which people would eliminate if they could—a criminal record.

A few years ago it was announced that anyone could write to the Federal Bureau of Investigation to see if they maintained a file on him or her. The FBI would reply—"yes" or "no." And if the FBI did not maintain a file on the requester, said Walter Cronkite, it would start one.

Churches are also the subject of records. Is your church legally incorporated? Does it have a bank account? Does it own land and have a deed which has been recorded? Does it pay wages on which tax is withheld? Has it elected to pay Social Security taxes? All of these activities result in records. Indeed, without records it would be impossible to have an orderly society. This paper, however, will focus on records kept on tax-exempt organizations in general and on churches in particular —records which are not made to facilitate any particular types of transactions, but which exist to aid government in supervising these organizations; the use to which these records are put, and the rationale of their creation.

Records Kept on Tax-Exempt Organizations

There are two major considerations which should be weighed when records are created on an individual or organization. One is the burden placed on the person or organization who is the subject of the record. For many individuals, this burden may be relatively light. An individual

111

establishing a credit rating may spend a limited amount of time filling out applications, and then provide most of the information by means of his financial activities, which are undertaken for their own sakes.

When an institution is required to submit information to a governmental agency, however, the costs may be significant. In 1976, the president of Columbia University estimated that the University spent "easily in excess of $1 million each year in meeting its various Federal reporting obligations."[1] No doubt the dollar figure has increased since that time.

A second aspect of the creation of a record is what happens to it after it is created: the manner in which it is stored, the persons who have access to it, and the uses to which the information may be put.

Until fairly recently, the records kept on tax-exempt organizations by governmental agencies were very sparse. Two factors have especially worked to change this: the advent of the computer, making it possible to store and manage large quantities of data, and the concept of the "public accountability" of exempt organizations.

At the root of the concept of "public accountability" is the notion that because tax-exempt organizations exist to benefit the public, they are "owned" by the public; and because they do not pay taxes, they are "subsidized" by the public. Because the organization is "public," the public—meaning the government—ought to have information on the organization's activities.

The "public ownership" theory taken to its logical extreme is illustrated by the receivership imposed on the Worldwide Church of God in an action brought by the California Attorney General's Office in 1979. Morton Jackson, who aided the Worldwide Church of God, called this concept "socialized religion . . . public ownership—and control—of the means of worship."[2] The fallacies of this theory are dealt with by Charles Whelan in his paper on page 57.

Another reason for imposing reporting requirements is the thought that fraud and waste will be diminished if the organization must make public reports, which appeals to advocates of consumer protection.

Most of the reporting requirements which have been imposed on tax-exempt organizations in recent years have not been applied to churches. The Senate in 1969 continued the exemption of churches from filing a certain reporting form "in view of the traditional separation of church and state."[3] As reporting requirements have been imposed on church-affiliated organizations not perceived to be as religious as churches, a fierce debate has emerged as to what kinds of institutions are subject to the religious constraints of the Constitution. Congress and the Internal Revenue Service have drawn the line more and more narrowly around the sanctuary.[4]

Consequently, the concern of churches over reporting requirements is not based for the most part on what they themselves must file, which is quite limited, but upon what their affiliated institutions must file, and also upon what churches perceive to be a trend that may result in the imposition of more reporting requirements upon churches.

Reporting requirements for tax-exempt organizations include the following forms to be filed with the Internal Revenue Service: the annual information return, the notice of entitlement to exempt treatment, and the annual return of unrelated business taxable income.[5] The Bureau of the Census distributes questionnaires to church-related institutions such as parochial schools. Furthermore, states and sometimes municipalities have their own reporting requirements. In New York State, for example, required reports include a registration statement upon the organization's formation, an annual report, and additional information from certain organizations soliciting funds.

In addition, there are certain federal and state reporting requirements relating to the employees of an organization, their compensation, and taxes withheld or paid on their behalf. (These requirements are beyond the scope of this paper.)

New York State recently instituted a requirement that organizations owning real property exempt from taxation file applications to maintain the exemption: a blue form describing the organization's purpose, to which organizational documents must be attached, and a yellow form for each parcel of property owned by the organization, describing in detail its use. Any property used as a manse, or home for clergy, is to be described using a special green form. The selection of manses for this distinction seems to result from an effort to detect property owned by "mail order ministers" not entitled to exemption. Shorter forms which update these applications must be filed by each organization annually.

New York City has recently ceased its practice of canceling water and sewer charges for organizations exempt from real property tax. Instead, the City has required organizations to submit separate applications for exemption from these charges. These applications require a detailed description of the organization and the use of its property. A certificate of incorporation must be attached.

This list of types of reporting requirements is not exhaustive. For instance, it does not include special reports which must be made by organizations subject to the supervision of a particular governmental department, such as a state department of education.

As mentioned previously, churches are often, but not always, exempted from various reporting requirements. In some cases, despite their exemption, churches may wish to file reports to assure their entitlement to certain benefits, or to insure that they are not investigated for a deficiency in their exempt status some years later.

Controversy has arisen over regulations issued by the Internal Revenue Service which define an "integrated auxiliary" of a church as an organization whose "principal activity is exclusively religious."[6] Tax-exempt church-related organizations which are not classified as integrated auxiliaries must file annual information returns with the Internal Revenue Service. Because the regulatory definition is so limiting, many church-related organizations are required to file these returns, even though the church may consider them integral to its mission and thus more properly exempted along with the church itself, as Philip Draheim points out in an earlier paper.

Recently, some technical advice memoranda have been issued by the Internal Revenue Service declaring that certain organizations did not qualify as integrated auxiliaries of a church. A technical advice memorandum is given to a particular individual or organization, and may not be cited as precedent. Two of these memoranda contain the following language:

> The rationale of the statute and the regulation is that a church-affiliated organization and an exempt non-affiliated organization providing the same services to the community should account to the public equally. The church-affiliated organization should not, solely because of its affiliation with the church, be excused from its duty to account.[7]

Processing of Information Held by Government

In order to understand more fully the significance of various reporting requirements, it is helpful to examine the manner in which this information is processed. Perhaps the most sophisticated processing system is the Business Master File maintained by the Internal Revenue Service. The current Business Master File results from the merging of the former Exempt Organization Master File and the Business Master File—and will be referred to here as the Master File. The Exempt Organization Master File as it existed prior to this merger will be referred to by the same name, without distinction.

The merger is only partially reflected in the Internal Revenue Manual, a manual for the use of Internal Revenue Service personnel which describes procedures. Further changes may arise as a result of the merger.

The Exempt Organization Master File was commenced in the summer of 1964, after questionnaires were mailed to about 500,000 organizations shown in the records of the Internal Revenue Service to be tax-exempt. Since that time, the Internal Revenue Service has added organizations to the File when it issued letters to them or received forms from them. Many churches have what are known as group exemption letters: letters stating that the main church body and those organizations it recognizes as affiliated with it are tax-exempt. The church body holding such a letter is included on the Master File, but its subordinates generally are not unless the subordinates are required to file exempt organization returns with the Internal Revenue Service. Churches or synagogues which have received individual determinations from the Internal Revenue Service are listed unless "affiliated with well-known religious denominations."[8]

The Master File consists of magnetic tape records stored and maintained at the National Computer Center. Each record on an exempt organization is divided into two parts. One is an "entity module" with data which describes the organization and its exemption; the other is a "return section" with information from returns filed by the organization and examinations of it.

The chart reproduced on pages 117 through 119 shows 31 data elements from the Master File which apply to an included organization.[9] Some of these elements are: a status code which indicates actual or potential deficiencies in the organization's tax exemption, a code indicating the amount of the organization's assets, a code for the organization's gross receipts as shown on its most recent return, and the year the most recent audit was conducted. One of the status codes indicates an intention by the Internal Revenue Service to conduct a pre-examination of a church which has never received a determination regarding its exempt status from the Service.[10]

You will note that data element number 19 consists of the organization's "activity codes." These are shown on the next chart, on pages 120–21. Organizations which submit applications to the Internal Revenue Service for tax exemption are required to list up to three activity codes which best describe the organization. (Churches and their integrated auxiliaries are not required to file applications for tax-exempt status, but they may wish to do so to assure their contributors of deductible contributions and to obtain special mailing rates more easily.)

An annual information return filed with the Internal Revenue Service is also required of various tax-exempt organizations, but not churches and their integrated auxiliaries.[11] This return formerly contained space for an organization to list up to three activity codes. The current version of the return does not require these codes to be listed, but does state that the organization must describe any *change* in its activities. The deletion may please the reporting organization, but this information is tracked just the same.

An examination of the chart of activity codes[12] shows that nine categories of religious activities are listed, including "mission" as one category and "missionary activities" as another—a fine distinction. There are four kinds of civil rights activities. And there are thirty-five codes under the heading of "Advocacy: Attempt to influence public opinion concerning" the Selective Service System, pacifism and peace, anti-communism, separation of church and state, and racial integration, among other issues. Big Brother, it seems, is interested not only in knowing your organization type, but in a very exact description of your issues of concern—for the computer.

The next chart, on pages 122 and 123, is a schedule of outputs which are regularly issued from the Exempt Organization Master File. As you can see, there are thirty-eight standard outputs which are distributed in time periods ranging from monthly to annually.[13] One of these outputs is an annual activity roster, produced on microfilm. This roster lists the names of all active organizations which have been classified under each activity code, and it lists the other activity codes of each organization as well. The roster is issued by district, and a microfilm copy for each district is sent to the "key district" which oversees the exempt organizations in the individual districts. Thus, a key district would annually receive a list of those organizations within its jurisdiction which were known to have as a principal activity the influencing of public opinion concerning racial integration, anti-communism, or various other issues. Some key districts might regard such organizations favorably; others might not.

The Master File is also able to produce special-purpose lists which combine various data elements within the Master File. An example of such a list is a "[n]ational listing of organizations on [the Master File] exempt under a specified exemption subsection with certain activity codes."[14] Thus, a special-purpose list could readily be produced which contained organizations exempt under Section 501(c)(3) of the Internal Revenue Code which engaged in missionary activities and attempted to influence public opinion on the use of tobacco. Special-purpose lists usually contain only the name and address of the organizations listed. On request, other data from the Master File may also be included.

Requests for special-purpose lists must be signed at the District Director or Division Chief level of the Internal Revenue Service. Members of the general public will be charged for such lists, as will governmental agencies which subscribe to such lists on a continuing basis.

What we have, then, is an extremely elaborate system which is capable of keeping track of the tax-exempt organizations in the country with a particular ideological persuasion. Furthermore, almost all of the information contained in the returns of exempt organizations filed with the Internal Revenue Service is open to public inspection. Some of this information includes, for organizations exempt under Section 501(c)(3) of the Internal Revenue Code, the names and addresses of directors and officers, the time they spend on their positions, and their compensation. An interested person, having learned of the existence of a particular organization through this amazing indexing system, could then contact the individuals responsible for the organization or take certain actions with respect to them.

In 1979, after the suicide of a woman who had been subject to rumors planted by the Federal Bureau of Investigation, the Director of the Bureau stated, "The days when the F.B.I. used derogatory information to combat advocates of unpopular causes have long since passed. We are out of that business forever."[15] One cannot help but wonder, however, what is the purpose of having a government agency maintain and regularly

Exhibit 15

BMF Data Elements   ◊

Element	Description
(1) Organization name	Organization's current name. This may be the organization's legal name, an abbreviation from the list of abbreviations, Exhibit 16, or an edited version of the organization's name to accommodate BMF.
(2) Name control	First four significant characters of organization's name, excluding "the" blanks, and special characters.
(3) Employer identification number (EIN)	Nine-digit number assigned to organization.
(4) Address	Street address, city, state, country, and ZIP code. When address has "in care of" entry, it is part of address.
(5) Other name	Other name of organization by which it is known (i.e., former name or "also known as").
(6) Status codes	Organization's current exempt status.
(a) 01	Unconditional exemption
(b) 02	Conditional exemption
(c) 03	Under reconsideration
(d) 07	Church filing 990–T
(e) 10	Pre-examination of a church
(f) 11	Organization filing Form 5578
(g) 12	Organization filing Form 5227/No exemption letter issued
(h) 20	Terminated/Out of business
(i) 21	Unable to locate
(j) 22	Revocation
(k) 23	Terminated under 507 (a)
(l) 24	Terminated under 507 (b)(1)(A)
(m) 25	Terminated under 507 (b)(1)(B)
(n) 26	Terminated/Merger
(o) 40	Filed return/No exemption on record
(p) 41	Failed to reply to solicitation for application
(q) 42	Reserved for future use
(r) 70	Denied exemption
(s) 71	Failed to establish exemption
(t) 72	Refusal to rule
(7) Status date	Month and year current status was established. Four zeros, in printout means it is an initial entry and status date goes back to time organization was created or formed.
(8) Prior status code	Organization's status code immediately preceding current status.
(9) Prior status date	Month and year prior status code was established.
(10) Ruling date (yr./mo.)	Month and year of ruling or determination letter recognizing organization's continued exempt status.
(11) Code subsections	Current code subsection and prior subsection, if applicable.
(12) District code	District office of jurisdiction.
(13) File Folder Number	District office code (National Office—50) of office issuing original ruling or determination letter.
(14) Deductibility code	Whether contributions are deductible 1=deductible 2=not deductible 4=deductible by treaty
(15) Deductibility year	If a year is shown, it represents year deductibility began where no prior status exists or the year it was last changed.
(16) Type of organiation	1=Corporation 2=Trust 3=Cooperative 4=Partnership 5=Association
(17) Classification codes	A further breakdown of Internal Revenue Code exemption subsections.
(18) Large Case Program Code	1=Yes 2=No
(19) Activity codes	Codes which reflect organization purposes, activities, operations or types. See Exhibit 24.

MT 7820–16

Exhibit 15 Cont. (1)

BMF Data Elements   ◊

(20) Foundation codes	3=Private Operating 4=Private Non-Operating 9=Suspense 10=170(b)(1)(A)(i) 11=170(b)(1)(A)(ii) 12=170(b)(1)(A)(iii) 13=170(b)(1)(A)(iv) 14=170(b)(1)(A)(v) 15=170(b)(1)(A)(vi) 16=509(a)(2) 17=509(a)(3) 18=509(a)(4)
(21) Affiliation code	1=Central (no group exemption) 2=Intermediate (no group exemption) 3=Independent 6=Central (group exemption)—except church or 501(c)(1) 7=Intermediate (group exemption) 8=Central (group exemption)—Church or 501(c)(1)
(22) Cross-reference EIN	EIN of related organization.
(23) Group exemption number	Number assigned to group exemption.
(24) Pension Plan Code	1=Organization has a plan 2=No plan
(25) Accounting period	Month (01-12) in which organization's accounting period ends.
(26) Filing requirements	A 26 Position field on the BMF representing the various filing requirements

Position	Return
1 & 2	941
3 & 4	1120
5	720
6	942
7	1041
8	1065
9	CT–1
10	940
11	943
12	990–C
13	990–T
14	1041–A
15	5227
16	990–PF
17	4720
18	990
19	709
20	706
21	4638
22	2290
23	11
24	11–B
25	11–C
26	730

(27) Asset code	Amount of assets shown on most recent return on EO/BMF.

Code	$ Amount
0	Blank or zero
1	1–4,999
2	5,000–9,999
3	10,000–24,999
4	25,000–99,999
5	100,000–499,999
6	500,000–999,999
7	1,000,000–9,999,999

Exhibit 15 Cont. (2)

BMF Data Elements

	Code	$ Amount
	8	10,000,000–49,999,999
	9	50,000,000 & greater
(28)	Income code	Amount of gross receipts shown on or computed from most recent return on BMF. (Code and Description same as Asset Class, Item (31).)
(29)	Asset code year	The year of the return from which the latest asset and income code was computed.
(30)	Latest year audited	Year of the return on which the latest audit was conducted.
(31)	Year of audit	Year the latest audit was conducted.

Activity Code Numbers of Exempt Organizations (select up to three codes which best describe or most accurately identify your purposes, activities, operations or type of organization and enter in block 7, page 1, of the application. Enter first the code which most accurately identifies you.)

Code		Code		Code	

Religious Activities
001 Church, synagogue, etc.
002 Association or convention of churches
003 Religious order
004 Church auxiliary
005 Mission
006 Missionary activities
007 Evangelism
008 Religious publishing activities
--- Book store (use 918)
--- Genealogical activities (use 094)
029 Other religious activities

Schools, Colleges and Related Activities
030 School, college, trade school, etc.
031 Special school for the blind, handicapped, etc.
032 Nursery school
--- Day care center (use 574)
033 Faculty group
034 Alumni association or group
035 Parent or parent-teachers association
036 Fraternity or sorority
--- Key club (use 323)
037 Other student society or group
038 School or college athletic association
039 Scholarships for children of employees
040 Scholarships (other)
041 Student loans
042 Student housing activities
043 Other student aid
044 Student exchange with foreign country
045 Student operated business
--- Financial support of schools, colleges, etc. (use 602)
--- Achievement prizes or awards (use 914)
--- Student book store (use 918)
--- Student travel (use 299)
--- Scientific research (see Scientific Research Activities)
046 Private school
059 Other school related activities

Cultural, Historical or Other Educational Activities
060 Museum, zoo, planetarium, etc.
061 Library
062 Historical site, records or reenactment
063 Monument

Scientific Research Activities
180 Contract or sponsored scientific research for industry
181 Scientific research for government
--- Scientific research (diseases) (use 161)
199 Other scientific research activities

Business and Professional Organizations
200 Business promotion (chamber of commerce, business league, etc.)
201 Real-estate association
202 Board of trade
203 Regulating business
204 Better Business Bureau
205 Professional association
206 Professional association auxiliary
207 Industry trade shows
208 Convention displays
--- Testing products for public safety (use 905)
209 Research, development and testing
210 Professional athletic league
--- Attracting new industry (use 403)
--- Publishing activities (use 120)
--- Insurance or other benefits for members (see Employee or Membership Benefit Organizations)
211 Underwriting municipal insurance
212 Assigned risk insurance activities
213 Tourist bureau
229 Other business or professional group

Farming and Related Activities
230 Farming
231 Farm bureau
232 Agricultural group
233 Horticultural group
234 Farmers' cooperative marketing or purchasing
235 Financing crop operations
--- FFA, FHA, 4-H club, etc. (use 322)
--- Fair (use 065)
236 Dairy herd improvement association
237 Breeders association
249 Other farming and related activities

Mutual Organizations
250 Mutual ditch, irrigation, telephone, electric company or like organization
251 Credit Union

Youth Activities
320 Boy Scouts, Girl Scouts, etc.
321 Boys Club, Little League, etc.
322 FFA, FHA, 4-H club, etc.
323 Key club
324 YMCA, YWCA, YMHA, etc.
325 Camp
326 Care and housing of children (orphanage, etc.)
327 Prevention of cruelty to children
328 Combat juvenile delinquency
349 Other youth organization or activities

Conservation, Environmental and Beautification Activities
350 Preservation of natural resources (conservation)
351 Combatting or preventing pollution (air, water, etc.)
352 Land acquisition for preservation
353 Soil or water conservation
354 Preservation of scenic beauty
--- Litigation (see Litigation and Legal Aid Activities)
--- Combat community deterioration (use 402)
355 Wildlife sanctuary or refuge
356 Garden club
379 Other conservation, environmental or beautification activities

Housing Activities
380 Low-income housing
381 Low and moderate income housing
382 Housing for the aged (see also 153)
--- Nursing or convalescent home (use 152)
--- Student housing (use 042)
--- Orphanage (use 326)
398 Instruction and guidance on housing
399 Other housing activities

Inner City or Community Activities
400 Area development, re-development or renewal
--- Housing (see Housing Activities)
401 Homeowners association
402 Other activity aimed at combatting community deterioration

Code
512 National defense policy
513 Weapons systems
514 Government spending
515 Taxes or tax exemption
516 Separation of church and state
517 Government aid to parochial schools
518 U.S. foreign policy
519 U.S. military involvement
520 Pacifism and peace
521 Economic-political system of U.S.
522 Anti-communism
523 Right to work
524 Zoning or rezoning
525 Location of highway or transportation system
526 Rights of criminal defendants
527 Capital punishment
528 Stricter law enforcement
529 Ecology or conservation
530 Protection of consumer interests
531 Medical care system
532 Welfare system
533 Urban renewal
534 Busing students to achieve racial balance
535 Racial integration
536 Use of intoxicating beverage
537 Use of drugs or narcotics
538 Use of tobacco
539 Prohibition of erotica
540 Sex education in public schools
541 Population control
542 Birth control methods
543 Legalized abortion
559 Other matters

Other Activities Directed to Individuals
560 Supplying money, goods or services to the poor
561 Gifts or grants to individuals (other than scholarships)
--- Scholarships for children of employees (use 039)
--- Scholarships (other) (use 040)
--- Student loans (use 041)
562 Other loans to individuals
563 Marriage counseling
564 Family planning
565 Credit counseling and assistance
566 Job training, counseling, or assistance

festival, pageant, etc.)
065 Fair
088 Community theatrical group
089 Singing society or group
090 Cultural performances
091 Art exhibit
092 Literary activities
093 Cultural exchanges with foreign country
094 Genealogical activities
--- Achievement prizes or awards (use 914)
--- Gifts or grants to individuals (use 561)
--- Financial support of cultural organizations (use 602)
119 Other cultural or historical activities

Other Instruction and Training Activities
120 Publishing activities
121 Radio or television broadcasting
122 Producing films
123 Discussion groups, forums, panels, lectures, etc.
124 Study and research (non-scientific)
125 Giving information or opinion (see also Advocacy)
126 Apprentice training
--- Travel tours (use 299)
149 Other instruction and training

Health Services and Related Activities
150 Hospital
151 Hospital auxiliary
152 Nursing or convalescent home
153 Care and housing for the aged (see also 382)
154 Health clinic
155 Rural medical facility
156 Blood bank
157 Cooperative hospital service organization
158 Rescue and emergency service
159 Nurses' register or bureau
160 Aid to the handicapped (see also 031)
161 Scientific research (diseases)
162 Other medical research
163 Health insurance (medical, dental, optical, etc.)
164 Prepaid group health plan
165 Community health planning
166 Mental health care
167 Group medical practice association
168 In-faculty group practice association
169 Hospital pharmacy, parking facility, food services, etc.
179 Other health services

domestic building and loan association, cooperative bank, or mutual savings bank
253 Mutual insurance company
254 Corporation organized under an Act of Congress (see also 904)
--- Farmer's cooperative marketing or purchasing (use 234)
--- Cooperative hospital service organization (use 157)
259 Other mutual organization

Employee or Membership Benefit Organizations
260 Fraternal beneficiary society, order, or association
261 Improvement of conditions of workers
262 Association of municipal employees
263 Association of employees
264 Employee or member welfare association
265 Sick, accident, death, or similar benefits
266 Strike benefits
267 Unemployment benefits
268 Pension or retirement benefits
269 Vacation benefits
279 Other services or benefits to members or employees

Sports, Athletic, Recreational and Social Activities
280 Country club
281 Hobby club
282 Dinner club
283 Variety club
284 Dog club
285 Women's club
--- Garden club (use 356)
286 Hunting or fishing club
287 Swimming or tennis club
288 Other sports club
--- Boys Club, Little League, etc. (use 321)
296 Community center
297 Community recreational facilities (park, playground, etc.)
298 Training in sports
299 Travel tours
300 Amateur athletic association
--- School or college athletic association (use 038)
301 Fund raising athletic or sports event
317 Other sports or athletic activities
318 Other recreational activities
319 Other social activities

Attracting new industry or retaining industry in an area
404 Community promotion
--- Community recreational facility (use 297)
--- Community center (use 296)
405 Loans or grants for minority businesses
--- Job training, counseling, or assistance (use 566)
--- Day care center (use 574)
--- Referral service (social agencies) (use 569)
--- Legal aid to indigents (use 462)
406 Crime prevention
407 Voluntary firemen's organization or auxiliary
--- Rescue squad (use 158)
408 Community service organization
429 Other inner city or community benefit activities

Civil Rights Activities
430 Defense of human and civil rights
431 Elimination of prejudice and discrimination (race, religion, sex, national origin, etc.)
432 Lessen neighborhood tensions
449 Other civil rights activities

Litigation and Legal Aid Activities
460 Public interest litigation activities
461 Other litigation or support of litigation
462 Legal aid to indigents
463 Providing bail
465 Plan under IRC section 120

Legislative and Political Activities
480 Propose, support, or oppose legislation
481 Voter information on issues or candidates
482 Voter education (mechanics of registering, voting, etc.)
483 Support, oppose, or rate political candidates
484 Provide facilities or services for political campaign activities
509 Other legislative and political activities

Advocacy
Attempt to influence public opinion concerning:
510 Firearms control
511 Selective Service System

568 Vocational counseling
569 Referral service (social agencies)
572 Rehabilitating convicts or ex-convicts
573 Rehabilitating alcoholics, drug abusers, compulsive gamblers, etc.
574 Day care center
575 Services for the aged (see also 153 and 382)
--- Training of or aid to the handicapped (see 031 and 160)

Activities Directed to Other Organizations
600 Community Chest, United Fund, etc.
601 Booster club
602 Gifts, grants, or loans to other organizations
603 Non-financial services or facilities to other organizations

Other Purposes and Activities
900 Cemetery or burial activities
901 Perpetual care fund (cemetery, columbarium, etc.)
902 Emergency or disaster aid fund
903 Community trust or component
904 Government instrumentality or agency (see also 254)
905 Testing products for public safety
906 Consumer interest group
907 Veterans activities
908 Patriotic activities
909 4947(a)(1) trust
910 Domestic organization with activities outside U.S.
911 Foreign organization
912 Title holding corporation
913 Prevention of cruelty to animals
914 Achievement prizes or awards
915 Erection or maintenance of public building or works
916 Cafeteria, restaurant, snack bar, food services, etc.
917 Thrift shop, retail outlet, etc.
918 Book, gift or supply store
919 Advertising
921 Loans or credit reporting
922 Endowment fund or financial services
923 Indians (tribes, cultures, etc.)
924 Traffic or tariff bureau
927 Fund raising
928 4947(a)(2) trust
930 Prepaid legal services plan exempt under IRC section 501(c)(20)

Schedule of EOMF Outputs

Output Title	Jan.	Feb.	Mar.	Apr.	May	June	July	Aug	Sept.	Oct.	Nov.	Dec.
List of Centrals	X	X	X	X	X	X	X	X	X	X	X	X
Register of Exempt Organizations (Standard List)	X	X	X	X	X	X	X	X	X	X	X	X
Mail Labels	X	X	X	X	X	X	X	X	X	X	X	X
EOMF Statistical Summary Table 1	X	Cum X	Cum X	Cum X	Cum X	Cum X	Cum X	Cum X	Cum X	Cum X	Cum X	Comp X
EOMF Returns and Foundation Data Tables 2.0 and 2.1	X	Cum X	Cum X	Cum X	Cum X	Cum X	Cum X	Cum X	Cum X	Cum X	Cum X	Comp X
EOMF National Recap Tables 1, 2.0, and 2.1	X	Cum X	Cum X	Cum X	Cum X	Cum X	Cum X	Cum X	Cum X	Cum X	Cum X	Comp X
EOMF Entity Analysis Table 3	X	X	X	X	X	X	X	X	X	X	X	X
EOMF Posting Activity and Returns Filed Data Table 4	X	Cum X	Cum X	Cum X	Cum X	Cum X	Cum X	Cum X	Cum X	Cum X	Cum X	Comp X
EOMF Return — Results of Examination Tables 5.0 and 5.1	Cum X	Cum X	Cum X	Cum X	Cum X	Cum X	Cum X	Cum X	Comp X	X	Cum X	Comp X
Transaction History (Microfilm)	X	Cum X	Cum X	Cum X	Cum X	Cum X	Cum X	Cum X	Cum X	Cum X	Cum X	Comp X
Returns Register	X	Cum X	Cum X	Cum X	Cum X	Cum X	Cum X	Cum X	Cum X	Cum X	Cum X	Comp X
Returns Delinquency Check	X	X	X	X	X	X	X	X	X	X	X	X
EIN Register (Microfilm)	X	Cum X	Cum X	Cum X	Cum X	Comp X	X	Cum X	Cum X	Cum X	Cum X	Comp X
EIN Register (KDO only)						Comp X						Comp X
Cumulative List	X			X		X			X			
Audit Classification Register		X			X				X			X
Active Entities by Entity Activity Codes Tables 6.0		X			X				X			X
EOMF Active Entities by Classification Codes Table 7		X			X				X			X
Group Exempt Roster		X							X			

Note: Outputs described above are produced after the last NCC posting cycle for the month in which the output is scheduled to be produced.

Exhibit 25 Cont.

Schedule of EOMF Outputs

Output Title	Jan.	Feb.	Mar.	Apr.	May	June	July	Aug.	Sept.	Oct.	Nov.	Dec.
Register of Status 09's	X						X					
EIN Assignment Purge Records (ENAF)	X						X					
D.O. Alpha Register	X						X					
Data Center Lobbying Tape							X					
National Alpha Register (Microfilm)	X											
National Cross Reference Register (Microfilm)	X											
Foundation Center Information Tape	X											
501 (c) (7) Discrimination Listing	X						X					
Private Foundation Listing	X											
Future Examination Year List										X		
Entities Not Required to File									X			
Activity Roster (Microfilm)												X
Form 990 SOI Tabulations												X
Form 990 PF SOI Tabulations												X
Private Schools — Filing Requirement No Return Filed (Listings)												X
Private Schools — Filed Return — Made Certification (Listings)												X
Private Schools — Filed Return — No Certification (Listings)												X
Private Schools — No Return Filed — Made Certification (Listings)												X
Census Gross Receipts Study			X				X			X		

Note: Outputs described above are produced after the last NCC posting cycle for the month in which the output is scheduled to be produced.

[The next page is 21,785-3.]

issue lists of organizations involved in matters of public controversy. This practice could lend itself to uses similar to those disowned by Mr. Webster—either by government or by members of the public.

This detailed description of the Master File is meant to show the potential of a sophisticated, computer-based information system. Any return filed, then, should not be considered merely as the paper submitted, but should be thought of in light of the information system to which it contributes. It is a data resource from which a wide variety of informational by-products can be spun. Furthermore, it should be noted that returns are only one of several sources of information for the Master File.

The Internal Revenue Manual lists sources of information for the Master File as follows: "information voluntarily furnished to the Service by exempt organizations on applications, amendments to articles, returns, etc., and information developed by Service personnel during an examination *or otherwise.*"[16] Consequently, an organization which had never filed anything with the Internal Revenue Service could still be listed on the Master File.

Information contained in this File is within the discretion of the Internal Revenue Service, and may be revised "without approval or consent of exempt organizations,"[17] according to the Internal Revenue Manual. The Manual also indicates that because of the increased reporting obligations recently imposed on churches and their affiliates, more of them will be listed on the Master File.

ERISA: A Case Study

Is there anything which can be done to stem the rising tide of reporting and disclosure requirements imposed on religious institutions? Something might be done through constitutional litigation in the courts, but the avenue of legislative reform should not be overlooked. What happened with the Employee Retirement Income Security Act of 1974, "ERISA," provides a good illustration.

When ERISA was adopted, it substantially altered the legal treatment of the nation's private pension plans. Every pension plan to which the new law applied needed to be amended as a result and became subject to stricter reporting and disclosure requirements.

If a pension plan covered by ERISA has more than 100 participants, the plan administrator generally must file an annual report with the Internal Revenue Service containing financial data. This report may be very complex and may have to be audited by an independent public accountant, depending upon how the plan is funded. The plan administrator must also distribute to participants summary plan descriptions, summary annual reports, summaries of material modifications, and individual benefit statements.

"Church plans" as defined by ERISA are not subject to the provisions of

ERISA unless they choose to be.[18] Church plans which do not make this choice must still meet certain standards of reporting and disclosure, but these are less rigorous than those imposed by ERISA, which must be one of the most complicated statutes in existence.

Under ERISA as initially enacted, "church plans" could only be offered to employees of churches themselves, and not to employees of "church agencies." The application of this definition was delayed, however, for plans already in existence on January 1, 1974.[19]

Final Treasury regulations issued in 1980 defined a church agency as "an organization which is exempt from tax under section 501 [of the Internal Revenue Code] and which is either controlled by, or associated with, a church."[20] If a church appointed a majority of the directors of an organization, for example, the organization would be considered controlled by a church. An organization was associated with a church if it shared "common religious bonds and convictions with that church."[21]

ERISA provided that until January 1, 1983, pension plans in existence on January 1, 1974, which were maintained by a church *and* one or more church agencies would still be considered church plans if they met the other requirements for church plans. No new church agency could join the plan after January 1, 1974. Furthermore, the plan had to be maintained by *both* a church and its agencies. If a plan only included employees of a church agency, it would not be considered a church plan under the interim provision.

After the passage of ERISA, many churches were concerned by what they saw as yet another governmental attempt to disregard the religious character of church-related institutions. In order to obtain exemption from ERISA's provisions after January 1, 1983, churches whose pension plans covered employees of both churches and church agencies would have to institute separate plans for each group of employees. Churches felt that they were being artificially dissected by statute.

The concerns of churches were addressed in a number of bills introduced in Congress to amend the definition of "church plan." Such a bill was finally attached as a rider to the Multiemployer Pension Plan Amendments Act of 1980, and became law.

Under the amended provision defining "church plan," an "employee of a church" includes a minister "in the exercise of his ministry, regardless of the source of his compensation," and also includes an employee of a tax-exempt organization which is "controlled by or associated with a church."[22]

Consequently, pension plans which cover both employees of churches and their affiliated institutions, and even plans which cover only employees of church-affiliated institutions, are church plans under the revised definition. The term "church agency" has been dropped, avoiding the addition of yet another ambiguous church-related term to the federal statutes.

Six years passed between the enactment of the original "church plan" definition in ERISA and its revision in a manner generally satisfactory to churches. The course of this definition shows that it is possible for churches to oppose the seemingly unstoppable tide of more regulation and compelled disclosure and reporting if enough sustained and determined effort is made in that direction. The result will not necessarily come easily or quickly, but it may come.

The "Incontestable Duty": Public Disclosure

An evaluation of reporting and disclosure requirements imposed on religious organizations should take two basic factors into account: the revolution in the handling of information which has resulted from use of the computer, and the special constitutional status of these organizations.

With the advent of advanced computer technology, the matter of the storage and handling of information has become an increasingly important subject. Threats to individual privacy have been recognized, and statutes have been enacted for its protection. Some of the most important of these statutory provisions have been enacted within the last ten or even the last five years. The Bill of Rights protects the privacy of individuals through the Third and Fourth Amendments, and, less directly, through the First and Fifth Amendments. There is a general recognition that people who seek to have their privacy protected are not just "evil people," but are asserting a valid and recognized right.

Senator Lowell Weicker Jr., who sponsored the privacy provisions of the Tax Reform Act of 1976, wrote:

> The linchpin of any totalitarian system is the information it has about individuals. The right to privacy is the very essence of freedom, not merely in a philosophical sense but also in a very practical sense.[23]

A former chairman of the United States Privacy Protection Commission stated:

> [I]t is widely believed that the balance of power in our society is becoming more and more dangerously weighted in favor of large institutions—government and industry alike. A chief reason is that they are the ones with the information.[24]

At the same time that there has been an expanded recognition of the need to protect individual privacy, there has been an incongruous move in the opposite direction, seeking to compel extensive disclosure and reporting of information by charitable institutions. This move is fueled by the recently popularized concept of "public accountability." Information which is recognized as a tangible and potentially harmful weapon against an individual is regarded as an almost immaterial commodity with respect to the institution. Persons express astonishment at the unwillingness of church-affiliated institutions to respond to disclosure under government compulsion. Is there something wrong? What is the organization trying to hide?

John Gardner, when Chairman of Common Cause, objected to a call by Carl Bakal for the creation of a new federal agency which would regulate charitable organizations, including religious organizations. Mr. Gardner stated:

> If a commission is given the powers that Mr. Bakal proposes, it would have a mighty lever over all kinds of voluntary associations, including those irritating groups that think the Federal establishment could be doing a better job. Indeed, a commission with the powers proposed could smother such critics. All experience tells us that if government has such powers, sooner or later it will use them.[25]

Mr. Gardner recognizes what many people do not: that government's attitudes towards charitable organizations are not always charitable.

In the same letter, however, Mr. Gardner stated: "As one who is identified with openness in all public matters, I can readily agree that there is room for improvement in statutory requirements for disclosure by charitable organizations."[26] The latter statement fails to recognize that compelled disclosure can result in some of the same evils over which Mr. Gardner expresses concern in regard to the creation of a federal commission.

For years, Representative Charles Wilson of California sponsored a bill, popularly known as the "Wilson bill," which would give the United States Post Office power to regulate fundraising by charities. (Mr. Wilson served as Chairman of the Subcommittee on Postal Operations and Services.) In the fall of 1978, Mr. Wilson was reprimanded for "official misconduct" for failing to admit that he received a gift of $1,000 from Tongsun Park of South Korea.[27] In the spring of 1980, Mr. Wilson became the third Representative in this century to be censured by the House of Representatives, and was removed from his subcommittee chairmanship.[28] Mr. Wilson was found to have violated House rules by taking improper cash gifts from a California businessman and by converting campaign funds to his personal use.[29] Perhaps he was not as zealous for governmental regulation of *private* charity.

Regardless of the requirements which may be imposed on charitable organizations—the general class in the tax law to which religious organizations belong—special considerations come into play where churches and their related institutions are concerned. Religion is protected by the First Amendment in a way that most other activities are not. Many people have one or more religions which they like. They also have one or more religions which they dislike. The same is true of government bureaucrats.

The First Amendment was adopted to prevent government officials from using their power to benefit the former or hinder the latter.

Conclusion

Information gives power over the entity which provides it. The degree to which government should be able to obtain such power over church-related institutions should not be left to the tender solicitude of would-be protectors of the supposedly incompetent public, but should be soberly considered in light of *all* its implications. People do not *have* to give to church-related institutions. But they *do* have to pay taxes which support government regulators. As the Supreme Court stated in *Buckley* v. *Valeo,* "compelled disclosure has the potential for substantially infringing the exercise of First Amendment rights."[30] The dimension of this potential for infringement must not be disregarded for the sake of trying to catch a few shysters.

Then, too, there is the matter of burden to be considered. Is it really necessary that the federal government receive information from Columbia University every year which costs the University over $1 million annually to produce?

Before church institutions comply with the ever-rising tide of government-compelled disclosure, they should give the matter some hard thought and intelligent action. The experience of churches with the Pension Reform Law, ERISA, shows that relief might not come quickly, but it can come.

Current Issues in Government Regulation of Religious Solicitation

BARRY A. FISHER

The legal status of religious solicitation[1] is intimately entwined with the development of the system of freedom of expression.[2] Indeed, the former might fairly be said to have begotten the latter, at least in part.[3]

> [D]uring the decades of the thirties and forties, the Jehovah's Witnesses, a sect "distinguished by great religious zeal and astonishing powers of annoyance," brought to the Supreme Court of the United States a large and varied number of issues about the exercise of freedom of speech and religion in public places. Indeed, in their robust evangelism, they appear to have stimulated the expression by the Court of a full chapter of constitutional law.[4]

Perhaps as a consequence, there has developed little in the way of a special branch of constitutional law that either inhibits or ratifies state regulation of religious solicitation. Instead, there is primarily a body of precedent governing speech in the public forum, which, although largely generated by religious solicitation, is applied to various types of expression without regard to subject matter.[5]

Disclosure of Church Finances

The Supreme Court's recent decision in the *Schaumburg* case[6] once again raised, albeit indirectly, the extent to which and the means by which churches desiring to engage in the solicitation of funds from the public may be required to disclose to the government details of their internal financial affairs. The Court has addressed questions of this kind infrequently, and in consequence, the state of the law in this area is uncertain. It will be examined briefly here in several different but related aspects.

The first context in which the question of disclosure arises is that of a prerequisite to obtaining a license or permit to solicit. For more than forty years, the Court has consistently and expressly declared that a governmental unit may require that one obtain a license before he may solicit,

129

and moreover, "to establish his identity and his authority to act for the cause which he purports to represent."[7] While the Supreme Court has never directly held this, it has repeated the formula so often that it has come to be regarded as constitutional gospel.

These pieces of information, in themselves, are relatively innocuous and do not often generate constitutional challenge,[8] but local governments have sometimes attempted to take the matter much further. When they do, they run into another oft-stated constitutional principle that, even where a license requirement may be imposed on the exercise of First Amendment-protected rights, the licensing authority must have little or no discretion to grant or deny the permit.[9] A financial disclosure requirement may violate this precept either explicitly, when the authority has express power to request whatever information it deems necessary, or implicitly, where the data specified by the ordinance is ill-defined.[10] In these situations, the government has the effective power to block solicitation campaigns of those churches which do not meet its own standards of financial probity, or it may use its authority, consciously or unconsciously, to interpose an overlong de facto waiting period between the time of application and the time when it is acted upon.

The courts have had little difficulty with problems such as those just mentioned. Other cases, however, are more problematical.

The specific issue which attracted the attention of the Supreme Court in *Schaumburg*[11] was the validity of the imposition of a requirement that prevents a charitable or religious organization from engaging in solicitation unless a minimum proportion of its receipts, there, 75 percent, is used directly for the organization's substantive purposes, or, conversely, unless the "cost" of the organization's solicitation program does not exceed a fixed percentage of receipts. Financial disclosure arises in the percentage limitation context because such requirements are typically policed by permitting governmental examination of the soliciting organization's books and records.[12]

The *Schaumburg* Court held that an absolute percentage requirement is unconstitutional (even as to non-religious, public-issue solicitation) since it is insufficiently related to the governmental interests claimed to justify it, the prevention of fraud and the protection of public safety and residential privacy.

Schaumburg, however, did not entirely settle the question of percentage limitation requirements. An earlier decision of the Fifth Circuit Court of Appeals, *National Foundation* v. *City of Fort Worth*,[13] had upheld an ordinance under which an applicant for a solicitation permit was deemed presumptively ineligible if his costs of solicitation were greater than 20 percent of the amount collected. Fort Worth's ordinance, however, differed from Schaumburg's in that under the former to exceed the 20 percent figure was not conclusive, but only shifted the burden to the applicant to show special facts or circumstances which made the limitation "unreasonable" as applied to him, and the court placed considerable weight on this feature of the law in the course of holding it valid. Thus an important question is the constitutional status of a Fort Worth-type law after *Schaumburg*.

The *Schaumburg* Court might well have doubted the vitality of *National Foundation* either on the fundamental ground that the Fifth Circuit misunderstood the applicability of the First Amendment to the general subject matter,[14] or on the more specific basis that the Fort Worth ordinance would have survived the actual analysis of *Schaumburg* in no better condition than did the Schaumburg ordinance itself. Indeed, as the single dissenting Justice in *Schaumburg* pointed out, it is difficult to imagine the former to be an "improvement" on the latter since the "not unreasonable" criterion in *National Foundation* certainly seems to constitute an "open-ended grant of discretion" creating serious "potential for abuse."[15] Under that approach, "Fort Worth's ordinance would be more, not less, suspect than Schaumburg's."

The Court, however, chose none of these alternatives. Instead, it went to some pains to distinguish the two ordinances. Arguably, the Fort Worth law was viewed in a relatively favorable light, since the Court noted that the Schaumburg ordinance totally prohibited solicitations by organizations not meeting the percentage limitation while that of Fort Worth offered the applicant an escape hatch.

No more can be said for certain than that the Court did not rule definitively upon the Fort Worth model one way or the other. Not surprisingly, therefore, the lower courts after *Schaumburg* have differed upon its effect. One federal trial court has stated in dictum that the presumption-with-flexibility "guideline" exemplified in *National Foundation* "is permissible,"[16] while a California state appellate court has flatly held unconstitutional an ordinance with a presumption set at the 85%-15% point.[17] While the California result seems on far firmer ground in terms of principle, the Court has left an opening, indeed a gaping hole, through which the opposite view may eventually emerge prevailing.[18]

An additional fact of potential importance in this debate is that *Schaumburg* itself involved public-issue charitable solicitations, not solicitations by a church for its religious purposes. By establishing, or, by the Court's lights merely reaffirming, the First Amendment status of charitable solicitations, the Court seems in effect to have placed such activities on the same constitutional plane as religious solicitations, the central value of which it had early recognized.[19] Under this view, if *Schaumburg's* apparent approval of the *National Foundation* formulation were to be realized in the charitable context, a flexible percentage limitation would be valid for purely religious solicitation as well.

But considerations specific to church fundraising could produce the opposite result. The religion clauses of the First Amendment, those guaranteeing the free exercise of religion and forbidding the establishment thereof, "chart a course that preserve[s] the autonomy and freedom of religious bodies. . . ."[20] Given the obvious importance of a church's ability to raise funds,[21] governmental action that impinges upon this process may well jeopardize these independent constitutional values.[22] Regardless of the validity of *National Foundation* as to other kinds of charitable organizations, the argument would run, the religion clauses would forbid even the governmental intrusion of a discretionary percentage formula where churches are concerned. The Fifth Circuit itself has recently chosen just this course.[23]

Even where financial disclosure is connected to a license or permit procedure, some courts have in effect balanced the nature and extent of the disclosure required and the public interest served by it against the burden on the religious organizations imposed by the provision at issue. For example, an ordinance was upheld which called for certain specific information about the organization to appear on a card which solicitors must exhibit to the persons they contact.[24] Since the data required to be disclosed were explicitly stated, and the person to whom a solicitation is made has an obvious interest in ascertaining the information concerning the cause to which he is asked to donate, the value to the public was held to outweigh the assertedly minimal burden visited upon the organization from which the disclosure was required.

But where the licensing authority has wide power to investigate into the financial status of the organization, that fact alone may easily violate the postulate that "disclosure must be reasonably related to legitimate objectives of the ordinance."[25] In this circumstance, the nexus between the required disclosures and the public interest designed to be served is highly attenuated, and the law will not be permitted to stand.

Under this analysis, conditions other than unbounded investigatory authority may well be similarly unconstitutional, as in a case where particular information is indeed specified by a law but has little or no connection to a proper public interest. The result in any given situation may well depend upon the degree of justification the court demands of the government. If the judicially-adopted standard is a relatively lax one, such as "reasonable relationship," the law will frequently be upheld,[26] but where it is stringent, such as "compelling interest," the provision will often fall.[27]

Interestingly, one of the most difficult problems in the area of disclosure would be posed by one of the simplest kinds of laws, one which might require disclosure of certain sequestered financial data of a church clearly related to solicitation, to be used as a public record with few, if any, overtly regulatory or prohibitory provisions. The problem is difficult because there is almost no constitutional doctrine that lends any guidance in its solution.

Schaumburg itself illustrates the issue. There, in the course of holding that the governmental interest in preventing fraud was ill-served by the absolute percentage limitation the village sought to justify, the Court noted that apart from the traditional "less restrictive alternative" of direct criminal prosecution,

[e]fforts to promote disclosure of the finances of charitable solicitations also may assist in preventing fraud by informing the public of the ways in which their contributions will be employed. Such measures may help make contribution decisions more informed, while leaving to individual choice the decision whether to contribute to organizations that spend large amounts on salaries and administrative expenses.[28]

In a footnote to this passage, the Court referred to the example of the Illinois (state) charitable solicitations statute[29] which "requires charitable organizations to register with the State Attorney General's Office and to report certain information about their structure and fundraising activities."[30]

Statutes such as Illinois' are common but they have tended explicitly to exempt purely religious solicitation. Even before *Schaumburg*, however, there has been significant legislative activity counter to this traditional exemption,[31] and the broad dicta of the recent Supreme Court decision may be expected to accelerate this nascent trend.

If such a statute were to be enacted, avoiding all other unrelated constitutional shoals, the question of its constitutionality would then be squarely presented. In that event, churches would be compelled to rely on the special status granted them under the religion clauses, just as they may have to with respect to percentage limitations. The outcome is difficult to predict, although concerns expressed in related contexts in a few recent cases[32] give at least some reason for a modicum of optimism. Arguments under both of the clauses would be employed: the church autonomy implicit in the free exercise clause and the prohibition against government "entanglement" with religion under the establishment clause[33] which could arise depending upon the particular statutory mechanism chosen.

Regulations of the Time, Place and Manner of Solicitation

Forty years ago the Supreme Court, bowing to "the unbeatable proposition that you cannot have two parades on the same corner at the same time,"[34] upheld a parade permit ordinance which limited municipal discretion in granting or denying permits exclusively to considerations of the time, place, or manner of the proposed expression.[35] But stating a much broader principle than this holding, the Court declared that when the regulation is not concerned with the content of expression, but only its circumstances, "the question in a particular case is whether that control is exerted so as not to deny or unwarrantedly abridge the right of [expression or] assembly and the opportunities for the communication of thought and the discussion of public questions immemorially associated with resort to public places."

"Of course, *Cox* v. *New Hampshire* did no more than give a general standard for accommodation of the conflicting interests,"[36] preserving order in and protecting the "primary purposes"[37] of public places and using them as fora for expression. *Cox* neither defines what factors are to be taken into account nor how they are to be evaluated.[38] Other Supreme Court decisions of the same vintage furnish some guidance, but they do not articulate concrete criteria that define "how heavy a burden of justification—and how large a sacrifice of other goals—to impose on government."[39]

The Court has, however, suggested that the government interest that is asserted to justify a regulation must be more than trivial. For instance, prevention of litter

> is insufficient to justify an ordinance which prohibits a person rightfully on a public street from handing literature to one willing to receive it. Any burden imposed upon the city authorities in cleaning and caring for the streets as an indirect consequence of such distribution results from the constitutional protection of the freedom of speech and press.[40]

Moreover, the balancing process must take into account whether the government may achieve its goal by a means that has a less drastic impact upon expression. If other effective means that do not affect expression exist, then the regulation "can serve no purpose but that forbidden by the Constitution, the naked restriction of the dissemination of ideas."[41]

However, in most cases the particular regulation challenged was chosen in the first place over whatever alternative a court might suggest, not because it would restrict expression, but rather because it was a more efficient means of achieving the state end.[42] For example, litter may be more effectively prevented by prohibiting the use of handbills than by punishing litterers; solicitation fraud may be more effectively prevented by advance screening of solicitors than by after-the-fact fraud prosecutions, the alternative suggested by the Supreme Court;[43] and a general prohibition of door-to-door canvassing will be a more effective means of protecting the privacy of householders than reliance upon "No Trespassing" signs, the court-mandated alternative.[44]

The Court assertion that the existence of a less restrictive alternative impeaches the purpose of a content-neutral regulation is consequently far too simplistic. An accurate statement of the principle that the Court has implicitly applied over the years might be that the marginally greater effectiveness of a challenged regulation relative to an alternative but probably less effective means of achieving the same end must be balanced against the burden (sometimes, the incremental burden) upon communication imposed by the regulation in question.[45]

Likewise, the marginal impact of the regulation upon expression must be factored into the equation. While the Court has declared in ringing terms that "one is not to have the exercise of his liberty of expression in appropriate places abridged on the plea that it may be exercised in some other place,"[46] a restatement of this portion of the inquiry might be that one cannot have his freedom of expression in appropriate places abridged *merely* on the plea that it may be exercised in some other place. "[A] time, place, and manner restriction cannot be upheld without examination of alternative avenues of communication open to potential speakers. . . ."[47]

Another variable in the equation is consideration of whether the regulation has a differential impact upon various groups in the society. "Like the proverbial ban on sleeping under the bridges of Paris, a ban on using loudspeakers or distributing handbills obviously falls with greater force upon the poor than upon those who can afford access to other methods of communication. . . ."[48] Consequently, the Court has scrutinized restrictions upon these means of communication with what seems to be special care,[49] although the weight of differential impact in relation to the other factors is far from clear.

Until recently, the closest that the Court had come to stating an analytic approach that could be applied by legislative bodies and lower courts in order to determine which regulations of expression are permissible was *Grayned* v. *City of Rockford.*[50]

> The crucial question is whether the manner of expression is basically incompatible with the normal activity of a particular place at a particular time. Our cases make clear that in assessing the reasonableness of a regulation, we must weigh heavily the fact that communication is involved; the regulation must be narrowly tailored to further the State's legitimate interest.[51]

While *Grayned* does suggest that the time, place, and manner inquiry must be undertaken "with the thumb of the Court . . . on the speech side of the scales,"[52] it does little more. Whether the weight on the other side must be overwhelming, for example, protection of residential neighborhoods from highly amplified sound that would be at least an extremely annoying invasion of privacy and could even cause physical pain,[53] or whether it need be merely a plausible, reasonable one[54] is not stated. Nor does *Grayned* allocate the burden of proof, either requiring the government to prove that the interest will be served and that no less restrictive alternative exists or the challenger to prove the opposite.[55]

Thus, courts faced with the question of time, place, and manner regulations as applied to religious solicitation were left to their own devices. For instance, although one court concluded that a curfew on religious solicitation was justified by governmental interests in preservation of the peaceful enjoyment of the home and prevention of crime,[56] two others reached the opposite result.[57]

The opportunity definitively to resolve these questions was, in the main, not taken in the Supreme Court's decision in 1981 involving religious solicitation by the International Society for Krishna Consciousness.[58] *Heffron* v. *International Society for Krishna Consciousness*[59] concerned the validity of a Minnesota State Fair rule that required religious literature distributors and solicitors, like commercial entrepreneurs, to conduct their activities only at an assigned location within the fairgrounds, a booth. The Hare Krishnas argued that while the rule might well be valid for the regulation of purely commercial activities,[60] it could not be justified under rigorous First Amendment standards.[61]

The Court found, first, that the case was unclouded by content or subject matter bias[62] or by discretionary authority to grant or to deny permissions to express ideas. Second, the Court declared that in order to be valid, a time, place, or manner restriction on expression must serve a "significant" governmental interest.[63]

The state interest found to be "substantial" in *Heffron* was crowd control and the prevention of congestion. That the exercise of First Amendment rights might, in some cases, have to be limited when balanced against real needs of crowd control is nothing new.[64] However, the Court misapplied the principle in *Heffron* since little or no evidence of an actual threat to this interest was found in the record or was even directly inferrable from it. The Court did not analyze evidence of congestion but instead merely recited statistics describing the crowd size, the area of the Fair, and the number of exhibitors and, in effect, accepted the conclusion of the Fair Manager that roving literature distributors and solicitors would be disruptive in this environment.[65] As Justice Brennan observed in his concurrence, the state relied upon, and the Court accepted as adequate, "a general, speculative fear of disorder" as a justification for restricting freedom of expression.[66]

As Justice Brennan also pointed out, the crowd control rationale is impeached by the facts that the state itself engaged in the distribution of leaflets at the fair and that it allowed unrestricted oral advocacy by unlimited numbers of people.[67] Both of these activities could be expected to be equally disruptive of crowds at the fair, if not more so.[68] Indeed, because of predictable differences in recipient reaction, "literature distribution may present even fewer crowd control problems than . . . oral proselytizing. . . ."[69]

Given this state of the evidence, which by itself does not even prove the existence of congestion, much less its exacerbation, the decision must rest upon the effect the Court perceived that potential hordes of literature distributors and solicitors would have. Not only is this spectre largely imaginary[70] but the opinion also seems to brush aside the possibility of a less-restrictive alternative means of avoiding it. While the Court did mention the possibility of "limiting the number of solicitors," it then dismissed it with a passing reference to the "other organizations" that would presumably possess the same rights as the Krishnas and to "the much larger number[s]" of persons exercising First Amendment rights that would result.[71] The Court, apparently, either ignored the possibility of a ceiling on the *total* number of literature distributors that could be accommodated at the fair[72] or else it illogically concluded that this device could not cope with the presumed hordes of solicitors.

The Court concluded its analysis with a declaration that alternative fora for expression must exist despite the effect of the challenged regulation in order for it to be valid.[73] Apparently, an otherwise constitutional time, place, and manner regulation may be forced to yield if it effectively blocks *all* expression.[74] While the recognition of this factor is welcome, the analysis of what constitutes an adequate alternative is considerably less than lucid. First, the Court noted that the state fair booth rule did not render the rest of the world unavailable as a forum,[75] a potentially meaningless observation since it would provide a basis for upholding *any* restriction on expression inasmuch as no jurisdiction can control what happens elsewhere, and some other place is presumably always available. Somewhat more to the point, the Court also observed that the Krishnas were not totally excluded from the fair itself since, first, they could orally propagate their views and, second, they could rent a booth.

While the possibility of oral proselytization at the fair is relevant, it is not especially meaningful, since a rule forbidding it would be virtually impossible to enforce[76] and would raise grave content regulation problems.[77] The primary point, therefore, seems to be that the fair provides its own mechanism for access, a booth available to all comers. The fair exists for the purpose of providing "a means for a great number of exhibitors temporarily to present their products or views, be they commercial, religious, or political, to a large number of people in an efficient fashion."[78] Since the fair "visitors are expected, and indeed encouraged" to pass by exhibitors' booths, everyone is afforded an opportunity to purvey their views to those who are interested.[79]

Heffron is a disappointment both for what it does not do and for what it does do. As to the former, *Heffron* does little if anything to resolve the analytical fuzziness of the time, place, and manner doctrine. How "substantial" the government interest must be, whether the government must prove that its interest is effectively served by the challenged regulation, how comparable any proposed alternative measures must be, and, most important, in what order and in what fashion these factors should be considered in relation to each other are questions not answered except perhaps by murky implication.

What *Heffron* does do is uphold a regulation of expression on the barest evidence of the actual existence of a governmental interest. In effect, the Court held that a rational basis, in this case crowd control, is sufficient reason to uphold a content-neutral restriction on expression. If *Heffron* is to be taken at face value on this point, then the "non-traditional" public forum[80] may have disappeared, since a rational basis for a restriction will probably always exist. Political agitators as well as religious proselytizers and solicitors would then be banished to the public streets and parks, places which the Court concedes have "immemorially . . . been used for assembly, communicating thoughts between citizens, and discussing public questions."[81]

Fortunately, *Heffron* contains an inherent limitation on the scope of its holding. The *Heffron* result is explicitly declared to be applicable only to "a limited public forum,"[82] a new constitutional construct. The fair is a limited public forum because it exists to attract an audience and to juxtapose it with an array of exhibitors of varied kinds. The very purpose of the fair and its entire structure is thus designed to bring together speaker and listener "in an efficient fashion." The booth rule is the major mechanism that fairs have historically employed to achieve this end,[83] and it therefore "serve[s] a substantial state interest." In light of the uniqueness of the fair as a forum and of the peculiar relationship of fairs to booth rules, whether any other place would also qualify as a "limited public forum" is open to substantial doubt.

Only in light of the "limited functions" of the fair, and its consequent status as a limited public forum did the Court conclude that the booth rule did not unnecessarily limit the right of expression. In contrast, in a more general public forum, the government interest is said to be only to assure the "availability . . . for their primary purposes of passenger . . . traffic" of the open spaces of a structure.[84] Whether a total prohibition of expression satisfies this exacting standard has been answered in a resounding negative by a host of courts.[85]

In sum, *Heffron* provides but limited guidance as to the future course of the law of the public forum. The streets and parks are still public fora where restrictions of expression can be imposed "only for weighty reasons."[86] In a "limited public forum" such as a fair[87] restrictions on expression can be imposed if there exists a reason to believe that a substantial state interest would otherwise be threatened. Other public facilities remain in an uncertain status[88] but, by the lower courts at least, they are treated as analogous to the streets and parks.[89]

Differential State Treatment of Religious Organizations

A case presently pending before the Supreme Court, *Larson* v. *Valente*,[90] provides an example of another area of constitutional law which is illuminated as a result of governmental efforts to regulate solicitation, one which is unique to problems arising from legislation directed to the collection of funds by religious, as opposed to charitable and other non-profit, organizations. In *Larson*, members of the Unification Church challenged the validity of the Minnesota charitable solicitations statute,[91] which, as amended in 1978, exempted some, but not all, religious organizations from a comprehensive scheme of registration, reporting, and disclosure. With minor exceptions,[92] the statute exempts from regulation those religious organizations which derive more than half their financial support from their own members or from their parent or affiliate organizations.[93] Conversely, therefore, the religious organizations which are made subject to the law's substantive requirement are those which receive more than half their funds from the public.

Both the district court,[94] and the Eighth Circuit,[95] held that this differential treatment of religious organizations contravened the establishment clause of the First Amendment. The court of appeals initially noted that the Minnesota statute provoked grave constitutional suspicion because of its seeming conflict with the establishment clause's interdiction of "laws which . . . prefer one religion over another" and the corollary that "[t]he government must be neutral when it comes to competition between sects."[96] This inherent difficulty was, moreover, greatly magnified by the fact that the court could perceive little, if any, relationship between the line drawn by the exemption provision and any significant state interest since, under the statutory criterion, a religious organization could collect an unlimited amount of money from the public and escape regulation, while another which received a quite small total sum unmatched by member contributions would be fully subject to regulation.[97] It thus held that under the Supreme Court precedents forbidding state favoritism among religions, "[t]he inexplicable religious classification" of the Minnesota law "would seem dispositive."[98]

As an historical matter, the problem of governmental preference in the religious area played an important, and perhaps decisive, role in the framing of the establishment clause.[99] The Supreme Court, however, has had little occasion to deal directly with the matter. What is arguably the closest modern approach appears in a 1971 case, *Gillette* v. *United States*.[100] There, over a lone dissent by Justice Douglas, the Court upheld the conscientious objector provision of the selective service act,[101] which relieves from conscription those with religious scruples in opposition "to participation in war in any form," rejecting a claim that because the statute had the effect of failing also to bar the drafting of religious objectors only to particular wars,[102] it resulted in a forbidden establishment.

The Court's analysis in *Gillette*, a case which, at least until *Larson*, has had little force in constitutional law,[103] centered on the fact that the conscientious objector statute did not "single out any religious organization or religious creed for special treatment," and worked no more than "a de facto discrimination among religions."[104] Formally at least, that observation did not end the inquiry, "for the Establishment Clause forbids subtle departures from neutrality, 'religious gerrymanders,' as well as obvious abuses,"[105] but, given the undemanding standard the Court announced, the result, to uphold the law, was virtually foreordained: In the de facto discrimination case, the "claimant . . . must be able to show the absence of a neutral, secular basis for the lines government has drawn." Since such a basis will almost always be present,[106] statutes which can be characterized as was that in *Gillette* will generally be permitted to stand.

This result is not particularly surprising because of the number and variety of laws which are neutral on their face but in application have differential effects on different religious organizations. Equally unsurprising is the fact that in *Larson* the state contends that *Gillette* is the dispositive precedent, and that under it the Minnesota solicitation statute's exemption must be upheld because the state's interest is indeed asserted to rest on a "neutral, secular basis."

Whether *Gillette* does control is, however, open to question. For in *Larson*, quite unlike the situation in *Gillette*, the statute at issue on its face discriminates among religious organizations, and the Court has never decided whether and, if so, under what circumstances, such an express inter-sectarian classification may be valid. The statute may very well be an example of an "obvious abuse" of which the Court spoke in *Gillette* rather than a mere "religious gerrymander," and, in any event, may be subject to a higher standard of justification than was the draft provision.

In regard to the latter, Minnesota in *Larson* asserts that the fifty-percent member-funded criterion is substantially related to the state's interest in preventing fraudulent solicitation, an interest which the Court has several times acknowledged in the abstract to be one appropriate to state concern.[107] Several premises, the validity of which is not obvious, are, however, necessary for this conclusion. One is that religious organizations which receive more than half their financial support from their members or from parent or affiliate organizations are in some meaningful sense more "controlled" by their members than are others. Moreover, even if this last point were to be granted, the state further claims that such organizations are less likely to engage in fraudulent conduct in connection with their solicitations. No support for these suppositions has been provided, and taken at face value they appear doubtful at best. At the least, an organization's incentive to act criminally would not appear to depend on the percentage of non-member contributions rather than on the absolute amount of such contributions, a variable for which the Minnesota law essentially does not account.[108]

Apparently, then, the state has presented no more than a rational basis for its classification and perhaps not even that. Moreover, both *Gillette* and the Court's general pronouncements on the necessity for government neutrality strongly suggest that a greater quantum of justification should be required to support an expressly discriminatory law.

Obtaining Information from Religious Bodies by Compulsory Process

EUGENE R. SCHEIMAN

One of the areas of church-state relations that has not received the attention it deserves is the attempt by government, or the use of governmental powers, to obtain information from churches or church workers under compulsory process, which can take the form of subpoena, administrative summons or court order. The party seeking such information may be a grand jury, a governmental agency, a Congressional committee, or private persons pursuing discovery in the course of civil litigation.

A close parallel to this problem is seen in the effort by news gatherers and members of the press and media to protect their confidential sources, editorial discretion and work-products from disclosure under compulsory process. Both church workers and news gatherers claim that such disclosure would impair their ability to perform their functions, which they insist are protected by the First Amendment's guarantees of freedom of religion and freedom of the press, respectively. That function is impaired when church or press is converted in any respect or to any degree into an arm of law enforcement or an instrument of government policy.

Grand Jury Subpoenas

The sharpest zone of such encounter between government and church workers centers on the work of the grand jury. The grand jury is considered one of the most important investigative bodies in our system of justice. In order to facilitate its functioning as an investigative body, the grand jury has been given almost unfettered powers. It may investigate a body of facts with no specific criminal charge in view, and its investigation need not be preceded by any definition whatsoever of the crime to be investigated or the person against whom eventual accusation may be made. The grand jury is not bound by the same rules of evidence as a criminal trial, and it operates in secret. Unlike most other judicial proceedings it is not an adversary proceeding in which both sides tell their story, but an *ex parte* or one-sided investigation to determine whether a crime has been committed and whether criminal proceedings should be instituted against any person.[1]

In view of these extremely broad powers, it is not surprising that a witness appearing before the grand jury has available to him considerably fewer rights than a witness or litigant in ordinary court proceedings. Speaking of such rights, the Supreme Court has noted that "it is a fundamental rule of law that the public has a right to every person's evidence."[2] And further, "we deal here not with the rights of a criminal defendant, but rather with the status of a witness summoned to testify before a body devoted to sifting evidence that could result in the presentment of criminal charges."[3]

Thus, in this situation there is, on one hand, a body endowed with enormous investigative powers and, on the other hand, churches and church workers supposedly protected by the First Amendment and some state statutes. I say "supposedly" because, as the cases illustrate, while state statutes in general recognize a priest-penitent privilege against compelled testimony, this protection is generally afforded only to members of the clergy, and even then only with respect to the content of confessions. And, perhaps more importantly, except in those cases clearly within the narrow confines of such statutory provisions, there is at present no clearly recognized privilege rooted in the First Amendment against compelled testimony. As the Supreme Court stated in *Branzburg* v. *Hayes,* a case concerning a reporter's claim that he was protected from appearing and testifying before a grand jury by reason of his First Amendment rights, "neither the First Amendment nor any other constitutional provision protects the average citizen from disclosing to a grand jury information that he has received in confidence."[4]

While paying lip-service to the existence of constitutional limitations on the use of subpoenas to churches and those performing church ministries, courts in general have not been willing to translate that constitutional consideration into a recognized basis for church officials and workers to refuse to testify before a grand jury. While generally recognizing that sincere claims of religious belief must be carefully weighed, the courts, in purportedly applying a balancing test, have generally avoided granting the privilege by weighing governmental needs and other factors more heavily than the asserted infringement. For example, in the case of *Smilow* v. *U.S.,* an appeal from a contempt conviction of a 17-year-old high school student who had refused to testify before a grand jury investigating an alleged fire bombing, the youth based his refusal to testify on free exercise grounds. His claim was that "as an observant and committed Jew, he must refuse to answer the grand jury or else suffer divine punishment and ostracism from the Jewish community as an informer." The Second Circuit Court of Appeals rejected the young man's assertion of privilege after finding that the free exercise interest of the witness had been outweighed by the government's demonstration of a "compelling state interest" in obtaining the testimony. In the weighing process, the court noted that there was strong reason to believe that the boy had vital and relevant information and that no claim had been made that the facts to be sought from the contemnor could conveniently be obtained from others.[5]

The compelling interest theory adverted to in *Smilow* was repeated by the court in a case entitled *In Re Subpoenas*. This case involved two church workers, one the national director, the other the secretary, of the Episcopal Church's National Commission on Hispanic Affairs, an official agency of the church established in 1970 with the goal of furthering ongoing work of the church among Hispanic people. Both workers were called to testify before a grand jury impaneled to investigate a series of violent acts and bombings in New York City for which the F.A.L.N. claimed responsibility. When served with the grand jury subpoenas, which sought both testimony and documents, the two workers filed a motion to quash based primarily on the grounds that the subpoenas violated their First Amendment rights to freedom of religion and association and threatened to disrupt their work as lay church workers as well as that of the Episcopal Church.

The motion to quash was denied on the basis of the court's belief that the petitioners did not fall within the scope of any recognized privilege. In so denying, however, the court was careful to note that the availability of a privilege not to testify was a matter of constitutional right, not simply of privilege granted by court or statute. Thus, the court noted that it was called upon to resolve a controversy which the movants asserted brought the powers of the grand jury into conflict with fundamental rights protected under the Constitution. In such circumstances, the court stated, courts have sought to perform the dual role of zealously protecting constitutional rights and of being alert to guard against abuses of the investigatory powers of the grand jury. In this balancing of conflicting interests, the court noted, it must also weigh the traditional powers of the grand jury to investigate into the possible commission of crime and the right of the public to every person's evidence except where a valid privilege is appropriately invoked.

The court further noted that "there can be little doubt under the cases that the First Amendment right to free association and freedom of religion reach within the closed doors of the grand jury chamber." Accordingly, when First Amendment rights are validly asserted on a motion to quash, the burden shifts to the government to demonstrate a "compelling interest" sufficient to outweigh the possibility of infringement.[6]

Not only federal courts but state courts have at least bowed their heads in acknowledgement of the existence of a free exercise privilege. Thus a New York appellate court in the case of *People* v. *Woodruff* recognized that sincere claims, even those based on unusual beliefs (the person in question was a member of Dr. Leary's drug cult), must be carefully weighed. Nevertheless, since the charges being investigated by the grand jury were serious, and the questions being asked were material, free exercise was subordinated to government need.[7]

Up to the present, then, grand juries have enjoyed almost unlimited power with respect to eliciting testimony from church workers with respect to their work in the church.

Administrative Summonses

Grand juries are not the only governmental bodies seeking information from churches and church workers. With increasing frequency, churches and their members have been served with informational demands by such government agencies as the Internal Revenue Service, the Equal Employment Opportunity Commission and state regulatory bodies. In addition, private parties using the courts for redress of private harms such as libel and invasion of privacy have become an additional intrusive force.

An example of a state administrative demand is found in a 1979 case, in which the Puerto Rican Department of Consumer Affairs subpoenaed documents of the Roman Catholic church in order to investigate operating costs at Roman Catholic schools in Puerto Rico and the effect of the inflationary spiral with respect to the cost of private education. The church was ordered to provide documents and books and to furnish information with respect to the school's annual budgets for the three previous years, the sources of its income, costs of transportation, student costs for registration, admission dues, activities, medical insurance, nourishment services, salaries paid to teachers, scholarships and the criteria upon which they were awarded, and a variety of other data. The lower court dismissed the complaint brought by the church seeking to enjoin the Secretary of Consumer Affairs of Puerto Rico from such investigation, ruling that it was faced with the sensitive and delicate task of balancing governmental dictates of social policy against a religious claim for exemption from requirements of general applicability.

The church appealed, and upon appeal the decision of the District Court was reversed, based upon a finding by the First Circuit Court of Appeals that there was indeed a First Amendment encroachment engendered by the Commonwealth's efforts to obtain the demanded information. The basis for the Court's decision was its belief that the Commonwealth action, even though aimed at private schools in general, constituted a palpable threat of state interference with the internal policies and beliefs of church-related schools. Reasoning further that the information sought was to be the basis of regulations affecting school tuition, the court recognized that future entanglement was inevitable. In conclusion, the court found that the countervailing interest of the state in seeking such information did not pose such weight as to justify a First Amendment encroachment.[8]

In *U.S.* v. *Holmes,* the Court of Appeals for the Fifth Circuit had before it an appeal from an order commanding the Bishop and Director of the Miletus Church to appear before an IRS agent and to produce the following: all records pertaining to cash receipts and disbursements, including, but not limited to, bank accounts, deposit slips, cancelled checks and the like, all balance sheets and other statements of financial condition covering the period from April, 1975, to December, 1977, all documents related to the organizational structure of the Miletus Church, all correspondence files for the two-year period, all records of the names and addresses of persons who were or had been officers, directors or trustees or ministers of the church, all minutes of meetings held by the above officers and directors for a two-year period, one sample of each brochure, pamphlet or hand-out program and other literature pertaining to the church, all records reflecting the names of any employees, associates or ministers of the church, all records reflecting the names of any other organizations that had been chartered as churches or integrated auxiliaries by the Miletus Church, all documents reflecting the principles, creeds, precepts, doctrines, practices and disciplines espoused by the church, and a variety of other documents reflecting income to the church.

The Court of Appeals in this instance had no trouble finding the summons in question to be too far-reaching although it also had no trouble in finding that a valid purpose was present in the issuance of the summons. Thus, though the Court vacated the summons on grounds of its being too broad, it went on to discuss the First Amendment implications of the matter, and held that requiring a church or its members to comply with a narrow summons in order to show entitlement to a tax exemption resulted in only an incidental burden upon free exercise. Balanced against that incidental burden was the substantial government interest in maintaining the integrity of its fiscal policy, and that interest, the court found, was sufficiently compelling to justify any incidental infringement of First Amendment rights occurring by reason of a narrowly drawn summons.[9]

That decision of the Fifth Circuit was followed by a decision of the Court of Appeals for the Eighth Circuit in a case entitled, *United States* v. *Life Science Church*. In that case, the Eighth Circuit was faced with exactly the same summons as had been served in the case before the Fifth Circuit. Again the Court found the summons too broad and vacated the lower court's judgment of enforcement, though leaving it open to the government to issue a more narrow summons if it cared to do so.[10]

Thus, the present state of law with respect to IRS summonses may be briefly summarized as permitting such summonses or subpoenas in an appropriate IRS investigation of a claim of tax-exempt status, so long as the summons or subpoena is properly narrow in scope and falls within certain restrictions of the tax code.

In contrast, however, is the case of *United States* v. *The Freedom Church*, decided by the First Circuit Court of Appeals in December, 1979, which, when faced with a summons similar to that in the two previous cases, refused to limit it, on the basis that the taxpayer failed to raise substantial issues in the court below. Thus, noting that counsel for the taxpayer had made only a "general objection" in the court below to the summons being "substantially over-broad," and that the words "general objection" constituted the entire argument below on the issues of First Amendment privilege and relevancy, the Court found against the taxpayer in each of its arguments and affirmed the lower court's order of enforcement.[11]

In the recent case of *Equal Employment Opportunity Commission* v. *Mississippi College,* the United States Court of Appeals for the Fifth Circuit was faced with an appeal by the EEOC of a District Court's denial of a petition seeking enforcement of a subpoena issued in connection with an investigation of a charge of discrimination filed against Mississippi College, a four-year co-educational liberal-art institution owned and operated by the Mississippi Baptist Convention. The summons was issued in connection with an original charge by an assistant professor that she had been discriminated against on the basis of sex in promotions, recruitment and pay, and a subsequent charge of racial discrimination. In investigating the charges, the EEOC issued a subpoena seeking both testimony and documents with respect to characteristics of each member of the college's faculty and administration, including race, sex, religion, job classification and pay, sources from which the college recruited faculty members, studies of faculty pay, promotional information, employment applications and other data.

The Court ruled that the college was subject to a charge of discrimination against women and blacks, although it noted that the exemption granted to religious institutions from certain provisions of Title VII must be construed broadly to exclude from the scope of the act any employment decision made by a religious institution on the basis of religious selection. Thus, the Court held that it was appropriate for the EEOC to investigate charges of racial and sexual discrimination, and that a properly narrow subpoena should and would be enforced.[12]

Civil Discovery Orders

Private citizens also may use the government as a means to elicit information from churches and church members. There is a case that is presently before the courts based on a claim of libel brought by a church member and his wife against three Elders of their church. The alleged libel arose from a letter signed by the three Elders charging the church member with acts against God's word and the well-being of the church. This letter of admonishment and rebuke had been drafted and approved at a meeting of church authorities and was hand-delivered by the three Elders to the home of the church member.

In pursuit of his action against the Elders, the church member served a subpoena requesting the Pastor of the church to produce records, papers and memoranda of his own and of the church. The Pastor, along with the church, moved in court that the subpoena be quashed and vacated because the issues presented in the action were based on purely ecclesiastical matters. The Court declined to quash the subpoena, ruling that the matter in question was not purely ecclesiastical but rather involved a question of whether or not a communication concerning the member's behavior constituted actionable libel, a civil, not ecclesiastical matter, and that communications made in the regular course of the church's business were not privileged from discovery. That decision was based in part on the court's interpretation of a state code which provided that no minister shall testify to or disclose "a confidential communication" entrusted to him in his professional capacity. The Court concluded upon its review of relevant cases that the privilege against disclosure was only properly invoked in those circumstances which were somewhat similar to that of a priest-penitent transaction. In this instance, because the communications were made to the minister not in his role as a confidant but rather as the head of the local church, the Court ruled that it was not the type of communication intended by the legislature to be protected nor traditionally protected by common law and was therefore discoverable.

Further, the Court ruled that the communications were not confidential since they involved more than the minister and one other party, and thus any confidential character was already dissipated. So the subpoena was not quashed, and the issue is on appeal.

Use of Clergy as Informants

A related issue is the use of confidential informants by the government. On February 9, 1981, an article appeared in *The New York Times* entitled "New Evidence Backs Envoy on His Role in Chile." The story was based on CIA documents and interviews with CIA and White House officials. The materials tended to support ex-Chilean Ambassador Korey's insistence that he had not personally been involved in the military coup overthrowing the Allende government. Included in the story were comments by Mr. Korey concerning CIA activity in Chile, and among such comments was the statement that, "with the full knowledge of Chile and the United States, millions in CIA and AID funds were allocated to Roman Catholic groups opposed to 'laicism, protestantism and communism.'" Also noted by Mr. Korey was the fact that the previous ambassador, on leaving Chile, provided him with the names of fifteen residents of Santiago whose companionship and friendship he particularly recommended. All, *among them three clergymen,* had been "funnels and instruments of important CIA programs."[13] Mr. Korey's remarks are not surprising to those who have long known that the government has made use of persons connected with church and missionary organizations, both to gather information and to implement foreign policy. However, such an open statement of fact is a surprise and should be of considerable concern to those church organizations distributing A.I.D. materials in foreign countries. The danger to the churches and church agencies involved cannot be too strongly stressed. If the foreign recipients of food or other material believe the churches or their agencies to be agents of the government, the churches' integrity could be compromised and the safety and lives of their personnel endangered.

In all fairness, it should be noted that the CIA has issued a policy statement dated February 11, 1976, as follows:

> Genuine concern has recently been expressed about CIA relations with newsmen and churchmen. The agency does not believe there has been any impropriety on its part in the limited use made of persons connected in some way with American media, church and missionary organizations. Nonetheless, the CIA recognizes the special status afforded these institutions under our constitution and in order to avoid any appearance of improper use by the agency, the Director of Central Intelligence has decided on a revised policy to govern agency relations with these groups.
>
> CIA has no secret, paid or contractual relationship, with any American clergyman or missionary. This practice will be continued as a matter of policy.
>
> The CIA recognizes that members of these groups may wish to provide information to the CIA on matters of foreign intelligence of interest to the United States Government. The CIA will continue to welcome information volunteered by such individuals.[14] [Open letter dated Feb. 11, 1976.]

(The Reagan Administration, however, is seeking to nullify most such self-restrictions of the federal intelligence agencies.)

How Subpoenas Should Be Resisted

Churches should consider some methods of resisting at least the intrusion by government into their affairs through use of the subpoena. Such subpoenas must be resisted if the integrity of the religious body is to be preserved. Thus, in each instance of intrusive subpoena, strong argument must be made in each court of original jurisdiction that any subpoena served upon those pursuing church religious work, whether members of the clergy or not, should meet the following minimum requirements in order to pass constitutional muster:

1. The government must clearly show that there is probable cause to believe that a church worker possesses information which is specifically relevant to a specified matter into which it has authority to inquire.

2. The government must clearly show that the information it seeks cannot be obtained by alternative means, *i. e.*, from sources other than the church or its workers.
3. The government must clearly demonstrate a compelling and overriding interest in each item of the information it seeks.

This minimal showing by the government is, of course, not the ordinary test required when the government seeks testimony. However, we are not dealing here with ordinary cases, but with those coming under the protection of the First Amendment. Church subpoena cases should no more be viewed merely as cases of the power and function of a grand jury, or of the reach of compulsory process against assertions of common law privileges, or of ordinary administrative investigations than a case involving the right of Jehovah's Witnesses to hand out pamphlets was viewed as a case concerning the power to keep streets clean and unlittered.[15]

When viewed in proper context, it is quite little to ask that the government meet the minimal tests outlined above before being permitted to intrude on grounds long considered inviolate. This position follows from the premise that if church personnel become sources of information for the government concerning those groups whom they are mandated by religious precepts to seek out and aid, and thus become in their view arms of governmental investigatory bodies, the churches' missions will, at best, become infinitely harder to achieve. This premise and theory must be urged upon each court reviewing a subpoena's validity.

Indeed, such motions should be vigorously pursued whenever resistance to testimony is based on religious or moral convictions. Upon each motion, the First Amendment arguments referred to above should be fully set forth to illustrate to the court the sincerity of the petitioner's belief and the undeniable foundation for it. In addition, affidavits of clergy and those performing lay ministries should be obtained attesting to the affiant's sincere belief that the giving of such testimony as is sought will endanger not only the petitioner's fulfillment of mission, but each and every mission.

In addition, while the motions to quash discussed above form the basis of the usual response to each particular government subpoena to church workers, some direct relief and certainly procedural protection may also be attained by a concerted effort made *now* to obtain specific rules to be mandatorily followed by those seeking to subpoena church workers on behalf of the government. Indeed, a willingness to consider such rules in the form of Attorney General's guidelines has already been indicated by the Department of Justice with respect to the press.

Such guidelines for church-directed subpoenas should take a "balancing test" approach. For example, prior to issuing a subpoena, U.S. Attorneys should be required to attempt to negotiate the subpoena with the religious body in question, then to take into consideration the seriousness of the crime being investigated, whether the information sought from the church worker is directly relevant to the investigation, whether the subpoena is for specific information or is a fishing expedition into church files, and whether there are alternative sources for the information other than the church worker. Failure to follow such guidelines should result in a government motion to quash its own subpoena.

If government agencies would adopt guidelines with respect to churches similar to those already adopted to protect the press, the tension now building between the government and various religious bodies would be measurably relieved. Such guidelines would also, to a great extent, free those religious bodies to continue their work among the poor and disadvantaged without the debilitating suspicion which inevitably follows the giving of testimony by church workers about their contacts and activities or even the suspicion that they *might* have given such testimony.

Government Restraint on Political Activities of Religious Bodies

WILFRED CARON

DEIRDRE DESSINGUE

JOHN LIEKWEG

This paper deals with Section 501(c)(3) of the Internal Revenue Code, which describes certain tax-exempt organizations and imposes restrictions both on lobbying and political campaign activities by such organizations. Since this assignment was accepted, the National Conference of Catholic Bishops has been sued by reason of what plaintiffs call "political activity" in violation of those restrictions.

Suit Against the Catholic Church

The suit was instituted in October of 1980 by multiple plaintiffs, the lead plaintiff being known as Abortion Rights Mobilization, Inc. It was commenced only against the federal government, in the person of the Secretary of the Treasury and the Commissioner of Internal Revenue, but in January the plaintiffs filed an amended complaint which included the National Conference of Catholic Bishops and the United States Catholic Conference as parties defendant.

Abortion Rights Mobilization, Inc. is described in the complaint as a tax-exempt organization dedicated "to the guarantee and implementation of the Constitutional Rights of women to choose to have abortions." Among the other parties plaintiff are other organizations and individuals who similarly support that cause; they include doctors and abortion clinics, clergymen who have religious beliefs that permit abortion, and Roman Catholics who assert that they oppose the Church's position on abortion.

The gravamen of the complaint is that the Roman Catholic Church in the United States has been "guilty" of repeated violations of the restrictions on political activity in Section 501(c)(3) by virtue of its pro-life effort, and that the Secretary of the Treasury and the Commissioner of Internal Revenue have overlooked those alleged violations, thus failing to discharge a ministerial duty enjoined upon them by law, namely, to revoke the tax-exempt status of the Church. It is also alleged that they showed partiality, in that, while the violations of the Catholic Church were being overlooked, there were other tax-exempt organizations (unnamed) engaged in the abortion controversy which became the targets of revocation or threats of revocation.

The plaintiffs assert that because they complied with the restrictions on political activity contained in Section 501(c)(3), they were disadvantaged in the abortion controversy by the government's alleged failure to enforce those restrictions against the Catholic Church. There is financial harm alleged by the doctors and abortion clinics. With regard to the Catholic plaintiffs, it is claimed that their contributions to the Catholic Church are "compelled," and that they have suffered injury because the contributions are used to support views which they oppose. And finally, with respect to all individual plaintiffs who have taxpayer and voter status, it is claimed that they are harmed because there was a violation of the Establishment Clause, and the alleged unequal enforcement of the Code distorted the political process and impaired the right to vote.

The plaintiffs ask the court to declare the Catholic Church's activities in violation of the Internal Revenue Code and the Constitution of the United States and to direct the Secretary and the Commissioner to revoke its tax exemption, assess and collect taxes due, and notify contributors of non-deductibility. An award of costs is sought, including attorneys' fees.

By the time this paper appears in print, the A.R.M. suit may well have been resolved, but the problems which it poses in a painfully concrete way will probably remain to plague all religious organizations. Let us consider what the present status of the law is.

Limitations on Lobbying

Exemption under Section 501(c)(3) of the Code is limited to organizations that do not, as a substantial part of their activities, engage in carrying on propaganda or otherwise attempting to influence legislation.[1] The Income Tax Regulations indicate that "action organizations" are not entitled to exemption under Section 501(c)(3).[2] An action organization is defined as one whose primary objective may be attained only through legislation or the defeat of proposed legislation, and which takes action by advocating or campaigning for the attainment of that primary objective rather than engaging in non-partisan analysis, study or research.[3] The Service has issued a few revenue rulings that shed some light on what will be considered non-partisan analysis, study or research. For example, the exempt status of an educational organization that engaged in non-partisan research with respect to court reform and disseminated that research to members of the public was not adversely affected by that activity.[4] Likewise, an organization that assisted local governments by performing research into common regional problems and did not advocate legislation to implement its findings was entitled to exemption under Section 501(c)(3).[5]

The rule that an organization exempt under Section 501(c)(3) may not engage, as a substantial part of its activities, in attempts to influence legislation gives rise to several questions. First of all, what is legislation? Second, what is an attempt to influence legislation? And, finally, what is substantial?

"Legislation" and "Attempt to Influence" Defined

Essentially, legislation includes ". . . action by the Congress, by any State legislature, by any local council or similar governing body, or by the public in a referendum, initiative, constitutional amendment, or similar procedure."[6] The Service makes no distinction between good and bad legislation. For example, the Service found that an organization that advocated legislation to protect and benefit animals was not entitled to exemption under Section 501(c)(3), even though there was little doubt that the legislation it advocated would have been beneficial to the public.[7] Likewise, in the *Christian Echoes* case[8] the court held that the religious motivation behind the legislative activity was not relevant to determining whether the organization was entitled to exemption under Section 501(c)(3).

Once legislation is defined, then what is an attempt to *influence* it? The regulations under Section 501(c)(3) provide that an organization that urges members of the public to contact members of a legislative body to propose, oppose or support legislation, or an organization that advocates adoption or rejection of legislation, is attempting to influence legislation.[9] The term applies both to lobbying directed toward legislators and to "grassroots" lobbying directed toward the public.

The Service has taken the position that even general appeals to the public without calls for specific action concerning legislation will constitute attempts to influence legislation. The *Roberts Dairy* case[10] involved distribution of literature by an organization to its members and to members of the public about disparities in the tax laws. The ultimate goal of the organization was a revision of the tax structure. This organization was held to be engaged in an attempt to influence legislation as a substantial part of its activities even though the organization had no lobby in Washington, and was not engaged in any direct lobbying activities. In the *Christian Echoes* case,[11] publications and broadcasts were directed to the public, appealing for action on certain issues. The court found that publications and broadcasts need not be addressed to specific legislation in order to be considered influencing legislation. In the *Haswell* case,[12] unsolicited congressional testimony and personal contacts with members of Congress and their staffs (including informal contacts at cocktail parties and luncheons) constituted attempts to influence legislation, causing the organization to be disqualified from exemption under Section 501(c)(3).

An organization will not be viewed as attempting to influence legislation only at the moment its lobbyist enters a legislator's office. The time and effort spent by the organization in formulating its legislative positions, studying them, discussing them, etc., will be considered part of its entire legislative program and thus will constitute attempts to influence legislation. This is what happened in the *League of Women Voters* case.[13]

Permissible Activities

You may ask then, what is *not* an attempt to influence legislation? If a group gives testimony in response to an invitation by a congressional committee, that will not be considered an attempt to influence legislation.[14] If it communicates with members of the legislature and merely discusses broad social, economic or similar issues rather than addressing the merits of any particular legislation, that will not be considered an attempt to influence legislation.[15]

On November 25, 1980, the Service issued proposed regulations under Section 4945 of the Code, which deals with taxable expenditures of private foundations.[16] Even though these regulations would not be applicable to public charities, their criteria may, in fact, be applied to public charities, since the Service seeks consistency in its definitions under the Tax Code. They present a three-factor test to decide whether communications with the public constitute attempts to influence the public with respect to legislation. First, communications are attempts to influence the public with respect to legislation only if they pertain to actions being considered by a legislative body (including legislation being considered, about to be considered in the near future, and proposed legislation).

Second, the communication must reflect a view on that legislation, either explicitly or implicitly. The communication will be deemed to reflect a view if it is selectively disseminated to persons likely to share a common view. The proposed regulations provide an example of this second criterion. State A is considering proposed legislation that would close hunting on state land. If a private foundation has prepared a detailed analysis of the proposed legislation but has not taken any position on the legislation, one would ordinarily say that the foundation has prepared a neutral analysis. However, if the foundation distributes the analysis to groups that are opposed to hunting, the communication will be deemed to have reflected a view on the proposed hunting legislation. Third, the communication must be distributed in a manner that will reach individuals as voters or constituents.

What Is "Substantial"?

Once it is determined that an organization is engaged in attempts to influence legislation, the final question to be answered is what is considered "substantial." Although the substantiality test has withstood repeated judicial challenges, it is a test whose imprecision has led many organizations to fear that too much discretion has been left in the hands of the Service. A simple percentage test as a way of determining what is and what is not substantial has generally been rejected by the courts. However, there are a few cases that provide some parameters concerning what will be considered substantial. The *Murray Seasongood* case[17] found that less than five percent of an organization's time and effort devoted to legislative activities was *not* substantial. In another case[18] an organization that spent from sixteen to seventeen percent of its budget for legislative activities was found to be engaged in substantial legislative activities.

Generally, the courts have applied a balancing test. To determine what is substantial is a question of fact; it must be answered by comparing an organization's purely charitable activities to its legislative activities.[19] In the *League of Women Voters* case[20] the court found that the League's main purpose and reason for being was to influence legislation, and it took into account all the time and effort that the League spent on formulating and discussing its positions, holding that it was engaged as a substantial part of its activities in influencing legislation.

To summarize, in order to determine what is substantial, the Service will consider all the facts and circumstances, balancing an organization's exempt activities against its legislative activities. The percentage of time, effort and money spent by an organization, while not determinative of substantiality, will be taken into account as indicative of the relative importance of an organization's legislative activities in its total program and whether they are central or merely incidental to its charitable activities.

The Conable Amendment

In 1976, Congress enacted Sections 501(h) and 4911 of the Code,[21] which clarify to some extent the inherent uncertainties of the substantiality test. Section 501(h) set up a spending limitation on lobbying expenditures by certain public charities. It created a sliding scale that allowed proportionately less spending for larger organizations. This is not directly relevant to churches, their integrated auxiliaries, and members of affiliated groups whose members include churches or integrated auxiliaries, because these groups, at their own request, were specifically disqualified from choosing to come under Section 501(h). These organizations are left with the uncertainties of the substantiality test. However, there are certain parts of Section 501(h) and Section 4911 that may be relevant in interpreting the definitions applicable to Section 501(c)(3) organizations generally.

Section 4911 of the Code defines what is influencing legislation and then provides five exceptions to the rule. Although Section 501(h) provides that organizations not covered by it or Section 4911 will not be affected by its definitions, still the Service may look to those definitions of "influencing legislation" in interpreting the same term as it appears elsewhere in the Code. Section 4911 lists five activities which will *not* be considered to be "influencing legislation": making available the results of non-partisan analysis, study or research; providing technical advice or assistance in response to written requests by governing bodies; appearing before or communicating with legislative bodies with respect to possible decisions that might affect the existence of the exempt organization (this is the so-called "self-defense" provision); communicating with an organization's bona fide members, unless the communication directly urges members to influence legislation or urges non-members to do so; and routinely communicating with government officials and employees.[22]

There are three problems that will continue to beset exempt organizations with respect to lobbying: defining what is substantial; defining what constitutes non-partisan analysis, study or research; and distinguishing between what the Service considers their exempt activities and the support or back-up activities undertaken as part of their legislative program.

Political Campaign Activity

In addition to the lobbying limitations, organizations exempt under Section 501(c)(3) are prohibited from participating or intervening in political campaigns on behalf of any candidate for political office.[23] The lobbying limitations do not prohibit *all* lobbying activity, but merely place a limitation on the amount of that activity. However, the restriction on political campaign activity is expressed in terms that may be construed as absolute. Any such activity may cause the loss of exempt status under Section 501(c)(3). Thus, organizations should understand with some certitude what kinds of activities are restricted.

The statute itself provides little guidance. Exempt status under Section 501(c)(3) is afforded only to organizations which "do not participate in or intervene in (including the publishing or distributing of statements) any political campaign on behalf of any candidate for public office."[24] This language was added to the Internal Revenue Code in 1954 during the Senate debate as an amendment offered by then Senator Lyndon Baines Johnson. Because it was added to the Code during the floor debate, there are no committee reports or other legislative history which shed light upon the intent of Congress.

Definitions and Examples

The regulations implementing the restriction on political campaign activity provide that *action* organizations are not operated exclusively for exempt purposes and cannot qualify for exemption under Section 501(c)(3).[25] An organization is an action organization if it participates or intervenes directly or indirectly in any political campaign on behalf of, or in opposition to, any candidate for public office.[26] A candidate for public office is defined as an individual who offers himself or is proposed by others as a contestant for an elective public office, including national, state or local offices.[27] Publication or distribution of written, printed, or oral statements on behalf of, or in opposition to, a candidate are activities constituting participation in a political campaign.[28] The following are some examples of activities which the Internal Revenue Service, in a series of revenue rulings, has considered included under the restriction in Section 501(c)(3).

In 1967 an organization which evaluated the qualifications of potential candidates for a local school board and then selected and supported a particular slate was found not to be exempt under Section 501(c)(3), even though its process of selection was completely objective and unbiased and was intended primarily to educate and inform the public.[29] The critical factor was the act of supporting a particular slate of candidates.

In another ruling, an organization whose primary activity was the rating of candidates for public office on a nonpartisan basis was held not to be entitled to exempt status under Section 501(c)(4).[30] It analyzed candidates' qualifications and rated them as average, good, or excellent. These ratings were disseminated to the public. The Service stated that comparative rating of candidates, even though on a nonpartisan basis, is participation or intervention on behalf of those candidates favorably rated and in opposition to those less favorably rated.

A 1976 ruling held that an organization which had directly approached candidates for public office with a request to sign or endorse a code of campaign ethics had engaged in activity constituting participation in a political campaign which may result, through the publication or release of the names of candidates who endorsed or refused to endorse the code, in influencing voter opinion.[31] It is important here to emphasize that the Service found the activity to be prohibited simply because of the possibility that voters might be influenced, even though the organization had not actively supported or endorsed any candidate nor had it released or publicized the results of its request to endorse the code.

The Service's concern with activities which might influence voters became more evident with the publication of Rev. Rul. 78-160, in which the Service denied exemption to a nonprofit organization which had sent a questionnaire to candidates for public office relating to topics of concern to the organization. The responses to the questionnaire were published without additional comment in its newsletter, which was distributed to numerous individuals and organizations. The Service held that the publication of candidates' views on topics of concern to the organization can reasonably be expected to influence voters to accept or reject candidates, and accordingly the questionnaire activity was found to be participating or intervening in a political campaign.[32]

The publication of this ruling caused such a public outcry that shortly thereafter it was revoked by the issuance of Rev. Rul. 78-248, in which the Service stated that whether an organization was participating or intervening in a political campaign on behalf of or in opposition to any candidate depended upon all the facts and circumstances of each case. The ruling then gave four examples of voter education activity, two of which were viewed as political campaign activity within the meaning of the statute. (1) In one of the examples, an organization sent a questionnaire to candidates and used the responses to prepare a voter guide which was distributed during an election campaign. The ruling stated that some questions evidenced a bias on certain issues, and that by using a questionnaire structured in this way the organization was participating in a political campaign in contravention of the provisions of Section 501(c)(3). The ruling did not define or give any examples of what constituted bias. (2) In the other example, an organization primarily concerned with land conservation published a compilation of incumbents' voting records on selected land-conservation issues of importance to the organization. The publication contained no express statements of support for or opposition to any candidate. In denying exemption, the Service stated that by concentrating on a narrow range of issues in the voter guide, which was widely distributed among the electorate during an election campaign, the organization was participating in a political campaign.[33]

Left unclear in the wake of Rev. Rul. 78-248 was whether organizations which take positions on legislation could ever publish the voting records of legislators during a campaign without jeopardizing their tax-exempt status. This question was partly answered in two rulings issued in 1980.

In a private letter ruling issued to an organization called Independent Sector, the Service held that certain lobbying activities, including the reporting of votes on proposed legislation and the presentation of testimony to the platform committees of the two major political parties, did not constitute participation in a political campaign.[34] The ruling emphasized that the activities were directed towards producing a legislative result.

In the second ruling, Rev. Rul. 80-282, it was held that an organization's publication of congressional voting records on a number of issues in its monthly newsletter after the close of the congressional session would not adversely affect its exempt status.[35] Significantly, the ruling stated that the votes would be published in a manner which indicated whether they were in accord with the organization's position on the issue. (This ruling echoed much of what was included in an earlier private letter ruling issued to the United Church of Christ, a ruling which it received only after it had filed suit against the IRS.)

Although these two rulings indicate that the Service is not inflexible on the question of voting records, they are narrowly drawn and should not be viewed as a major retreat from Rev. Rul. 78-248, which is still viable and will continue to be a source of controversy and uncertainty. One of the primary difficulties with the ruling is its lack of a clear objective test for determining when an organization is engaging in political campaign activity. An "all-the-facts-and-circumstances" test provides little guidance, and the use of such subjective words as "biased" even less. The vagueness of the ruling causes serious constitutional problems.

Constitutional Infirmities

When the government regulates in an area affecting First Amendment freedoms, it must do so with specificity.[36] Vague laws may serve as a trap for the innocent by not providing fair warning and by fostering arbitrary and discriminatory enforcement. They also tend to inhibit protected expression by inducing citizens to steer far wider of the restricted zone than if its boundaries were clearly marked.[37] The failure of Rev. Rul. 78-248 to provide specific, objective standards has a chilling effect which can only serve to inhibit the free and open discussion of public issues by religious groups.

What is evident from Rev. Rul. 78-248 is the Service's continued concern with publications and activities which have the potential to influence the voting public. The danger inherent in this approach is clear. Religious groups and other organizations often have strong opinions on a number of issues which may be raised during political campaigns. Any publication or dissemination of these opinions will obviously have some impact on the public, and this is to be expected. One of the reasons for publishing materials is to influence persons receiving the materials. A flaw in the approach which the Service seems to be taking is its failure to distinguish between discussion of issues and candidates, on the one hand, and intervention in campaigns on behalf of candidates, on the other.

The necessity of making this distinction in interpreting laws regulating political expression was explained in *Buckley* v. *Valeo*, where the Supreme Court invalidated on First Amendment grounds the limitations on certain political campaign expenditures imposed by the Federal Election Campaign Act of 1971 as amended in 1974:

> For the distinction between discussion of issues and candidates and advocacy of election or defeat of candidates may often dissolve in practical application. Candidates, especially incumbents, are intimately

tied to public issues involving legislative proposals and governmental actions. Not only do candidates campaign on the basis of their positions on various public issues, but campaigns themselves generate issues of public interest.[38]

In order to save a provision in the Act from invalidation on grounds of vagueness, the Court in *Buckley* held that the phrase "advocating the election or defeat of a candidate" must be construed to apply only to communications that expressly advocate the election or defeat of a clearly identified candidate for office. This construction, said the Court, would restrict application of the Act to express words such as "vote for," "elect," "defeat," or "vote against."[39]

In applying and interpreting Section 501(c)(3), the IRS should pay heed to the words of the Supreme Court. The restriction on political campaign activities must be construed narrowly and should be limited to communications that in express terms are clearly made on behalf of or against a candidate for office. This construction is necessary to insure that religious groups will not be inhibited in their protected right to discuss public issues and candidates.

In addition to vagueness problems, Rev. Rul. 78-248 is constitutionally suspect on another ground. By favoring publications containing voting records on a broad range of issues over publications limited to a narrow range of issues, the ruling, in effect, makes a distinction based on the content of the publications. The case law is clear that the First Amendment prevents governmental regulation of the content of communications except in narrow circumstances (e.g., obscenity, libel).[40] Implicit in Rev. Rul. 78-248 is the concept that an organization which desires to publish voting records must do so with respect to a broad range of issues, even though its interests may be more limited. The effect of the ruling is that loss of exempt status may depend on the content or range of issues discussed in the publication. Practically speaking, it discriminates against groups with a narrow range of concerns.

Views of the Roman Catholic Church

A pamphlet was issued recently by the United States Catholic Conference entitled *Political Responsibility: Choices for the 1980's*. In it there is a section that speaks about the role and responsibility of churches. Of course there is great diversity of opinion as to what that ought to be, but this pamphlet states the views of the bishops of one church.

There is a section entitled "The Church and the Political Order," in which the point is made that its mission in society is to establish Gospel values as part of the fabric of society in all institutions for the common good of all. This view of the Church's ministry and mission requires it to relate positively to the political order. Since social injustice and the denial of human rights can often be remedied only with the assistance of governmental action, concern for social justice and human development necessarily requires persons and organizations to participate in the political process in accordance with their own responsibilities and roles. Lest that be misunderstood, at the bottom of page 7 is this statement:

> As the 1971 Synod of Bishops pointed out: "It does not belong to the Church, *insofar as she is a religious and hierarchical community*, to offer concrete solutions .in social economic and political spheres for justice in the world." [Footnote deleted. Emphasis added.] At the same time, it is essential to recall the words of Pope John XXIII:
>
> > . . . It must not be forgotten that the Church has the right and duty not only to safeguard the principles of ethics and religion, but also to intervene authoritatively with her children in the temporal sphere when there is a question of judging the application of these principles to concrete cases.
>
> The application of gospel values to real situations is an essential work of the Christian community. Christians believe the Gospel is the measure of human realities. However, specific political proposals do not in themselves constitute the Gospel. . . .
>
> We specifically do not seek the formation of a religious voting block; nor do we wish to instruct persons on how they should vote by endorsing candidates. We urge citizens to avoid choosing candidates simply on the personal basis of self-interest.

There is misunderstanding in many quarters of what most religious groups really are trying to do. We could do a far better job of improving the understanding of the people in government. And if we did that, we might have more success with our legal situation. Thus, I propose at the outset that we redouble our efforts to assure that we are correctly perceived.

Are the Restrictions Constitutional?

The restrictions on political activity in Section 501(c)(3) must be viewed in the light of constitutional guarantees of the right to petition, the right of free speech and the free exercise of religion. Although free speech and the right of petition are cardinal values in and of themselves and have independent worth, in the case of religious groups they are the instruments of the transcending values protected by the guarantee of religious liberty. When one conceives of a church's mission as just outlined, surely the right to petition and the right to speak freely are in service to the even more fundamental exercise of religious freedom.

The restrictions of Section 501(c)(3) on constitutional freedoms is a crude reality that holds those freedoms hostage by a threat of governmental retribution for their lawful exercise. At the threshold we have the question of whether these restrictions on lobbying and political activity are constitutional. Only a few cases have treated the issue, and the U.S. Supreme Court has not yet ruled. In our view, they are unconstitutional and there is some reason for optimism as to what might be the result if a proper case posing this question were to come before the Supreme Court of the United States.

Redress Through Litigation

One of the procedural obstacles to litigating the constitutionality of Section 501(c)(3) is the so-called Anti-Injunction Statute which is co-terminous with a counterpart provision in the Declaratory Judgment Act. Together they withhold declaratory and injunctive relief in tax cases except in proper cases under Section 7428 of the Code, which provides some relief for tax-exempt organizations. It permits application to a court for declaratory relief once the Secretary of the Treasury (and that should be understood to mean the IRS on an appropriate level) has issued a determination which the particular organization believes is erroneous. However, the statute allows the Secretary 270 days in which to reconsider a determination before the tax-exempt organization may go to court and seek declaratory relief. Moreover, there is uncertainty as to when that period begins to run. When this is combined with the rule that the tax-exempt organization must exhaust its administrative remedies with IRS before seeking judicial redress, there emerges a clear prospect of an intolerable delay which justifies doubt of the practical efficacy of Section 7428.

The Anti-Injunction Act provides that, with certain exceptions irrelevant to this discussion, no suit for the purpose of restraining the assessment or collection of any tax shall be maintained in any court by any person. The Supreme Court has held that the language is to be taken quite literally, and has rejected efforts to circumvent these statutes based on a contention that the challenge is not merely to the collection or assessment of a tax, but to the lawfulness of the regulation or conduct. It appears that no judicial exception will be made except in a rare case where irreparable injury is demonstrated and it is clear that the government could not succeed. The meaning of the latter requirement is unclear since the cases speak both of a "probability" of success by the government and a requirement that it appear the government could not prevail "under any circumstances." Because no case has met these tests, it is very difficult to know what they mean. In sum, there are substantial procedural hurdles in the way of litigation challenging the constitutionality of Section 501(c)(3). I would note that the same hurdles do not exist with regard to a defense to a suit of the kind brought against the Church by Abortion Rights Mobilization, Inc. That suit could prove providential.

The practical dilemma of churches is this. They are obliged to surrender either precious constitutional freedoms or their tax-exempt status, which is so important to their ability to accomplish their religious and social mission. The grip of this vise tightens perceptibly when one ponders the vagueness of the restrictions in Section 501(c)(3) and the relevant IRS rules or regulations. What clarity does not restrict, vagueness threatens and chills. By any reasonable measure, this situation breaches the proper limits of the Constitution and offends basic fairness. More important, to the extent it stifles freedom, it adversely affects the good of a free society.

Another Approach

Whatever may be the hurdles to a litigated resolution to these important issues, there is another approach which involves few obstacles for open-minded and fair people. There ought to be an intensification of dialogue with appropriate representatives of government on this question. Let us urge a reexamination and reassessment of these infringements of constitutional liberty, one (on political campaign activity) born of mundane political ambition, and the other (on lobbying) born of a rationale which lacks contemporary cogency. Let people of good will admit that the old principle which decried the so-called public subsidy of legislative and political activity must yield to the present realities, which include deductible contributions to political campaigns, contributions from public funds to qualified presidential candidates, deductible lobbying expenses, and so forth. Let people of good will take note of the evolution in Establishment Clause cases whereby the principle of "benevolent neutrality" toward religion has replaced the bankrupt and often pernicious rhetoric of "separation."

Finally, as we encourage constructive dialogue, let us invite attention to the lack of logic that surrounds obsolete theory and rank injustice. In the well-known *Christian Echoes* case, the Court expressed the view that tax exemption for organizations operated exclusively for charitable, religious and educational purposes is granted because of the benefit their activities confer on the public. It reasoned that the government is compensated for the loss of this tax revenue by its relief from the need to use public funds to confer the same or similar benefits. Thus, there is judicial recognition of an unquestionable public good accomplished by tax-exempt organizations. On the other hand, we also have another public good in the form of the constitutional freedoms of religion, speech, and petition. What do the restrictions in Section 501(c)(3) do? They set these two goods in opposition, one against the other. There is something terribly wrong with this result. It is bad jurisprudence, deplorable sociology and outrageous illogic.

Litigation is one appropriate avenue to the amelioration of this condition, but even better is dialogue which looks to reason and fairness as the means for achieving equity and justice. This is more appropriate to the values we profess and the institutions we represent.

The Use of Legal Process
for De-Conversion

SHARON L. WORTHING

"There's no use trying," [Alice] said: "one *can't* believe impossible things."

"I daresay you haven't had much practice," said the Queen. "When I was your age, I always did it for half-an-hour a day. Why, sometimes I've believed as many as six impossible things before breakfast."[1]

The subject of the coercive change of an individual's religious beliefs brings us to a surreal world. It is characterized by two related techniques. One is called deprogramming—the forcible breaking of an individual's religious affiliation; the other is a particular use of conservatorship proceedings in court. The basic element which both of these share is the involuntary restraint of the targeted individual.

On this stage, a host of self-proclaimed experts assert that they have the elixir to dispel religious illusion and dispense theological sanity. We are told of "thought control," "mind manipulation," "borderline personalities," "psychological kidnapping." A group of obedient professionals follow in their train, embellishing with learned phrases the rougher language of the self-proclaimed experts.

A book coauthored by Ted Patrick, the initiator of "deprogramming," states that this process "may be said to involve kidnapping at the very least, quite often assault and battery, almost invariably conspiracy to commit a crime, and illegal restraint."[2] That is the raw truth, in this instance admitted, but in most cases glossed over or denied.

In a search for a means to put people through deprogramming without running the risk of criminal prosecution, certain individuals have seized upon the use of conservatorships. A conservatorship proceeding is one in which a court gives one adult authority over the person or property of another adult, the "conservatee," even though the conservatee has not been recognized as legally incompetent. The proceeding was developed to protect senile persons from exploitation. As used by deprogrammers, however, the grant of a conservatorship order becomes the court-ordered means to subject an individual to mental coercion and physical intimidation—in an unsupervised setting—in an intense effort to make him or her recant.

Among the claims commonly purveyed to the public by advocates of deprogramming is that there are 3,000 to 5,000 so-called "cults" in the nation—evil religions that no sensible person would want to get involved with. In fact, Ted Patrick, when pressed, offered a list of about fifty groups, some of which would be considered quite innocuous by most people—yet the huge figure continues, uncorrected by reality. The untutored observer thus finds himself confronted by an enormous problem which is seemingly beyond control.

Another postulate of the deprogramming advocates is that no one ever becomes old enough to make his or her own decisions in matters of religion. California Judge Vavuris, who granted conservatorship orders to parents of members of the Unification Church so that they could be put through deprogramming, said, "The child is the child even though a parent may be 90 and the child 60."[3] This could be called the doctrine of perpetual religious infancy.

A third assumption is that individuals who join unpopular religions are not there of their own free will, but only because they have been "psychologically kidnapped." No one, it is thought, would willingly join such a religion, so that the apparently voluntary adherence must have been brought about by some strange kind of mind manipulation. As Professor Richard Delgado expressed it at a meeting chaired by Senator Dole, "In the cult joining process, [legally adequate knowledge and capacity] are maintained in inverse relationships, so that when capacity is high, knowledge is low. Conversely, when knowledge is high, capacity is reduced. . . . A convert thus never has full capacity and knowledge simultaneously. One or the other is impaired by cult design."[4] According to this reasoning, the choice to adhere to a disfavored religious organization cannot be a voluntary one, so that coercion to break the affiliation is justified.

Given the assumptions that there are hordes of mindless zombies in thousands of cults who have been magically tricked into joining against their wills—and are not old enough to make their own religious decisions in any event, no matter how old they may be—there has been a call for the state to allow the use of force to get the individuals out of such organizations. These individuals are considered to be outside the ordinary protections which the Constitution affords; having been classified as "non-persons," they are not covered by the Bill of Rights.

Even without the extra effort of setting up a state-sanctioned method, deprogrammers have had a very easy time of it with the authorities for the most part. After the police intervened to prevent the attempted abduction of a young man by Ted Patrick and the young man's parents in New York, the police let Ted Patrick walk from the police station without so much as asking his name. Patrick, who cheerfully admits that he instigates the forcible seizing of his subjects, has had remarkable success with law enforcement agencies and courts across the country, as he relates in his book.[5]

Nevertheless, many persons are not as bold as Ted Patrick, and seek a legal cover for their deprogramming activities. In New York State, a bill setting up a special temporary conservatorship proceeding, expressly designed to be used against members of unpopular religions, actually passed both legislative houses in the last-minute rush in June of 1980. Governor Carey vetoed the bill, stating that it would "ultimately prove to be both unworkable and unconstitutional."[6]

Under this New York temporary conservatorship bill, specified relatives, including grandparents, could obtain an *ex parte* preliminary order of temporary conservatorship over the person and property of an individual upon a showing that "reasonable cause exist[ed] to believe" that the individual had

> become closely and regularly associated with a group which practices the use of deception in the recruitment of members and which engages in systematic food or sleep deprivation or isolation from family or unusually long work schedules; and that such person for whom the temporary conservator is to be appointed has undergone a sudden and radical change in behavior, lifestyle, habits and attitudes; and has become unable to care for his welfare and that his judgment has become impaired to the extent that he is unable to understand the need for such care.[7]

One can imagine the grandmother of a young man who had joined the Marines trying to persuade a judge that her grandson had been deceived when recruited, had an unusually long work schedule, had radically changed his formerly easygoing lifestyle, and didn't even know that anything was wrong.

Once a person had obtained such a preliminary order—and he could go to justices anywhere in New York State to do so—he would be authorized to take forcible physical custody of the targeted individual in *any state in the Union* with the help of a police officer who could use "whatever reasonable force [was] necessary." The target—or proposed temporary conservatee—need not be informed of anything, or given the right to communicate with anyone, until the next regular session of the court granting the preliminary order. This could be several days. At this next session, the judge could amend the preliminary order "to provide for the psychological and/or psychiatric treatment of the proposed temporary conservatee."

What the bill did, then, was to provide state authorization and support for private inquisitions. The total period for which an individual could be held under the proceedings described in this bill was three-and-a-half months. At the end of that time, there was nothing to prevent the person who had sought the order, if still faced with a recalcitrant relative, from starting over again. An individual could literally be locked up for years, unsupervised by any competent professional. This power goes far beyond any powers granted even over individuals who are adjudicated to be incompetent.

A California appellate court threw out the temporary conservatorship orders issued by Judge Vavuris, mentioned earlier. The California conservatorship statute at that time allowed such orders for individuals "likely to be deceived or imposed upon by artful and designing persons." The appellate court stated that although these words

> may have some meaning when applied to the loss of property which can be measured, they are too vague to be applied in the world of ideas. In an age of subliminal advertising, television exposure, and psychological salesmanships, everyone is exposed to artful and designing persons at every turn. It is impossible to measure the degree of likelihood that some will succumb. In the field of beliefs, and particularly religious tenets, it is difficult, if not impossible, to establish a universal truth against which deceit and imposition can be measured.[8]

Other court decisions, however, have not found the issue so clear when asked to impose penalties against those engaging in deprogramming activities.

It appears, then, that conservatorship proceedings can result in extreme limitations on personal liberty, often without due process of law, on the basis of thinly supported psychological theories. Such slender reeds ought not to be used to permit activity which otherwise would be subject to heavy criminal penalties.

Then there is the idea: "Why not allow it? Only those strange people whom we don't like are going to be hurt by it—no one will ever go after respectable folk like us." This is not true either in the course of history or in the case of deprogramming. An Episcopalian and a Roman Catholic have been put through deprogramming. The wife of a man who served as president of Free Minds, Inc., an "anticult" group, complained, "The Way, International, believes that Jesus Christ is not God and also denies the Holy Trinity!"[9] She saw something very wrong with defending the rights of such people. Once a means of persecution gets going, it is really impossible to keep it in a tight box so that it affects only those people who "deserve" it.

By the granting of conservatorship orders which allow an individual to be kidnapped and held against his will, courts are intervening in the lives of these individuals in an unconstitutional fashion. Although the impact of such intervention falls initially upon the individual rather than the institution, it will also be felt by the institution and impair its ability to function. Consequently, it is yet another form of government intrusions in religious affairs.

In the words of Lord Acton,

The most certain test by which we judge whether a country is really free is the amount of security enjoyed by minorities. Liberty, by this definition, is the essential condition and guardian of religion. . . . [10]

If the courts were to leave the Constitution intact but merely start deleting various categories of people from its protections, the Bill of Rights would soon lose all meaning. It would be merely a paper instrument admired as a decorative ornament by those who did not need it. It is always a very dangerous thing for a society to create a special category of persons who, though not incompetent, are exempted from rights that belong to all.

When Is Governmental Intervention Legitimate?

MARVIN BRAITERMAN

DEAN M. KELLEY

Introduction: Two Important Truths

In the church-state field, there are two important truths that must be kept in perspective. The primary truth is that *religion is not an appropriate object of governmental regulation.* Its important work does not thrive when government clumsily attempts to foster, direct, modify, regulate, inspect, license, organize, standardize or certify it. In the case of religion, at least, for government even to try to "help" is to hinder and distort. That is the primary truth toward which these proceedings have been directed. But if it were the only truth to be contemplated, a conference of this size might not be necessary. There is another and countervailing truth that must be held in tension with it, and that truth is that *there are some respects in which government can and should regulate religious activities.*

They are very limited, but they exist. Under what circumstances government is justified in regulating religious activities is the subject of this paper. Its perspective is that the primary truth must not be eclipsed by the secondary truth. The role of government suggested here—with respect to religion, at least—is very *minimal.* In all really close cases, the doubt should be resolved in favor of religion, not government. The primary truth should prevail, and government should keep out.

There will be no lack of advocates of greater government intervention; not only are many public servants so inclined, but many within the religious community itself seem prepared to "pre-shrink" their own claims to fit what they believe to be the public good or what they think to be the public's expectations. We will not do that. We take it to be our task to assert the maximum freedom for religion, the minimum responsibility for government toward it. It will be hard enough to maintain the needed "free space" for religion without its advocates pre-shrinking it before it has even been asserted or defended.

I. Government Can and Should Regulate Some Activities Claimed to Be Religious or Actually Religious

A. Relatively Uncontested Interventions

Most people would not challenge the right and responsibility of government to protect the health and safety of all inhabitants, at least from the kinds of "clear and present danger" generally recognized by all. The "war powers" of government, for instance, are quite sweeping in military emergencies and take precedence over most other considerations. Though these powers are not as broad and unconstrained as government has sometimes assumed them to be, and though there will always be boundary disputes about what constitutes an "emergency," how long it may be considered to last, and what long-term measures it justifies, most would concede the over-riding necessity for government to act quickly, effectively and vigorously to defend the nation from external attack.

The role of government with respect to internal threats to public health and safety is somewhat more circumscribed. Though genuine crises such as fire, flood, earthquake, epidemic or other natural disaster may justify peremptory measures, the "police power" is subject to certain constraints, such as those which distinguish the war powers from those legitimately exercised by civil authorities even in domestic disorders.[1] The point is that ultimately government can and must do whatever is genuinely necessary to enable an ordered society to survive. But within that perimeter, certain important rights must be respected, and foremost among those is the right to free exercise of religion.

1. A "Parade of Horribles"

To anchor one end of the spectrum, one need only cite a handful of stories from recent issues of *Religious News Service*:

a. "Bishop" DeVernon LeGrand of Brooklyn was convicted in 1977 of murdering several of his female followers and sinking their weighted bodies in an upstate lake.[2]

b. Ervil LeBaron, leader of a recusant sect of Mormons still practicing polygamy in the remote fastnesses of southern Utah, was convicted of the slaying of the leader of a rival sect.[3]

c. "Bishop" Robert A. Carr of the Church of God and True Holiness in North Carolina pleaded guilty to the charge of holding several of his followers in "involuntary servitude" by compelling them to work in a poultry processing plant and confiscating their wages.[4]

d. The "Jonestown Meltdown" in Guyana. Many recent interventions by government in religious activities have been sought to be justified by reference to various notorious scandals and tragedies allegedly connected to religion, chief among which is the terrible disaster in Jonestown, Guyana, where over 900 people committed suicide (or in some instances were probably murdered). What sort of government intervention does "Jonestown" justify?

i. There is a tremendous social power in religious movements like "the People's Temple." Politicians tried to exploit that power for their own aggrandizement. It is hard for a human being to try to be a messiah without suffering an ego-overload. When that person is lionized—or victimized— by the political order, the dangers of such overload are vastly increased. One should approach such high-commitment communities in the same way one would approach a dynamo or an atomic pile rather than barging in as Congressman Ryan did with reporters, TV crews and dissident former members. The "meltdown" that followed is testimony to the perils of incautious governmental intervention. (It does not necessarily mean government should not have intervened at all.)

ii. How does the government prevent its recurrence? Fortunately, such meltdowns are extremely rare. To predicate public policy on the possibility of very rare events is unwise. How does the government prevent the recurrence of the Chicago fire, the San Francisco earthquake, the Johnstown flood or the nuclear malfunction at Three Mile Island? Some preventive measures can be taken where human care can prevent human error. But *government cannot forfend against all possible eventualities*, since that is an open-ended, and thus infinite, class, and it would never get anything else done about more real and imminent problems.

iii. "Jonestown" was not only outside the jurisdiction of the U.S. law and Constitution within which our deliberations are focused, but much is unknown about what actually happened there. Its rarity, its distance, and its unknownness all suggest that it is not a suitable basis for formulating governmental policy that is to apply to the other 99 percent of religious organizations, which are generally stable, all too innocuous, and deplorably law-abiding. Rabbi Maurice Davis asserted at the hearings conducted by Senator Dole on "cults" in 1979: "The road of the cults leads to Jonestown!" Statistically speaking, the opposite is true. Almost any other outcome is more likely than mass suicide.

2. The Same Threshold of Evidence Must Be Met

Surely no one would contend that the government should not have intervened in these scandalous cases and enforced the criminal laws that apply to everyone, whether they claim to be actuated by religion or not. In all such cases, however, the same threshold of evidence must be met for governmental investigation, arrest, indictment and conviction as in non-religious cases, no more, no less. Religious leaders or adherents should no more be subjected to surveillance, investigation or arrest on the basis of mere suspicion or allegation than anyone else.

In this connection one must question some of the quaint modes of law enforcement on the West Coast:

a. The Los Angeles Police Department has recently been discovered to have infiltrated Indian sweat-lodge ceremonies (an indisputably religious activity); the LAPD sought to justify this infiltration by asserting that the American Indian Movement (AIM) is a "violent" organization.[5] At what point was it "violent"? In occupying "Wounded Knee"? Does that justify such surveillance of all members of that organization forever after? Even during sacramental activities?

b. The Attorney General of California in 1978 obtained a court order *ex parte* placing the Worldwide Church of God in receivership on the basis of unsubstantiated charges by six dissident members; those charges —among them that church leaders were "siphoning off" millions of dollars of church funds for their own personal aggrandizement—the Attorney General has never attempted to prove, nor to give the persons charged their chance to prove their innocence in court; some charges —that church properties were being hastily sold off far below their market value to line the leaders' pockets—were recognized by the court granting the receivership order to be completely unfounded.[6]

c. Since the Attorney General of California has claimed jurisdiction over churches as "public trusts," some constables in that state have not felt it necessary to obtain a search warrant before entering a church to hunt for contraband since—in their words—"It's a public place!"[7]

3. Should Not Religious Bodies Meet the Same Threshold of Qualification as Other Applicants?

A corollary of the foregoing might be the reciprocal concern on the part of government that religious bodies meet the same threshold of qualification for various civil categories as other applicants. In how many areas of law or civil administration are applicants allowed to qualify on the basis of their own self-serving and unsupported assertion, it is often asked. One answer might be: in cases where that is the best or only evidence. Persons applying for marriage licenses do not have to adduce documents or witnesses to prove that they wish to get married. Conscientious objectors to military service are often the only witnesses to their asserted convictions. The best testimony to such applications is often the continuing behavior of the applicant after the application is granted. In any event, it seems unlikely that the few claimants to the status of religion whose claims might be fraudulent would seriously distort or dislocate the functioning of civil society.

B. Areas of Contest: Use of the Police Power to Safeguard Public Health, Safety, Order, Morals, Good

1. Boundaries of "Public Health and Safety"

How far the courts should go in allowing government to safeguard "public health and safety" is a significant boundary question where such safeguarding impinges on freedom of religion.

a. Adult Jehovah's Witnesses have been upheld in refusing blood transfusions for themselves that violate their conviction that such transfusions are the same as "eating blood" prohibited in the Bible, even when such refusal has resulted in their own deaths. Courts have usually overruled that objection when made by a parent on behalf of a minor child, holding that what adults may choose to their own damage they may not choose for another, even their own offspring.

b. Christian Scientists have sometimes been upheld in refusing vaccinations or inoculations which violate their religious rejection of the germ theory of disease, both for themselves and their minor children, except in cases of highly contagious diseases or an incipient epidemic in which their susceptibility to infection might endanger others. [8]

c. Adherents of the Native American Church have been exempted from California laws forbidding the use of peyote as a dangerous substance because Indians have historically used peyote in their religious rituals, and the state had not shown an interest outweighing the claim of religious liberty sufficient to justify prohibiting it as to religious usage, [9] but other claimants of more recent provenance have not fared as well. [10]

2. Protecting People from Themselves

To what degree does the responsibility for safeguarding public health and safety justify government in attempting to protect people from their own weaknesses, predilections, impulses? That is a question much broader than the church-state field, and has confronted everyone obliged by law to don a crash-helmet or a seat-belt before travelling in certain vehicles. There is some current agitation for the "de-criminalization" of what are rather simplistically denoted "victimless" crimes, as though the perpetrator were not in some respects a victim, not to mention his/her dependents, insurance carrier, and the public servants who have to clean up the remains.

3. Protection of "Public Morals," "Public Order," "Public Good"

The scope of the police power has often been characterized as encompassing "public health, safety and morals," and other terms such as "the public good" or "public order" have been used as well to justify government intervention in private conduct. "Health and safety" are usually more objective, factually grounded considerations than these other terms. In items a, b and c above, we moved from matters more clearly of health and safety (a and b) to considerations of "morals" (c). That is, blood transfusions and smallpox vaccinations are more obviously matters of life and death than the use of peyote or marijuana, which fall more in the category of "morals," something strongly believed to be improper or wrong by many, yet whose potential for harm is less immediately visible. If hallucinogens were to be shown scientifically to produce brain damage or genetic mutations, for instance, regulation of their use would move from the realm of public morals to that of public health and safety (as did cigarette smoking not long ago).

Whether government may intervene in private conduct claimed to be religious is a special question under the broader one of the scope and application of the police power, and it has traced its own unique course through American jurisprudence, which is of central interest to this inquiry. The question may be posed as follows: If government by law requires or prohibits some action, may an individual be exempted from that law because it interferes with his/her religious belief or practice?

The protection of the free exercise of religion as an independent constitutional right was vitiated early on by a doctrine that distinguished belief from action and gave virtually no rights to the latter in conflict with positive law.

a. Religious Belief Is Free, But Not Action

In the 19th Century, the Supreme Court said in *Reynolds* v. *U.S.*, Mormons could "believe" in plural marriage (polygamy), so long as they did not practice it.[11] Within twelve years, the Supreme Court enlarged that infringement on religious practice in *Davis* v. *Beason*,[12] which upheld a statute of the Idaho Territory requiring applicants for the right to vote to subscribe to an oath that they were not members of any organization which "teaches, advises, counsels or encourages" its members to commit the crime of bigamy—a kind of Smith Act in the field of "subversive" religion that did for "free exercise" what *Dennis* v. *U.S.*[13] did for the rest of the First Amendment sixty years later—compelled a person to forswear certain affiliations as a condition of citizenship rights.

The common perception of the Mormon polygamy cases today is that they prohibited only overt criminal acts. After all, Reynolds was convicted for being a practicing polygamist. But the actual reach of state power over religious exercise, as embodied in *Davis* v. *Beason*, goes much further in the belief/action doctrine. Davis was not convicted of bigamy but of taking a false oath that denied that he was a member of the Mormon Church. Thus, it was asserted, except for passive belief, the state could prohibit anything in the religious area that offended public policy, including advocacy, encouragement and membership, if the particular religious doctrine shocked "the moral judgment of the community . . ." or offended "the common sense of mankind . . ."[14]

The belief/action distinction was advanced in spite of the fact that "exercise" is an *action* word, used expressly in the First Amendment solely to characterize freedom of religion. A wooden adherence to the teaching of the two Mormon polygamy cases would render the free-exercise clause a dead letter, conferring no independent rights to act or practice and no protection against collateral sanctions where beliefs were unpopular enough to incur the wrath of repressive legislation.

b. Progress Sub Silentio

Over the succeeding few decades, some eccentric religious practices began to be tolerated and protected, but without much recognition that the First Amendment's free-exercise clause conferred any special rights. *Pierce* v. *Society of Sisters*[15] held that a state law requiring parents to send their children to public schools only was unconstitutional. In recent years, *Pierce* has been viewed as protecting the freedom of parents to educate their children in private schools, including religious schools. To that extent, it is treated as a case that supports an exemption from general (compulsory education) law because of the claims of free exercise. But that is "development of doctrine." *Pierce* was based on the protection of the property rights of private schools (including military academies as well as religious schools). As late as 1965, Justice Douglas characterized *Pierce* as a freedom-of-speech case, protecting "freedom of inquiry, freedom of thought and freedom to teach."[16]

It is an axiom of constitutional history that times of war are times when civil liberties suffer retrenchment and restraint. Claims and rights of iconoclasts and dissenters are drowned out by the orthodox din of patriotic fervor. World War II may have been typical in this respect, but one significant decision of the Supreme Court was an exception. In *West Virginia* v. *Barnette*[17] the Court exempted a school child of Jehovah's Witnesses' persuasion from compliance with a state law that required all children in the schools of the state to join in a compulsory salute to the flag. That decision overruled one of exactly opposite effect three years earlier,[18] which, relying on the belief/action dichotomy of *Reynolds*, had held that "the mere possession of religious convictions which contradict the relevant concerns of a political society does not relieve the citizen from the discharge of political responsibilities." Justice Frankfurter, writing for the Court in *Gobitis*, had treated the duty of a school child to execute the rites of flag worship as a heavy "political responsibility," against which religious convictions were a "mere possession"!

Justice Jackson, writing for the Court in *Barnette*, explained that *Gobitis* erred in assuming that the issue was whether people had to be excused from the flag salute on religious grounds. Actually, he pointed out, the issue was whether government could compel a faith or belief in anything—an issue of freedom of expression applicable to state prescription of any orthodoxy—in "politics, nationalism, religion or other matters of opinion."[19] This was an important step along the way to a new principle beyond the belief/action dichotomy. But it achieved its important advance without any express recognition that the free-exercise clause standing alone can exempt anybody from anything.

c. The "Compelling Interest" Test: Braunfeld and Sherbert

The first explicit breach in the belief/action doctrine was the cluster of cases concerning Sabbath observance which the Court delivered in the 1960's. In *Braunfeld* v. *Brown*,[20] an Orthodox Jewish shopkeeper whose religious convictions compelled him to close his business on Saturday sought an exemption from Pennsylvania's Sunday-closing laws. Braunfeld lost his case, but the plurality opinion of Chief Justice Warren conceded that there are cases where exemptions from laws of general application could be justified on free-exercise grounds. However, *Braunfeld* wasn't such a case, since the appellant would suffer only an economic and not a criminal penalty for closing his store on Saturday.

The dissenters, including Justices Brennan and Stewart, disagreed, saying that the economic penalty was sufficient to grant Braunfeld a constitutionally based exemption on free-exercise grounds. In the course of that dissenting opinion, Justice Brennan argued that, because the Sunday-closing law was in fact such a heavy burden on Braunfeld's exercise of his religion, it should stand only if Pennsylvania could show that it was necessitated by a "compelling state interest." As it turned out, the justices in the plurality found that there *was* a compelling state interest, while Justices Brennan and Stewart did not, characterizing the interest of Pennsylvania in closing Braunfeld on Sunday as a matter of mere administrative convenience, which they deemed trivial compared to the consequences to Braunfeld. But there was now a majority of the Court in favor of the proposition that, in an appropriate case, free exercise possessed an independent and specific force beyond mere toleration of passive belief which might confer rights not otherwise available under expanded interpretations of freedom of speech or the First Amendment generally.

It took only two more years for the Court to find a case in which free exercise would justify an exemption. *Sherbert* v. *Verner*[21] reversed a decision that denied unemployment compensation to a Seventh-day Adventist who refused to accept a job that would require her to work on her Sabbath, Saturday. Justice Brennan, writing for the Court, found that the South Carolina decision imposed a substantial burden on the appellant's right to free exercise of her religion. Then he found that no compelling state interest was served by the burden thus imposed by the state.

Sherbert began to clarify the concept of "compelling state interest" against which claims for exemption on free-exercise grounds must be weighed. The state must show more than a "rational relationship to some colorable state interest." Indeed,

> In this highly sensitive constitutional area, only the gravest abuses, endangering paramount interests, give occasion for permissible limitation.

South Carolina had asserted that to allow such an exemption would invite feigned religious claims that would fraudulently dilute the unemployment compensation fund. Justice Brennan held that this allegation was not sustained by the evidence, but that, even if it had been, it would not justify such a substantial infringement of religious liberty. And South

Carolina would still have to demonstrate that no alternative form of regulation was available that did not infringe rights protected by the First Amendment.

d. The Burden on the State Grows Heavier

Over the years, the burden to be met by the state in showing a "compelling state interest" that would outweigh the claims of free exercise has grown more difficult for the state to meet. "Administrative convenience" (as characterized by the dissenters, at least) was deemed adequate to justify the Sunday closing law upheld in *Braunfeld*, but the effort to exclude claims for unemployment compensation that might be fraudulently based on feigned Sabbatarian beliefs was not deemed compelling in *Sherbert*. And the compulsory education law of Wisconsin requiring two years of public schooling beyond the eight accepted by the Amish was found less than compelling in *Wisconsin* v. *Yoder*.[22]

Though the process of balancing free exercise of religion against compelling state interest has become rather clearly defined, the canons of what constitutes a *compelling* state interest are less settled. Just as the Constitution is what the judges say it is, so that state interest is compelling which the majority of justices on the Supreme Court at the time believe to be so. Here is the frontier where the struggle for religious liberty goes on. Every effort should be made to frame free exercise cases in the way that most vigorously asserts the importance of allowing people to embody their religious beliefs in action. And every effort should be made to demonstrate to the Court that religious liberty outweighs in importance—not just to the practitioners of religion, but to society as a whole—almost every countervailing interest the state can assert short of clear and present danger to public health and safety that can be averted in no other way.

C. Other Areas of Contest

1. Government as Protector of Consumers—of Religion?

Recently governments have taken on a new role as protector of consumers against the chicanery of mendacious merchants and stretch-penny manufacturers, a laudable role when effectively done. The standards for judging the merchantability of a vacuum cleaner or a TV set are relatively straightforward and objective. The criteria for "Truth in Lending" and "Truth in Advertising" are also more or less obvious.

a. The Ballard Standard

But when government undertakes to protect consumers from fraud in the field of religion, the task is less clearcut, since one person's "fraud" is another one's "faith." In *U.S.* v. *Ballard*, the Supreme Court held that religious teachers could not be put to the proof of their teachings in a court of law:

Freedom of thought, which includes freedom of religious belief, is basic in a society of free men. . . . It embraces the right to maintain theories of life and of death and of the hereafter which are rank heresy to followers of the orthodox faiths. Heresy trials are foreign to our Constitution. Men may believe what they cannot prove. They may not be put to the proof of their religious doctrines or beliefs. Religious experiences which are as real as life to some may be incomprehensible to others. Yet the fact that they may be beyond the ken of mortals does not mean that they can be made suspect before the law. Many take their gospel from the New Testament. But it would hardly be supposed that they could be tried before a jury charged with the duty of determining whether those teachings contained false representations. The miracles of the New Testament, the Divinity of Christ, life after death, the power of prayer are deep in the religious convictions of many. If one could be sent to jail because a jury in a hostile environment found those teachings false, little indeed would be left of religious freedom. The Fathers of the Constitution were not unaware of the varied and extreme views of religious sects, of the violence of disagreement among them, and of the lack of any one religious creed on which all men could agree. They fashioned a charter of government which envisaged the widest possible toleration of conflicting views. Man's relation to his God was made no concern of the state. He was granted the right to worship as he pleased and to answer to no man for the verity of his religious views.[23]

The Court remanded the case for trial, not of the truth or falsity of the Ballards' views, but of their sincerity in promulgating them. Justice Jackson would not even have admitted that. In dissent, he added:

All schools of religious thought make enormous assumptions, generally on the basis of revelations authenticated by some sign or miracle. The appeal in such matters is to a very different plane of credulity than is invoked by representations of secular fact in commerce. . . .

The chief wrong which false prophets do to their following is not financial. The collections aggregate a tempting total, but individual payments are not ruinous. I doubt if the vigilance of the law is equal to making money stick by overcredulous people. But the real harm is on the mental and spiritual plane. . . . The wrong of these things, as I see it, is not in the money the victims part with half so much as in the mental and spiritual poison they get. But that is precisely the thing the Constitution put beyond the reach of the prosecutor, for the price of freedom of religion or of speech or of the press is that we must put up with, and even pay for, a good deal of rubbish. . . .

I do not doubt that religious leaders may be convicted of fraud for making false representations on matters other than faith or experience, as for example if one represents that funds are being used to construct a church when in fact they are being used for personal purposes. But that is not this case. . . . I would dismiss the indictment and have done with this business of judicially examining other people's faiths.[24]

The courts have tended to follow Justice Jackson's dictum in avoiding judicial examination of religious doctrines and tenets, but government still tends to see itself as guardian of the public's purses, even in the area of religion. It is prone to try to justify the use of some form of prior restraint on grounds of preventing fraud, thus offering a weak justification for sweeping governmental regulation that has the potential to become a cure that is worse than the disease.

b. There Are Some Remedies for (Some) Fraud

Even though punitive, overdrawn or overbroad prior restraints that chill First Amendment rights are not justified even to prevent fraud, some ordinary remedies are appropriate. So-called "common law fraud" may be the basis of an action by a victim of some flim-flam in the name of religion. A person charged with breach of contract for failure to pay a debt can claim fraud as a defense. Likewise, a person who has paid money to another can seek to recover it through a suit for damages grounded either in contract or tort against an individual or corporate perpetrator on the charge of fraud.

In appropriate situations, fraud may also incur criminal prosecution. Various statutes provide criminal penalties for such things as fraud, false pretenses, conspiracy to defraud, etc. Such criminal fraud can incur the usual penalties of fine, imprisonment or both. Corporations and/or individuals can be prosecuted. The usual rules of criminal law and procedure apply: criminal intent, the burden of proof and the presumption of innocence, for example.

However, neither civil nor criminal cases involve continuing or prospective sanctions beyond the direct and specific relief afforded to the victim in a civil case or to the state in a criminal proceeding. The activity of the perpetrator of a fraud with respect to future conduct or damage to other victims is not policed or deterred beyond the case itself. That's the rub. In an age of growing consumer consciousness and consumer law, all this is feeble stuff indeed—not far beyond the olden indifference of the common law that yawned at many sharp practices in the field of commerce with the cynical benediction of *caveat emptor*. That benighted doctrine is slowly eroding under the impact of remedial legislation and administrative regulation, even though the traditional spirit still shrouds some American courtrooms.

Not surprisingly, many people crave stronger medicine to cure the ill of fraud. Where there are no contrary public policy considerations to constrain zealous law reform and law enforcement (aside from the ordinary principles of due process), government can proceed apace to protect the innocent potential victims of fraud. But where the prevention or punishment of fraud involves the entanglement of government with religion, the otherwise limited remedies of the common law may be all that are available to victims or potential victims. Law reform that authorizes a more activist role for government may need to exclude or curtail its writ where it encounters the free exercise of religion or its non-establishment.

There will probably be some victims of fraud in the field of religion who will go uncompensated. There will be some fraud that the government might have been able to prevent or punish if constitutional constraints had not intervened. Those losses must be charged to the large account of injuries that in an imperfect world the law cannot reach without wreaking larger harms than it seeks to remedy.

c. Should Attorneys General Monitor Religious Fund-Raising?

A committee of Attorneys General has been pressing for adoption in those states not thus far blessed with it of a "model statute" that would authorize the Attorney General to protect the public against fraudulent charitable solicitations. Whatever the merits of that step may be with respect to secular charities, it is of dubious value (and constitutionality) as applied to religious solicitations. The Supreme Court has recognized that many solicitations have other purposes in addition to raising money, purposes protected by the First Amendment from all but the most minimal kinds of state regulation. If the Village of Schaumburg (Illinois) could not impose a 25 percent ceiling on fund-raising costs because it impaired the freedom of speech of representatives of Citizens for a Better Environment who wished to spread the gospel of ecology as well as collect contributions,[25] how much more inappropriate it is for governments to restrict solicitations that bear a religious message!

The model statute would require all organizations that solicit charitable contributions from the public to register with the Attorney General (often with a filing fee running to $50 each year) and to report annually—if not oftener—in great detail their costs, receipts, payments to beneficiaries, principal officers, consultants, their salaries, etc., and within each state innumerable lesser jurisdictions seek to impose their own additional requirements. This may enable the Attorney General to pose as the ever-vigilant guardian of the public weal without incurring the expense or risk that pursuing organized crime might entail, but it is not apparent that the public good is enhanced to a degree commensurate with the effort and expense involved—most of which are loaded on the soliciting charities, thus vastly increasing the very "pipeline" costs which the Attorneys General like to criticize and diminishing the "payload" available for the charitable purpose.

(One of the arguments behind the model statute is that it is not designed to punish, but to expose. The Attorney General is not trying to tell charities how to raise or spend their money, but simply to inform the public about where it goes so that donors can make their own decision on the basis of full information. To that argument we will return in the next section.) How many contributors want to look before they give, or go to the trouble of consulting the public records of disclosure the Attorney General is so anxious to maintain? Even if such reporting requirements may keep honest some solicitors who otherwise might not have been, or provide data for a few circumspect donors, they cannot entirely eliminate the already-small element of chicanery in the charitable field nor greatly reduce the large number of what Justice Jackson called "overcredulous people" nor make their money stick by them. The problem of *caveat donor* is not solved by the Attorney General's intervention, and another array of problems is created, some of constitutional dimensions, as we have seen.

The Attorney General is not without recourse, as has been noted, against the kinds of fraud that do not have as an essential element the claims of human "faith or experience," concerning which honest people may and do intensely differ. Of course, prosecution of such fraud requires some active gathering of evidence rather than just filing reports and banking registration fees, but investigation of actual crime is more the prosecutor's function than imposing vast regimens of reportage on law-abiding citizens.

It cannot be denied that there are some sticky distinctions to be made in attempting to apply the tests of fraud to religious solicitations. If a self-anointed "prophet" raises money to "feed the hungry" and uses it to supply the (spiritually) hungry with copies of his inspired teachings, is that "fraud"? And if someone gives $100,000 to a religious group to send Bibles to the heathen, but finds that that particular $100,000 went to pay for an executive jet for the founder, has that donor been defrauded? Especially if another $100,000 of undesignated money went for Bibles for the heathen? Rather than engage in theological hair-splitting, the prosecutor might do well in close cases to err on the side of mercy and devote his/her efforts to the apprehension of criminals who make no pretense of charitable purpose.

2. Government as Regulator of "Lobbyists"

Another recent development is the effort by certain states[26] to require all "lobbyists" to register with the state and to disclose the amounts they expended, the purposes served, and the sources of their funds. Whatever the merits of this course with respect to commercial lobbyists seeking to advance their own private interests, it poses significant obstacles to citizens' groups seeking to exercise their rights to "assemble and petition the government for redress of grievances."[27] And such obstacles are doubly obnoxious when imposed on citizens' groups acting out of religious obedience to advance the cause of morality (as they see it) for the common good rather than their own personal profit.[28]

In this area, as in that of charitable solicitations just discussed, the argument is made that the government is not trying to stifle freedom of speech, press, religion, assembly or petition but simply to make its exercise more visible. When someone addresses a legislator and urges his or her vote for or against a particular bill, he or she is entitled to know what is behind the urging, whether the effort has been financed by others, for how much, and by whom, runs the argument. It is maintained that private groups which try to affect public policy, just as those who try to raise money from the public, must be made more "accountable" to the public, and disclosure is a simple way to do it. What harm is there, we are asked, or what limitations on First Amendment freedoms, in simply publishing an organization's financial transactions so that all may see it has "nothing to hide"? And religious groups seem all too anxious to prove that they have "nothing to hide"! But this characterization of the situation is predicated upon some serious misconceptions.

It assumes: (a) that legislators are *obliged* to vote, or donors to contribute, as they are adjured to by lobbyists or solicitors; (b) that private groups must be made "accountable" to the public; and (c) that the way to do this is by mandatory disclosure required by government. A legislator may want to ask a lobbyist who pays the bills for his/her lobbying, and perhaps even ask a government agency to verify the answer; otherwise the legislator need not assign much weight to what the lobbyist says. The legislator is presumably a grown person and can make mature judgments about whose testimony should be taken seriously without elaborate and voluminous data-gathering in advance that creates more problems than it solves.

Much lobbying disclosure regulation seems aimed less at exposing the machinations of General Motors or General Electric than it does at sparing legislators the full impact of the robust working of the democratic process. Legislators seem able to steel themselves quite well to the blandishments of great corporations seeking their own profit, but wince at the approach of citizens' groups seeking to promote the public good. They insist that individual voters—especially those from their own district —are always welcome, but not organized bands of "outsiders"—as though their votes did not affect the fortunes of people outside their own districts. But to limit citizen action to individuals acting in dispersion is of course to condemn it to futility, since only organized effort is likely to be informed, timely, and effectively focused. (Perhaps futile is precisely what some people think citizens' action groups should be.)

The way to make private, voluntary citizens' groups "accountable" is not to compel them to report to the Attorney General or the Sergeant-at-Arms of the legislature, but to ask them to establish their bona fides by (voluntarily) producing audited financial records, references, and other pertinent data as needed. That's what one does when hiring an architect or buying a work of art: one examines the person or object, consults knowledgeable experts in the field, and makes an informed choice. One does not necessarily need the intervention of the Attorney General to do that. It may be helpful to have laws about "Truth-in-Advertising" in commercial matters, but in areas of public policy, charitable purpose and—above all—religious faith, the Attorney General is no better guide than anyone else, and mass mandatory disclosure simply produces a fog of undifferentiated data-overload.

Whatever may be the merits of mandatory disclosure with respect to commercial lobbyists and professional fundraisers, or even with respect to secular citizens' organizations and public charities, it is a pernicious device as applied to religious groups. It is pernicious because it encourages in the public mind the erroneous notion that religious organizations are obliged to account to the public or to a public official for their beliefs or their (lawful) activities. Certainly religious groups ought to be accountable, and they are, but not to the public or to public officials. They are accountable to their members and contributors. They are accountable in the sense that no one is *required* to give money to church or synagogue. If they do not like the way it is run, they can take themselves and their money elsewhere—and they often do. If they continue to support it by their voluntary gifts and efforts, that is no one else's business, least of all the Attorney General's.

> Man's relation to his God was made no concern of the state. He was granted the right to worship as he pleased and to answer to no man for the verity of his religious views. [29]

Churches and synagogues should resist being placed in the position of having to report routinely to civil authorities on their religious activities. *Voluntary* disclosure of a religious group's finances to its members and contributors is a wise and constructive policy for all such groups, though some choose another policy, and persons who knowingly join and support a group that does not voluntarily disclose its finances have no basis to demand something that wasn't in their contract of membership to begin with.

But *mandatory* disclosure of a religious body's internal affairs to the public or to civil authorities is inappropriate for three reasons:

i. It conduces to the mistaken notion that such bodies are "public" entities, with all the consequent errors noted earlier:

(a) The monstrous "public trust" concept asserted by the Attorney General of California;[30]

(b) Police entering church premises without a warrant on the ground that "it's a public place";[31]

(c) The insistence by some press representatives (and even by some of their counterparts within religious groups) that all religious gatherings should be "open meetings" because they are "accountable to the public"!

ii. It contradicts the truth recognized by the Supreme Court as being rooted in the Constitution: that there should not be "excessive entanglement" between government and religion.[32]

iii. Any religious organization worthy of its calling might well have undertakings that would be wrong to disclose because of pastoral confidentiality, the privacy rights of individuals, and other reasons. (One of us recalls that as a pastor he often assisted families in need in the parish out of his discretionary fund—expenditures that he was directed by the

Official Board that set up the fund not to divulge to anyone, even themselves.)

3. Government as Arbiter of Disputes Within Religious Groups Over "Temporalities"

The Supreme Court has repeatedly held that civil courts are not to scrutinize the "doctrines and tenets" of religious bodies.[33] The reason that courts might occasionally be tempted to do so is that religious bodies have their being in a material, social and legal world, to which they are anchored by the "temporalities" of their existence: real property, mortgages, contracts, trusts, insurance policies, bank accounts, articles of incorporation, etc. When they rely upon civil or secular mechanisms to authenticate or regularize their interest in or title to these temporalities, as to some degree they must, they subject themselves to the jurisdiction of the civil government, and when internecine disputes break out which cannot be resolved within the religious community, to the arbitrament of civil courts.

Three lines of cases have developed which seek to minimize the courts' concerning themselves with religious doctrines and tenets in resolving such disputes. (a) One line holds that when there is a dispute over property within a hierarchical church, the civil courts will simply enforce the decision of the highest ecclesiastical tribunal within that body to which the issue has been taken.[34] (b) Another line recognizes that statutes may be drawn to accommodate particular ecclesiastical polities, but that even when an international entity is involved, neither court nor legislature can impose upon a religious body a structure of authority or polity other than it has chosen for itself,[35] since the structure of authority within a religious body is usually inextricably intertwined with theological doctrine.

(c) A third line, the most recent, relies upon "neutral principles of law" to resolve disputes over property: deeds, trust instruments, etc., which are thought to be free of theological bias.[36] The use of such supposedly "neutral principles" sometimes has the effect of "congregationalizing" a hierarchical polity by granting control of local church property to a dissident local congregation in defiance of the higher judicatory to which it was formerly attached. This can occur when the property deed gives title to local trustees without an explicit provision of control by the superior church body, and may actually contravene the hitherto generally accepted self-definition of authority within the religious body. In such a case, the "neutral principles of law" are neutral on the side of local dissidents and against the rest of the religious body. which has defined itself as having a regional, national or world locus of decision-making.

On the other hand, civil courts have sometimes imposed upon churches a hierarchical character they have not chosen for themselves, as when both state and federal courts ruled that the United Methodist Church is a suable entity and would have to answer suit growing out of the bankruptcy of the Pacific Homes related to one of its regional jurisdictions (which *was* answering suit). The persons responding to the suit on behalf of the denomination insisted that it had no central, continuing body or officer able to answer suit, but the court held that it must respond anyway![37]

Religious bodies will need to take whatever steps are necessary to effectuate their own chosen self-definition of authority throughout their temporalities, so that "neutral" principles of law do not operate to repose decision-making authority elsewhere than they intend.

4. Religious Bodies' Utilization of Government Funds

A special case of religious entanglement with government through "temporalities" occurs when a religious body is the recipient of public funds through a governmental grant, contract or purchase-of-services arrangement. As the Supreme Court has observed (quoting Justice Jackson again):

> If the state may aid these religious schools, it may therefore regulate them. Many groups have sought aid from tax funds only to find that it carried political controls with it. Indeed, this Court has declared that "it is hardly lack of due process for the Government to regulate that which it subsidizes." Wickard v. Filburn.[38]

So when a religious body accepts government money, it should not expect to be impervious to government intervention to the degree it might otherwise have been (which is not by any means complete, as we have seen). But it may still seek to keep the arrangement one "at arm's length," however.

The National Council of Churches, which receives extensive federal grants for refugee resettlement, overseas relief, employment training of incarcerated veterans, energy education, etc., has acknowledged the government's right to a full accounting for the use of that money, but has contended—thus far successfully—that government auditors should not enter upon ecclesiastical premises to make direct audits of ecclesiastical books of account. Instead, it has offered two alternatives: (1) that audits be performed by private auditors, such as Arthur Anderson, Inc., its regular auditor, and made available to the government, or (2) that all books of account and other records pertaining to the government grant programs, and those only, will be made available to government auditors for inspection at the offices of the National Council's legal counsel. (It has no objection to on-site inspections by government officers at the various projects it operates which are not on ecclesiastical premises.) This may not be a fool-proof arrangement, or it may be superficial, but it is an effort to preserve an arm's-length relationship.

The converse of this special situation is seen in the recognition by a federal circuit court that if Roman Catholic parochial schools are, as the

Supreme Court has held,[39] too religious to receive public funds, they are likewise too religious to be subject to regulation by a federal agency.[40]

5. Government as Definer of What Is "Religious"

If religion is to be accorded an appropriately unique status in law, what entities should be entitled to that status and who should determine that entitlement? Some would insist that government should not be allowed to define what is religious, and that is partially correct. But since the unique status of religion is a category of the civil law, the civil magistrate will have the ultimate and unavoidable responsibility of determining who is entitled to be classified in that category. The magistrate should do so, however, without attempting to construct a new definition of religion (or adopting an old one), which would have the effect of freezing future forms of religion in the molds of the present or the past.

Rather, the magistrate should simply *recognize* the religious entities that were here, and acknowledged as such, long before there was a United States or a First Amendment, and with them their progeny, replicas, and functional equivalents. In another place,[41] one of us has spelled out in some detail how the magistrate can determine whether new claimants to the name of "religion" qualify. Suffice it to say here that the test entails, not the testimony of outsiders, but whether adherents derive from it, over time, the functional benefits of religion, i.e., an explanation of the ultimate meaning of life. And the magistrate need not decide whether a group meets the test until it has been around for a while —perhaps thirty, forty or fifty years, which is the mere twinkling of an eye in the life-span of a religion.

But there is no need for the magistrate to accord the (somewhat limited) civil benefits of being a "religion" to groups that are palpable "put-ons" that admit to being designed to serve solely as tax shelters! The Internal Revenue Service is seeking to crack down on "mail-order ministries" such as the Universal Life Church—a form of government intervention of which we can heartily approve. In its effort to do so, however, the IRS has developed a list of 13 marks, traits or evidences, not all of which, it generously recognizes, need be met by a group claiming to be a religion:

1. A distinct legal existence;
2. A recognized creed and form of worship;
3. A definite and distinct ecclesiastical government;
4. A formal code of doctrine and discipline;
5. A distinct religious history;
6. A membership not associated with any other church or denomination;
7. A complete organization of ordained ministers ministering to their congregations and selected after completing prescribed courses of study;
8. A literature of its own;

    9. Established places of worship;

   10. Regular congregations;

   11. Regular religious services;

   12. Sunday schools for the religious instruction of the young;

   13. Schools for the preparation of its ministers. [42]

(This definition or description is not only very conventional but also circular, in the sense that a group's government is "ecclesiastical" and its history "religious" *if* the group is a "religion," which is what the description was supposed to determine!)

Though this description is not part of any regulation—yet, and has no legal standing, it represents the type of exercise that government ought not to get into because it merely offers a facade which bogus religions can readily counterfeit while it fails to accommodate some real but unconventional religions.

II. Is Religion "Above the Law"?

A. Both Government and Religion Are Under the Constitution

There are those who will insist, after sensing the general thrust of this conference, that religious organizations should not think themselves to be "above the law." It is to correct that idea that this paper has been prepared. Indeed religious groups are *not* above the law, *but neither is the government.* Both are bound by the same law, and one of its most basic elements is the First Amendment with its two clauses about "religion," which creates a special category *under the law* for that mode of human behavior which both government and religions are obliged to respect. Sometimes that special status seems to work to the advantage of religious groups, as when it exempts them from the requirement of reporting to government agencies or entitles them to credential chaplains for the armed services, prisons or hospitals. At other times it seems to disadvantage them, as when it disqualifies them for various kinds of public support or subsidy.

But aside from the rather limited benefits and disabilities required by the law, religious groups and their members are not above or outside the law and should not be thought to be so, by themselves or by government. If they violate the law, they cannot expect to go unpunished on the plea that they are "religious." Neither should government officers or agencies make exceptions for them that the law does not recognize or require. We all know clergy who expect to be let off for traffic violations or who demand special treatment under foster-home or child-custody laws because they are ordained, and we all know of public servants who accede to these demands, and both are wrong.

But there are special categories in the law that apply solely to religion and its organizational embodiments, sometimes providing a blanket exception, immunity or exemption from laws that apply to all others. These are designed, not to abrogate the law, but to accommodate it to the unique status accorded "religion" by the First Amendment. Among them are (in the Internal Revenue Code alone):

a. "Churches, conventions or associations of churches" (which, of course, includes synagogues) is the first class in the catalog of organizations contributions to which are deductible from taxable income (Section 170(b)(1)(A)(i));

b. They are given mandatory exception from the presumption of being "private foundations" (Section 508(c)(1)(A));

c. They are given mandatory exception from the requirement that Section 501 (exempt) organizations must file annual informational returns (Section 6033(a)(2)(A));

d. IRS is limited in the auditing or examining it may undertake of such organizations (Section 7605(c));

e. They are disqualified from electing to rely on Section 501(h) to engage in limited direct-interest, and even more limited grass-roots, "lobbying." (This is not because lobbying is forbidden to them but because they requested not to be included in a provision they consider unconstitutional.)

B. Should Government Have a Maximal or a Minimal Role Toward Religion?

Some would contend that there should be no such categorical exemptions for religion as such, since they feel that it affords one particular kind of activity and organization an almost "extraterritorial" status within the terrain of laws applying to everyone else. This is another way of insisting that religion should not be above or outside the law. Advocates of this view would hold that religious liberty is at best an attribute of persons, not of groups, and it is sufficient to stay the application of a particular law to particular persons only if and after it is shown to have an actual effect of infringing their religious freedom. No blanket exemptions should be accorded in advance of such a showing to whole organizations on the supposition that the law *might* at some future time affect the religious liberty of their members.

This view would be one attributing a *maximal* role to government in relation to religion. It is the course James Madison might have recommended if he had said: "It is sufficient to take alarm after the government has experimented with our liberties, and then only if the experiment really turned out very badly." But that is not what James Madison said. He wrote in the famed *Memorial and Remonstrance*: "It is proper to take alarm at the first experiment on our liberties." The place to halt such experiments is at the threshold, and the way to halt them is by placing the entire area where they might occur "out of bounds" for government. That counsel, which we may attribute to at least one of the Founders, and a formative one in the architecture of our liberties, envisions a *minimal* role for government with respect to religion, and that is the one which we emphatically advocate for the (continuing) public policy of this nation.

C. Inadequate Rationales for Government Intervention

There are several ways in which the jurisprudence of the United States in its more primitive periods or levels has sought to justify government intervention.

1. Earliest was the dichotomy between "belief" and "action,"[43] which has been rather generally discredited and neglected (except by Attorneys General seeking to justify their interventions), though nowhere expressly repudiated or overruled. Religious groups cannot afford to concede that action motivated by religious belief is not entitled to some degree of protection under the First Amendment (see page 175 above).

2. The idea that only individuals have rights and groups cannot claim them, either on behalf of their members or on their own behalf, is one that appeals to some people on first blush, but the U.S. Supreme Court has recognized that groups also have some rights as groups,[44] and church property cases have recognized the right of church bodies to determine their own affairs (within certain still-controverted limits) without civil courts weighing their doctrines and tenets. Religious bodies cannot afford to concede that the treatment by civil courts of their structures of internal authority over real property does not have important religious implications and consequences.[45] It is integral to their *religious* duty.

3. The lower courts in California which granted and reviewed the *ex parte* receivership over the Worldwide Church of God sought to justify the Attorney General's intervention by insisting that the receiver would have authority only over the *finances* of the church, not over its ecclesiastical affairs, and that the court could easily distinguish the one from the other.

> . . . I just don't think ecclesiastical matters have anything to do with the financial aspects of the operation out there.
>
> I can see a clear delineation between what is ecclesiastical and what is not, but it has no reference whatsoever to financial matters.[46]

This, too, is a dichotomy that religious bodies cannot afford to concede. How a religious body raises, invests and expends its funds cannot be divorced from its religious purpose, ministry and mission, and government cannot intervene in the one without affecting the other. That does not mean that government never has a right to scrutinize the financial dealings of a church, but the threshold of its intervention should not be *lower* than that required in the case of a commercial corporation (as the

Attorney General of California would have had it under his theory of "public trust"), but much *higher*. Indeed, the same "compelling interest" test should apply here as in other "free exercise" areas.[47]

4. A distressing stain on the First Amendment jurisprudence of the United States is the curious decision of the Tenth Circuit Court of Appeals in *Christian Echoes National Ministry* v. *U.S.*,[48] which upheld the revocation of Billy James Hargis' tax exemption for alleged lobbying and electioneering with this remarkable dictum:

> In light of the fact that tax exemption is a privilege, a matter of grace rather than right, we hold that the limitations contained in Section 501(c)(3) withholding exemption from nonprofit corporations [which engage in lobbying] do not deprive Christian Echoes of its constitutionally guaranteed right of free speech. The taxpayer may engage in all such activities without restraint, subject, however, to withholding of the exemption, or, in the alternative, the taxpayer may refrain from such activities and obtain the privilege of exemption.[49]

The Tenth Circuit delivered its singular opinion without ever citing the Supreme Court's definitive decision on tax exemption of churches, *Walz* v. *Tax Commission*, decided two years earlier, and asserted what the Supreme Court has never said, that tax exemption of religious bodies is a privilege rather than a right, contradicted the Supreme Court's explicit holding that their tax exemption is not predicated upon the supposed social welfare services they perform, and flatly violated the Supreme Court's oft-repeated insistence that even a privilege (assuming *arguendo* it to be that) cannot be conditioned upon the abandonment of rights guaranteed by the Constitution.[50] It also characterized tax exemption as a "subsidy," which the Supreme Court had explicitly denied in *Walz*, and preferred churches which remain silent on public issues over those which speak out on them! Nevertheless, the Supreme Court did not take the case to correct these egregious errors, and the Tenth Circuit decision still hangs like a sword of Damocles over the efforts by churches to influence public policy on moral issues.[51]

Religious bodies cannot afford to concede that their tax exemption is dependent upon their refraining from petitioning the government for redress of grievances, nor can they permit the government, by that means or any other, to silence them on issues of moral importance to the nation.

5. Another ominous course being pursued by government at present is the contention that tax exemption is also conditioned upon conformity to what the government may characterize as "public policy."[52] Religious bodies cannot afford to allow tax exemption to be used as a carrot to cajole or a stick to coerce them into behavior deemed acceptable by the incumbents of government office at a given moment.

If and when religious bodies show by prevalent misbehavior that they need more careful regulating, then will be time enough to propose closer strictures in the law. But the burden of proof should be upon those who seek to justify such regulation, not upon religious bodies to resist it, and the burden should be a heavy one. It should not be deemed to have been met by pointing to a few isolated instances of supposedly scandalous behavior on the part of a few leaders or adherents of religion, particularly when most such instances could be dealt with by careful but conscientious application of existing law.

D. Religious Liberty Involves Some Risks

Between the two truths with which we began—(1) that religion is, by and large, not a proper object of governmental regulation, and (2) that there are some (very limited) respects in which government can and should regulate religious activities—there may be some gaps where the regulatory zeal of government will be kept at bay by constitutional restraints, and in some of them, some ills befall which might have been punished or prevented had the First Amendment's solicitude for the free exercise of religion not barred the way. But as we said earlier, "those losses must be charged to the large account of injuries that in an imperfect world the law cannot reach without wreaking larger harms than it seeks to remedy."

Yet it is important to realize that those ostensible harms, at their worst and most notorious, are not as pernicious or extensive as sensationalized reports or alarmist predictions might suggest. They represent but a tiny fraction of the total range of otherwise law-abiding religious behavior, and public policy should not be predicated upon the aberrations of a very few to the hurt of the very many if remedies more tailored to the actual ills can be applied, as we have suggested in many cases that they can.

In close and disputed cases, let public policy err on the side of minimizing the role of government in regulating religion rather than to engage in first experiments upon our liberties. And what if a few ills do go uncorrected? As Justice Jackson observed, with freedom comes the risk that it will be misused. Certainly there is always the danger that some hanky-panky will go on under the facade of religion, but that may be the price we pay for freedom.

We should not allow ourselves to be panicked by a few notorious scandals—such as the Pallottine Fathers or the Jonestown Meltdown —into draconian measures that will trammel the freedom of the 99 percent of religious activities that are legitimate and sincere without greatly inconveniencing the 1 percent that are not. It may be better in marginal cases to let the tares grow with the wheat until the harvest, or as Gamaliel the Pharisee put it:

> . . . let them alone, for if this plan or this undertaking is of men, it will fail; but if it is of God, you will not be able to overthrow them. You might even be found opposing God![53]

Many of the most vigorous and stable religious bodies in the nation might have been stamped out at their inception had the outcries of suspicion and alarm at that time stampeded the government into imprudent measures (as almost happened with the Mormons in the 19th century). But instead they were given room to grow or wither as their own efforts enabled them, and some have enriched not only the lives of many followers, but the religious vitality of the American people.

The Founders of the nation knew that they were taking risks when they wrote the First Amendment. We should be no less confident than they that the freedom of religion thus safeguarded was well worth the risk and that, by and large, it will be fairly and productively employed for the important purposes for which it was erected. What they were not willing to risk was permitting government to experiment with their liberties.

Concluding Remarks by the Chairperson

WILLIAM P. THOMPSON

We have now come to the end of an absorbing and informative experience. We have heard some of the leading observers and thinkers on church-state issues bring us up to date on recent developments that cover a wide range of legal and political encounters between governments and religious organizations. We have heard perceptive comments from them and from the floor. And now we may be asking ourselves, "Where do we go from here?"

First and foremost, we go back to our sponsoring bodies to acquaint them with the main lines of what we have learned. This has not been an exposure for our own edification alone, but for the bodies that sent us, and we must find ways to share with them what they need to know.

It may not always be easy to impress upon our colleagues in the great religious bodies we serve that there are greater issues at stake than the institutional prudentialities of the moment, but we must be insistent to point out that important precedents are being set by the decisions made each day that can affect all of us far into the future.

And those decisions are often shaped by localized or short-term considerations that do not take account of the wider picture, the deeper principles, the longer prospect. Sometimes a local pastor, rabbi or congregation will set the course of great events, and do so through impulse, expediency or inadvertence, in a way that cannot later be rectified except at great expense, if at all.

We who labor in the law know how often a case can be "queered" at the trial level by a local attorney inexperienced in the particular field of law involved, so that even the most illustrious appellate counsel cannot salvage much at higher levels because necessary evidence or objections were not gotten into the trial record at the beginning.

The same is true in the matters we have been considering here. A local congregation, confronted by a new governmental requirement, may either acquiesce when they should resist, or take a stand of adamant resistance when they "don't have a leg to stand on." Or to avoid over-reacting in the wrong direction, they may consult an attorney known to them, who may be very capable at handling wills and mortgages, but is a babe-in-the-woods at constitutional law, and even less well-versed in that particular branch of constitutional law that deals with the religion clauses of the First Amendment.

Such an attorney, when faced with a suit for libel against a church leader for comments made in the course of ecclesiastical admonition, may treat the case as a standard defense to the charge of libel rather than fighting the threshold issue of whether civil courts have jurisdiction to scrutinize the content of ecclesiastical admonitions at all. By the time the case comes to national attention on appeal, it may be too late to raise the threshold issue of jurisdiction because trial counsel has already conceded it by answering on the merits, and the precedent may then be set that action for libel will lie against clergy seeking to admonish fractious adherents—an appalling impairment of religious liberty!

The point I wish to make is that we are all defenders in common of a precious stronghold with a long and ragged perimeter. A bad mistake by any one of us at any point along that line may admit the "enemy" to an entire salient, and we will all be losers thereby because of the fault or neglect of one.

It therefore behooves us to know what is happening all along the line, to secure the best defense we can in any sector that is under attack, and to try to fit our efforts, wherever we may be, into a common strategy and mutual reinforcement, lest we be picked off one by one.

Do not be confused by the military analogy. I do not mean to suggest by it that government is the "enemy" carrying on a purposeful plan of attack, because I do not believe that to be so. In that respect, a better image might be that of a ship at sea in a storm, where all hands seek to patch any leak that might let in the ineluctable but impersonal pressure of the ocean. I used the military analogy only to suggest that a coherent, long-range strategy might be conceived and applied by the defenders so that they could do more than simply react to the attacks and sieges initiated by others. The analogy also breaks down because we do not have any over-all commander to coordinate our efforts, nor do we want one: that would be a cure as bad as the complaint.

We must rely on mutual respect, voluntary cooperation, and a shared understanding of the situation and the cause at stake. This conference has been an excellent example of that approach. We have worked together, with remarkably cooperative spirit and remarkably little friction, to do something jointly that we all felt urgently needed doing, and that is what I covet for us in the future.

We will continue to disagree with one another on various issues, but we share a common commitment to the over-all defense of religious liberty, which permits each of us to carry out his or her faith-group's obligation to God as each group understands it.

But there are perils in such easy-going voluntarism as well. Sometimes the trumpet will sound the alarm and we will be preoccupied with other matters, and the struggle will be lost. Those of us of Scotch-Presbyterian heritage are only too mindful of the historic vulnerability of the proud Highland clans, who could rarely subordinate their independence to follow a common leader, even of their own choosing and for the brief span of a battle, and so were regularly trounced by the less dashing but more disciplined English.

I am not suggesting that we should subordinate ourselves to some "general," however briefly, but that we need to be forewarned about the hazards we face, forearmed with resources to meet them, and steadfast in our determination not to be distracted, dissuaded or deflected from defending the religious liberty that is so crucial for all of us.

For if we do not take cognizance of our shared predicament, the inexorable pressures of the impersonal environing society will confine the free exercise of religion to the sanctuary, the synagogue, the sacristy, the narrow sanctum of worship and sacrament—the same parameters allowed religion in the Soviet Union and the People's Republic of China.

As we have been informed in these three days, religious bodies have responded to government intervention in several ways:

1. *Acquiescence.* The Board of Church and Society of the United Methodist Church acceded, perhaps rightly, to the Internal Revenue Service's insistence that the Board could not extend the benefit of its tax exemption to coalitions that it did not control.

2. *Compliance under Protest.* Some religious bodies have acceded to the ruling or directive of a government agency, but have accompanied their compliance with a formal statement of protest or objection, setting forth the reasons they felt the order was incorrect or unjustified. (It is not clear whether this is legally different from the preceding.)

3. *Remonstrance.* This is the commonest first step in all cases, and should precede any other outcomes. In most instances, civil officials have been willing to discuss the grounds of their actions before finalizing them. In many instances, they are unaware of the First Amendment implications of those actions with respect to religious bodies. In a distressing number of instances, they continue to treat religious bodies as though no special category were created for them by the First Amendment at all.

4. *Avoidance.* Sometimes the religious body withdraws from the field temporarily in order to preserve its right to challenge the government's decision at a later date. When the National Council of Churches was unable to persuade the Attorney General of Massachusetts that its direct-mail fund appeal for the "Due Process of Law Fund" was a "religious purpose" under the Massachusetts exemption for religious campaigns from its registration and reporting requirements, the National Council (on advice of counsel) ceased all solicitations in the Commonwealth of Massachusetts in order to preserve its right to challenge the Attorney General's interpretation of the Massachusetts law.

5. *Legislative Revision.* On several occasions, religious bodies have been able to secure modification of the law to clarify contested areas. Outstanding examples include:

a. The National Council of Churches and the U.S. Catholic Conference jointly proposed to the House Ways and Means Committee that the "loophole" permitting churches to avoid paying tax on income from trade or business unrelated to their exempt purpose should be closed because it gave them an unfair commercial advantage over taxpaying competitors, and in the Tax Reform Act of 1969, it was done;

b. A broad coalition including the same two bodies obtained exclusion of churches from the "Conable Bill," which became Section 501(h) of the Internal Revenue Code in 1976. This section permits public charities to do a limited amount of direct-interest lobbying without losing their exemption, and the churches considered it an inadequate patch on an essentially unconstitutional limitation on citizen action;

c. A wide coalition of religious bodies in California recently secured passage of the "Petris Bill," which repealed the powers of the Attorney General to exercise discretionary supervision over religious bodies (he can still enforce any and all pertinent portions of the civil and criminal law with respect to any and all persons or groups in the state, including religious bodies, but only after meeting the same threshold standards of evidence that apply in all other cases).

6. *Litigation.* Several bodies have taken their problems to court, as we have heard. When a mutual understanding between a religious body and a government agency cannot be reached, it is appropriate to seek adjudication of the difference. That's what courts are for. But one must be sure one's hands are clean and one's affairs in good array before going into court, or one may be worse off after than before.

7. *Civil Disobedience.* Other bodies have simply refused to comply with governmental directives, and indeed that is the only way to get into court on some issues: as a defendant. Both as plaintiff and defendant there are important problems and perils to be encountered, which we have glimpsed in these proceedings. Sometimes a religious body may feel that it is just not equipped to take on extensive litigation at a particular time, and so accedes rather than fights. I would hope that, before such a decision is made, others of us would be consulted to see if there is some way in which we can share the burden of defending our mutual interests, as the Southern Baptist seminaries did. Any one of us ought not to find it necessary to "go it alone" when the outcome of decisions taken by that one may profoundly affect us all. That seems to me to be the counsel of elementary prudence, but it is not easy to achieve, since we have no common mechanism of mutual defense.

I am concerned that—having been aroused and edified here—we will subside back into our own various preoccupations and lose the possibility of mutual assistance and support that this conference anticipates for lack of a means or mechanism to realize it. Therefore, I offer a few minimal suggestions, which are not far beyond what some of us are doing now, though at present only on a haphazard basis:

1. There is a need for a way to keep one another informed of new

developments as they occur, so that we do not learn about them too late to be of help. I suggest that our Planning Committee is an already smoothly functioning mechanism to meet that need. If you encounter a problem or situation that we all should know about, contact your representative on the Planning Committee, and he or she can let the others know about it, and they can spread the word through their own networks.

2. You have seen and heard upon this platform some of the ablest and most outstanding scholars and advocates in the field of First Amendment law. (There are not as many such specialists in this country as we need, and this conference is designed to help prepare additional ones.) But if you need expert advice on a problem you encounter, these are persons you can turn to with some confidence that you will not be led astray. But do not expect them to help you out for free. Most of them will be willing to hear your statement of the problem and your questions without charging you for that time. But finding answers in a responsible way takes some research and analysis, and that is highly skilled work. You should expect to pay for it. They will often give you an estimate beforehand of what it is likely to take to get your questions answered, but even that is difficult, as one doesn't always know in advance what hidden mazes the research will uncover that need to be explored before the answer is secure. Which brings me to my third point:

3. Don't expect to be safe without cost. Competent defense of anything precious isn't cheap. We should all anticipate the need for increased legal expenses in the future, and each organization represented here should begin to budget—if it does not do so already—a substantial fund for legal services. If it isn't used in the current year, save it for the next.

4. Do not be shy about coming to one another's aid, since even the defeats suffered by those we may consider rivals will often afflict us all, for we dwell under a common jurisprudence, whether we like it or not. For instance, the National Council of Churches has entered friend-of-the-court briefs in cases involving Billy James Hargis, one of its sharpest critics, and the Church of Scientology, a group whose standing as a religion is not universally accepted. It did so, not to embrace these defendants or testify to their theological merits, but to defend the principles at stake in their respective cases, since our liberties are most likely to be lost, not in the instances of attack on the most *respectable* and *secure* but upon the most *vulnerable*, whose cause may be controversial, unpopular, or repugnant. But that is where the battles for our civil liberties occur. We must learn to distinguish between the party and the principle and say, as did Voltaire, "I disagree with what you say, but will defend your right to say it."

A case in point is the suit against the Roman Catholic Church for its alleged political activities in opposition to abortion. Many of us would disagree intensely on the merits of that subject—some on one side, some on the other—but that does not mean we want to see that church or any other *silenced,* or that we will stand idly by when it is under attack for preaching and acting in support of what it believes to be the course of morality for all. We will continue to dispute the issue of what the public policy of the nation ought to be with respect to abortion—and other issues. But we will stand side by side with that church, or any other religious body, when its right to speak and act is challenged.

Some of us believe that it is unconstitutional to take away a religious body's tax exemption for doing what religious bodies are *supposed* to do: namely, to proclaim the course of morality as that body sees it and to denounce immorality at the top of its voice. We need *more* of that forthrightness today, not *less*. With tongue in cheek, I might suggest that tax exemption should be withdrawn from religious bodies that are *not* doing this, rather than from those that *do*.

It may not be wise at this stage to "make a federal case" of the Abortion Rights Mobilization suit against the Roman Catholic Church. But if it goes to trial, others of us may have a chance to show our solidarity with an embattled religious group. In this and other cases, we must make it clear that we will not stand mute and let secular forces whittle away the most vulnerable. And, finally:

5. There may come a time when we will need to gather again to learn how the struggle goes and where the line wears thin. In that day I hope we will be as well served as we have been this week. Let us in conclusion express our appreciation to all who have made this conference possible, and bid each other farewell until we meet again.

Notes

INTRODUCTION

1. This ratio is obtained by counting the cases included in *Toward Benevolent Neutrality: Church, State, and the Supreme Court* by Robert T. Miller and Ronald B. Flowers (Waco, TX: Markham Press Fund, 1977), a compilation of the important church-state decisions of the Supreme Court, which cites eight cases prior to 1940 and thirty-six since, plus at least four more since that volume was published, such as *McDaniel* v. *Paty*, 1978; *Jones* v. *Wolf*, 1979; *NLRB* v. *Catholic Bishop of Chicago*, 1979; *St. Martin's Evangelical Lutheran Church* v. *S. Dakota*, 1981.
2. Franklin Littell, *From State Church to Pluralism* (Garden City, NY: Doubleday & Co., 1962), p. 32.
3. *Yearbook of American and Canadian Churches*, 1980, lists total church membership in U.S. of 133,748,776 as of 1978, out of a total population of 203,000,000.
4. See D. M. Kelley, *Why Churches Should Not Pay Taxes* (NY: Harper & Row, 1977), ch. 4, for further discussion of this point.
5. Fortunately, that has already been done to some degree, at least for Protestants, in Thomas G. Sanders, *Protestant Concepts of Church and State* (NY: Holt, Rinehart and Winston, 1964); and for Roman Catholics in Luigi Sturzo, *Church and State* (South Bend, IN: University of Notre Dame Press, 1962); Pius Augustin, O.S.B., *Religious Freedom in Church and State* (Baltimore: Helicon, 1966); and for Lutherans in Albert G. Huegli, ed., *Church and State under God* (St. Louis, MO: Concordia, 1964).
6. See Littell, *From State Church to Pluralism*, op. cit.

GOVERNMENT AS BIG BROTHER TO RELIGIOUS BODIES

1. *Keyishian* v. *Board of Regents*, 384 U.S. 589, 604 (1967).
2. *State of Vermont* v. *LaBarge*, 134 Vt. 276 (1976); *State of Ohio* v. *Whisner*, 47 Ohio St. 2d 181 (1976); *State of North Carolina* v. *Columbus Christian Academy*, No. 78-CVS-1678 (N.C. Super. Ct., Sept. 5, 1978), judgment vacated No. 114, Spring Term, 1979 (N.C. Sup. Ct., May 4, 1979); *Rudasill* v. *Kentucky State Board of Education*, 589 S.W. 2d 877 (1979), *cert.* denied, ___U.S.___, 64 L. Ed. 2d 792 (1980); *State of North Dakota* v. *Shaver*, 294 N.W. 2d 883 (1980); *State of Ohio* v. *Olin*,___Ohio St. 2d___(Dec. 30, 1980); *State ex rel. Douglas* v. *Faith Baptist Church*, ___Neb.___(Jan. 30, 1981).
3. I use the phrase, "religious conviction." You can always spot a secularist judge when he employs the term, "religious scruples."
4. 98 U.S. 145, 166 (1879).
5. *Grace Brethren Church* v. *California*, No. CV 79-93 MRP (C.D. Cal., Sept. 21, 1979).
6. *New Jersey-Philadelphia Presbytery* v. *New Jersey State Board of Higher Education*, 482 F. Supp. 968 (D.N.J. 1980).
7. *E.g.*, Standard IV: "Major safeguards for quality education are . . . a profusion for a high degree of self direction. . . ."
8. I use the term, not in the technical sense of one sued by a "plaintiff," but in the broader sense of one against whom state regulation is sought to be enforced and who may, as in the *Rudasill* case, be forced to seek an injunction against the state (and therefore be a plaintiff) in order to protect his rights.
9. 460 F. Supp. 1337 (1978).
10. Ohio Revised Code, Section 4112.01, *et. seq.*
11. 483 F. Supp. 266 (N.D. Iowa, E.D. 1980).
12. *State* v. *Williams*, 253 N.C. 337 (1960).

13. Marshall, C. J., in *Brown* v. *Maryland,* 12 Wheat. 419, 439 (1827).
14. James Madison, *A Memorial and Remonstrance, II,* Madison 183–191. (Emphasis supplied.)

WHO OWNS THE CHURCHES?

1. *Watson* v. *Jones,* 80 U.S. (13 Wall.) 679.
2. *Cantwell* v. *Connecticut,* 310 U.S. 296.
3. *Everson* v. *Bd. of Education,* 330 U.S. 1.
4. *Presbyterian Church* v. *Hull Church,* 393 U.S. 440.
5. 393 U.S. at 449.
6. 393 U.S. at 451.
7. *Serbian Orthodox Diocese* v. *Milivojevich,* 426 U.S. 696 (1976).
8. *Jones* v. *Wolf,* 443 U.S. 595.
9. 443 U.S. at 604.
10. 443 U.S. at 602.
11. *Ibid.*
12. Footnote 8 of *Jones* v. *Wolf.*
13. State of Maine, Supreme Judicial Court Sitting as the Law Court, Law Court Docket No. Ar-80-14.
14. Brief of Appellants, pp. 2–3.
15. Petition, p. 35.
16. Petition, p. ii.
17. See, for example, *Lemon* v. *Kurtzman,* 403 U.S. 602 (1971), and *Wolman* v. *Walter,* 433 U.S. 229 (1977).

FRONTIER ISSUES OF TAX EXEMPTION FOR RELIGIOUS ORGANIZATIONS

1. As a matter of statutory law, all organizations described in Section 501(c)(3) of the Internal Revenue Code of 1954, as amended, *including* religious organizations in general but *excluding* churches in particular, are required (i) to apply to the Internal Revenue Service within the first 15 months of existence for recognition of tax-exempt status and (ii) to file with the Internal Revenue Service annual tax information returns. Thus, an organization claiming to be a "church" need not follow these procedures, so that it would not be threatened directly unless it went voluntarily to the Service with a request for clarification of its status or, alternatively, through informal means the Service "caught up" with the so-called church and commenced an audit.
2. Treas. Reg. Section 1.501(c)(3)-1(c)(2).
3. It must be noted that recently the Court of Appeals for the District of Columbia voided the regulatory definition of "educational" as being unconstitutionally vague and broad. *Big Mama Rag, Inc.* v. *U.S.,* 631 F.2d 1030 (D.C. Cir. 1981).
4. *Western Catholic Church* v. *Commissioner* 73 T.C. 196 (1979) aff'd without published opinion, 631 F.2d 736 (7th Cir. 1980) *cert.* denied _____ U.S. _____ (1981), *The Southern Church Universal Brotherhood Assembled Inc.* v. *Commissioner* 74 T.C. 1223 (1980), *Basic Bible Church* v. *Commissioner* 74 T.C. 846 (1980), *Bubbling Well Church of Universal Love, Inc.* v. *Commissioner* 74 T.C. 531 (1980), *People of God Community* v. *Commissioner* 75 T.C. 127 No. 8 (1980), *Church of the Transfiguring Spirit, Inc.* v. *Commissioner* 76 T.C. 1 (1981), *McGahen* v. *Commissioner* 76 T.C. 468 No. 41 (1981).
5. Treas. Reg. Section 1.501(c)(3)-1(a)(i).
6. Cf. *McGahen* v. *Commissioner, supra,* in which the Court stated on facts similar to *Basic Bible Church* that eligibility will not necessarily be denied where one individual controls the application of the organization's funds *for religious purposes,* but [there can be no] exception to the statutory prohibition against the inurement of the organization's funds *for personal purposes.* Such circumstances, where a single individual controls the use of the organization's funds for his own and his family's support, require close scrutiny to determine if there has been a violation of the private inurement prohibition of Section 170(c)(2) or Section 501(c)(3).

7. *Church of the Transfiguring Spirit, Inc.* v. *Commissioner, supra.*
8. See *Universal Life Church, Inc.* v. *U. S.*, 372 F. Supp. 770, at 775 (E.D. Calif. 1974).
9. 41 T.C. 719 (1964) at 729.
10. 4 B.T.A. 61 (1926).
11. 22 T.C.M. 1435 (1963).
12. 44 AFTR 2d 79-5190 (D.D.C. 1979).
13. One major distinction between the situation in *Beth-El Ministries* and Walden III is that in the former, in order to be a staff (i.e., full) member, all one's possessions and salaries, if any, had to be committed to the community. Beth-El then provided food, clothing, shelter, medical care, recreational facilities and a parochial school for its members. In Walden III there was no similar *quid pro quo.* Another major distinction is that while communitarian living is a fundamental religious belief of Walden III, there is no indication of a similar credo at the foundation of Beth-El Ministries.
14. 356 U.S. 30 (1958).
15. S. Rep. No. 552, 91st Congress, 1st sess. (1969), reprinted in 1969 (Vol. II) U.S. Code Cong. & Ad. News at p. 2311.
16. 330 F. Supp. 1150 (D.D.C. 1971), aff'd *per curiam sub nom. Coit* v. *Green,* 404 U.S. 997 (1971).
17. *Id.* at 1163.
18. *Id.* at 1164.
19. Rev. Rul. 71-447. 1971-2 C.B. 230.
20. See Rev. Proc. 72-54, 1972-2 C.B. 831, superseded by Rev. Proc. 75-50, 1975-2 C.B. 587.
21. 330 F. Supp. at 1169. In *dictum* the Court noted that "such a problem may never arise; and if it ever does arise it will have to be considered in the light of the particular facts and issues presented and in light of the established rule . . . that the law may prohibit an individual from taking certain actions even though his religion commands or prescribes them." *Id.* at 1169.
22. 1975-1 C.B. 158.
23. 436 F. Supp. 1314 (E.D.N.C. 1977).
24. *Id.* at 1319.
25. 639 F.2d 147 (1980).
26. *Bob Jones University* v. *Simon,* 416 U.S. 725 (1974).
27. 468 F. Supp. 890 (D.S.C. 1978.)
28. Apparently, the government took the position that an organization's principal activity governs the category into which it must be placed for purposes of Code Section 501(c)(3). Bob Jones University was both religious and educational in nature but, since the Court determined it to be principally religious, under the government's own theory, it was deemed by the Court to be a religious organization under Code Section 501(c)(3).
29. 468 F. Supp. at 896-7.
30. *Id.* at 898.
31. *Id.* at 905
32. 639 F.2d 147 (1980)
33. *Id.* at 150
34. Brief for the Appellant on Appeals from the Judgment and Orders of the United States District Court for the District of South Carolina in an action entitled *Bob Jones University* v. *United States of America* (Case Nos. 79-1215 and 79-1216) at p. 14.
35. 639 F. 2d 147, at 152.
36. *Id.* at 158, 159.
37. For a discussion of circumstances in which governmental intervention might be justified, see Braiterman, Marvin, and Dean M. Kelley, "When Is Governmental Intervention Legitimate?" at pp. 170 below.
38. As noted earlier, the government, in its brief on appeal in the Bob Jones University case, stated that "churches and similar religious organizations are concededly not subject to the non-discrimination condition on federal charitable tax benefits."

THE IRS CRACKS DOWN ON COALITIONS

1. See and compare Treas. Reg. § 1.501(c)(3)-1(d)(2) (1959); Rev. Rul. 67–71, 1967-1 C.B. 125; Rev. Rul. 75-384, 1975-2 C.B. 204; *Riker* v. *Commissioner*, 244 F.2d 220 (9th Cir. 1957).
2. See Treas. Reg. § 1.501(c)(3)-(1)(ii) (1959).
3. See 78 Cong. Rec. 5959 (1934).
4. See I.R.C. § 162 (a) and (e), adopted Oct. 16, 1962.
5. See I.R.C. § 501(h)(s) wherein churches are excluded as disqualified organizations.
6. *U.S.* v. *Ballard*, 322 U.S. 78 (1944) at 87.
7. See *Universal Life Church, Inc.* v. *U.S.*, 372 U.S. 770 (1974).
8. *Seasongood* v. *Commissioner*, 227 F.2d 907, 1956-1 U.S.T.C. Par. 9135 (6th Cir. 1955).
9. See *Haswell* v. *U.S.*, 500 F.2d 1133, 1974-2 U.S.T.C. Par. 9591 (Ct. Cl. 1974), *cert.* denied, 419 U.S. 1107 (1975).
10. *Slee* v. *Commissioner.* 42 F.2d 184, 2 U.S.T.C. Par. 552 (2d Cir. 1930) at 185.
11. See *Christian Echoes National Ministry* v. *U.S.*, 470 F.2d 849 (10th Cir. 1972), *cert.* denied, 414 U.S. 864 (1973)
12. See Haswell, *loc. cit.*
13. 122 F.2d 108 (3d Cir. 1941).
14. See also Rev. Rul. 66-258, 1966-2 C.B. 213, where a political questionnaire was proper, and charitable status was not jeopardized because it was nonpartisan.
15. *First National Bank of Boston* v. *Bellotti*, 435 U.S. 765 (1978).

CONCORDIA COLLEGE CHALLENGES THE IRS

1. Regulation § 1.6033-2 (g)(5), 42 Fed. Reg. 767 (1977).
2. The legislative history of the phrase "integrated auxiliaries" in Section 6033 is well-described in " 'Church' in the Internal Revenue Code: The Definitional Problems," by Charles M. Whelan, 45 Fordham Law Review 885, March, 1977.
3. S. Rep. No. 91-552, 91st Cong., 1st Sess. 52 (1969).
4. See "Government and the Mission of the Churches: The Problem of 'Integrated Auxiliaries' " by John W. Baker, September, 1977 Staff Report, Baptist Joint Committee on Public Affairs, to appreciate the apparent significance of Regulation Section 1.6033-2, as finally adopted, as compared with the Proposed Regulation promulgated on February 11, 1976.
5. "Taxation and the Free Exercise of Religion," Papers and Proceedings of the Sixteenth Religious Liberty Conference, October 1977.
6. See Sharon L. Worthing on page 114 for a technical advice memorandum in which the IRS spells out the "secular counterpart" rationale.
7. It is instructive that the phrase "convention or association of churches" is never used in the Code without being part of the larger phrase, "church or convention or association of churches." That Treasury regards the phrase "convention or association of churches" as being inseparably linked with the word "church" in the larger phrase is evidenced by its treatment of the term "integrated auxiliary" as also applying to conventions or associations of churches (see Reg. Section 1.6033-2(g)(5) (iii).
8. Hearings before the Senate Finance Committee on HR 8300, 83rd Cong., 2nd Session 1028 (1954).
9. S. Rep. No. 1622, 83rd Cong., 2nd Sess. 30 (1954), emphasis added.
10. Hearing before the Senate Finance Committee on H.R. 8920, 81st Cong., 2d Sess., 216; language in brackets supplied.
11. Section 421(a)(1)(A) of the Internal Revenue Code of 1939; this language was recodified without change as Section 511(a)(2)(A) of the Internal Revenue Code of 1954; the exemption in that Section has since been revoked, except to the extent set forth in Section 512(b)(14).
12. *WHYY, Inc.* v. *Borough of Glassboro*, 393 U.S. 117 (1968).
13. For one such approach, see " 'Church' in the Internal Revenue Code: The Definitional Problems," Charles M. Whelan, 45 Fordham Law Review 885, March 1977.
14. *Everson* v. *Board of Education*, 330 U.S. 1 (1947), reiterated in *McCollum* v. *Board of*

Education, 333 U.S. 203 (1948), *McGowan* v. *Maryland,* 366 U.S. 420 (1961), and *Torcaso* v. *Watkins,* 367 U.S. 488 (1961), by a unanimous court.
15. *Walz* v. *Tax Commission,* 397 U.S. 664 (1970), *Lemon* v. *Kurtzman,* 403 U.S. 602 (1971), and its progeny.
16. *St. Martin Evangelical Lutheran Church, et al.* v. *State of South Dakota,* U.S. Supreme Court No. 80–120, October Term, 1980. The Supreme Court has since ruled in favor of the church, holding that schools not separately incorporated are entitled to the exemption given the church.

A BAPTIST SEMINARY RESISTS THE EQUAL EMPLOYMENT OPPORTUNITY COMMISSION

1. Civil Action No. 4-77-141. The Commission's authorization for this was based on 28 U.S.C. Section 1345, Section 706(f)(3) of Title VII of the Civil Rights Act of 1964, as amended by the Equal Employment Opportunity Act of 1972, 42 U.S.C. Section 200e-5(f)(3) and Section 709(c) of Title VII, 42 U.S.C. Section 2000e-8 (c) (1970 Ed. Supp. V).
2. *EEOC* v. *Southwestern Baptist Theological Seminary,* "Plaintiff's Pre-Trial Brief," Civil Action No. 4-77-141, p. 3. U.S. District Court for the Northern District, Texas, Fort Worth Division. Cases cited in this regard included: *Polish National Alliance of the United States* v. *NLRB,* 322 U.S. 643, 64 S.Ct. 1196, 88 L.Ed. 1509 (1944), [1 EPD Section 9605]; *Mitchell* v. *Pilgrim Holiness Church Corp.,* 210 F.2d 879, (C.A. 7, 1954) *cert.* denied, 347 U.S. 1013, 74 S.Ct. 867, 98 L.Ed. 1136 (1954); and *McClure* v. *Salvation Army,* 460 F.2d 553 (5th Cir. 1972).
3. *EEOC* v. *SWBTS,* p. 4.
4. The following cases are cited: *Whitney* v. *Greater New York Corporation of Seventh-Day Adventists,* 401 F.Supp. 1363 (S.D.N.Y. 1975); *NOW* v. *Santa Clara College,* ____F.Supp.____, 16 FEP Cases 1158–59; and *EEOC* v. *Pacific Press Publicity Association,* 535 F.2d 1182.
5. *EEOC* v. *SWBTS,* "Plaintiff's Pre-Trial Brief," p. 6.
6. Section 709(c) of Title VII, 42 U.S.C. Paragraph 2000e-8(c); cited in *EEOC* v. *SWBTS,* p. 1.
7. *Ibid.,* p. 254; see also Jim W. Jones, "Seminary Awaiting Ruling," *Fort Worth Star Telegram,* 28 March 1979.
8. *EEOC* v. *SWBTS,* "Trial Transcript," p. 253.
9. *Ibid.,* p. 6; see also *EEOC* v. *SWBTS,* Pre-Trial Order, par. 6, Stipulated Facts, sub-part 2; "Admission of Fact No. 1."
10. *EEOC* v. *SWBTS,* "Plaintiff's Post-Trial Brief," p. 2.
11. *Lemon* v. *Kurtzman,* 403 U.S. 602 (1971). The first two were enunciated earlier in *Board of Education* v. *Allen,* 329 U.S. 263, 20 L.Ed.2d 1060, 1065, 88 S.Ct. 1923 (1968).
12. *EEOC* v. *SWBTS,* "Plaintiff's Post-Trial Brief," pp. 6–7.
13. *McClure* v. *Salvation Army,* 460 F.2d 553 (5th Cir., 1972), *Whitney* v. *Greater New York Corporation of Seventh-Day Adventists,* 401 F.Supp. 1363 (S.D.N.Y., 1975); *NOW* v. *Santa Clara College,* ____F.Supp.____, 16 FEP Cases 1158–59 (1975); and *Marshall* v. *Pacific Union Conference of Seventh-Day Adventists,* ____F.Supp.____, 14 EPD Section 7806 (C.D., Calif., 1977); for stay denied, 454 U.S. 1305, 54 L.Ed.2d 17, 98 S.Ct. 2 (1977).
14. *McClure* v. *Salvation Army,* at 558. The Court further declared, "Both the language and the legislative history" support the contention that "the exemption permits a religious organization to discriminate only on the basis of religion;" *ibid.*
15. *EEOC* v. *SWBTS,* "Plaintiff's Post-Trial Brief," p. 9.
16. 440 U.S. 490, 59 L.Ed.2d 533, 99 S.Ct. 1313 (1979).
17. *EEOC* v. *SWBTS,* "Plaintiff's Post-Trial Brief," pp. 12–13.
18. 396 F.Supp. 597, 601 (D.S.C., 1975); cited in *EEOC* v. *SWBTS,* "Plaintiff's Post-Trial Brief," p. 13.
19. 42 U.S.C. Section 2000 d.

20. *EEOC* v. *SWBTS*, "Plaintiff's Post-Trial Brief," p. 13. The Commission entered the Compliance Survey of June 1, 1977 (Plaintiff's Exhibit S) conducted by the Veterans Administration which concluded with the following statement: "The Title VII activities of the Southwestern Baptist Theological Seminary are under the jurisdiction of the Department of Health, Education, and Welfare. It is the school's stated policy that enrollment is open to all persons without regard to race, creed, color, or national origin. During the course of this survey no evidence of non-compliance with Title VII was noted." *EEOC* v. *SWBTS*, "Plaintiff's Response to Defendant's Post-Trial Brief," p. 1.

21. See *EEOC* v. *SWBTS*, "Brief of Defendant," pp. 4–22.

22. 426 U.S. 736, at 755–59; 49 L.Ed.2d 179, at 193–95; 96 S.Ct. 2337 (1976), cited in *EEOC* v. *SWBTS*, "Brief of Defendant," p. 22.

23. 397 U.S. 664, 668–80, 25 L.Ed.2d 697 (1970).

24. *EEOC* v. *SWBTS*, "Brief of Defendant," p. 24.

25. *Legislative History of the Equal Employment Opportunity Act*, p. 1227; cited in *ibid.*, p. 25.

26. *Ibid.*, p. 1228.

27. *Ibid.*, p. 1255.

28. *NLRB* v. *Catholic Bishop of Chicago*, 440 U.S. 490, 59 L.Ed.2d 533, 99 S.Ct. 1313 (1979); cited in *ibid.*, p. 27.

29. *EEOC* v. *SWBTS*, "Defendant's Brief," p. 37.

30. 426 U.S. 606, 49 L.Ed.2d 151, 96 S.Ct. 2372, rehearing denied, 429 U.S. 873, 50 L.Ed.2d 191, 97 S.Ct. 191 (1976).

31. 409 U.S. 896 (1972).

31b.*EEOC* v. *SWBTS*, "Defendant's Brief," p. 42. It was noted as early as *Watson* v. *Jones* (1872) that, "The Supreme Court began to place matters of church government and administration beyond the purview of civil authorities"; cited in *ibid.*, p. 39.

32. *EEOC* v. *SWBTS*, Civil Action, No. CA4-77-141-E, January 18, 1980.

33. *Ibid.*, "Memorandum and Court Order," p. 5.

34. *Ibid.* See *McClure* v. *Salvation Army*, 460 F.2d 553 (5th Cr., 1972); *EEOC* v. *Mississippi College*, 451 F.Supp. 564 (S.D. Miss., 1978) appeal docketed, No. 78-3123 (5th Cir., September 27, 1978).

35. *EEOC* v. *SWBTS*, "Appellate Brief for the Equal Employment Opportunity Commission," Cause No. 80-1370, U.S. Court of Appeals for the Fifth Circuit.

36. *Alabama State Federation of Labor* v. *McAdory*, 325 U.S. 450, 461 (1945); *Associated Press* v. *NLRB*, 301 U.S. 103, 132 (1937); *Broadrick* v. *Oklahoma*, 413 U.S. 601 (1973); *United States* v. *Raines;* 362 U.S. 17, 21 (1960); all cited in *EEOC* v. *SWBTS*, "Appellate Brief for the EEOC," p. 15.

37. *EEOC* v. *SWBTS*, "Brief of Appellee," pp. 2–3.

38. *Kedroff* v. *St. Nicholas Cathedral*, 344 U.S. 94, 73 S.Ct. at 150 (1952); *Kedroff* was followed by *Serbian Orthodox Diocese* v. *Milivojevich;* cited in *EEOC* v. *SWBTS*, "Brief of Appellee," pp. 32–33.

39. 651 F.2d 277 (5th Cir., 1981).

40. 659 F.2d 1075 (5th Cir., 1981).

41. Petition for *certiorari* was filed in U.S. Supreme Court, December 15, 1981.

THE POTENTIAL IN RECENT STATUTES FOR GOVERNMENT SURVEILLANCE OF RELIGIOUS ORGANIZATIONS

1. New York Times, Dec. 13, 1976, at 23, col. 1.

2. Jackson, *Socialized Religion: California's Public Trust Theory,* Philanthropy Monthly, Oct. 1980, at 17.

3. Senate Comm. on Finance, 91st Cong., 1st Sess., Tax Reform Act of 1969, Compilation of Decisions Reached in Executive Sess. 53 (Comm. Print 1969).

4. See Worthing, *"Religion" and "Religious Institutions" Under the First Amendment,* 7 Pepperdine L. Rev. 313 (1980).

5. For an expanded treatment of the role of the Internal Revenue Service in overseeing tax-exempt organizations and churches, see Note, *The Internal Revenue Service as a Monitor of Church Institutions: The Excessive Entanglement Problem*, 45 Fordham L. Rev. 929 (1977).

6. Treas. Reg. Section 1.6033-2(g) (1971). This controversy is discussed in Whelan, *"Church" in the Internal Revenue Code: The Definitional Problems*, 45 Fordham L. Rev. 885 (1977).

7. Internal Revenue Serv., National Office Technical Advice Memorandum No. 8048010; Internal Revenue Serv., National Office Technical Advice Memorandum No. 8046004.

8. 4 Internal Revenue Manual (CCH), Exempt Organization Master File Handbook Section 220 (2)(a) (1982).

9. 4 Internal Revenue Manual (CCH), Exempt Organization/Business Master File Handbook Exh. 15 (1982).

10. *Id.* Section 440(5).

11. I.R.C. Section 6033(a).

12. This chart appears in Internal Revenue Service Instructions for Form 1023, Application for Recognition of Exemption under Section 501(c)(3) of the Internal Revenue Code 8 (1981).

13. This chart appears in 4 Internal Revenue Manual (CCH), Exempt Organization Master File Handbook Exh. 25 (1982).

14. *Id.* § 622(16)(a).

15. Rawls, *F.B.I. Admits Planting a Rumor To Discredit Jean Seberg in 1970*, N.Y. Times, Sept. 15, 1979, at 1. col. 2, 6, col. 3.

16. 4 Internal Revenue Manual (CCH), Exempt Organization Master File Handbook § 220(4) (1982) (emphasis added).

17. *Id.* § 220(3).

18. *See* I.R.C. Section 410(d).

19. 29 U.S.C. Section 1002(33)(C) (1976), amended by 29 U.S.C.A. Section 1002(33)(C) (West Supp. 1981).

20. Treas. Reg. Section 1.414(e)-1(d)(2) (1980).

21. *Id.*

22. 29 U.S.C.A. Section 1002(33)(C)(ii) (West Supp. 1981).

23. Weicker, *Attacks on Privacy*, N.Y. Times, July 21, 1980, at A17, col. 2.

24. Linowes, *Must Personal Privacy Die in the Computer Age?* 65 A.B.A.J. 1180, 1184 (1979).

25. Gardner, Letter, *Don't Mess with Our Country's Charities*, N.Y. Times, Nov. 8, 1979, at A22, col. 4.

26. *Id.*

27. Hunter, *House Ethics Panel Finds Wilson Erred*, N.Y. Times, Apr. 17, 1980, at A20, col. 1.

28. *Rep. Charles H. Wilson Censured by House for Violation of Its Rules*, N.Y. Times, June 11, 1980, at A16, col. 1.

29. Hunter, *Censure Proposed for Coast Democrat*, N.Y. Times, Apr. 25, 1980, at A17, col. 1.

30. 424 U.S. 1, 66 (1976), quoted in *Surinach v. Pesquera de Busquets*, 604 F. 2d 73, 78 (1st Cir. 1979).

CURRENT ISSUES IN GOVERNMENT REGULATION OF RELIGIOUS SOLICITATION

1. As used herein, "religious solicitation" refers to requests for donations of funds for the support of a church or church-supported charitable or educational projects, propagation of religious doctrine, distribution of religious literature, or similar activities relating to the general public. The collection of money at religious services from members or at least worshippers is a practice that is probably as old as the settlement of the country and one which has enjoyed virtual immunity from regulation. See *Murdock* v. *Pennsylvania*, 319 U.S. 105, 111 (1943) ("passing of the collection plate in church" viewed as a paradigm of the free exercise of religion). The recent departure from this norm by the California Attorney General, see *Younger* v. *Faith Center, Inc.*, 2 Civil No. 56574 (Cal. App. Aug. 20, 1980) (unpublished); Worthing, *The State Takes Over A Church*, Annals Amer. Acad. Polit. & Soc. Sci., Nov. 1979, at 136 (Worldwide Church of God), recently remedied by the legislature, 1980 Cal. Legis. Serv. 5082, ch. 1324 (West) (amending Cal. Corp. Code Sections 9142 and 9690, and repealing *id.* Section 9230), can

only be viewed as an aberration. This discussion therefore will be confined to the legal status of religious solicitations from non-members.

2. The phrase was coined by Professor Thomas I. Emerson of Yale Law School. T. Emerson, *The System of Freedom of Expression* (1970).

3. The "central meaning of the First Amendment . . . , that debate on public issues should be uninhibited, robust, and wide open," *New York Times Co.* v. *Sullivan*, 376 U.S. 254, 273, 270 (1964), developed entirely apart from the religious expression environment. For a summary of the history of this concern of freedom of expression together with some probing comments, see G. Gunther, *Cases and Materials on Constitutional Law* (10th ed. 1980).

4. Kalven, *The Concept of the Public Forum: Cox* v. *Louisiana,* 1965 Sup. Ct. Rev. 1 (footnotes omitted).

5. See, *e.g.*, *Schneider* v. *New Jersey*, 308 U.S. 147 (1939) (appeal by Jehovah's Witness pamphleteer decided together with three other cases involving a labor dispute, a protest of the administration of government, and a meeting to discuss international events).

6. *Village of Schaumburg* v. *Citizens for a Better Environment*, 444 U.S. 620 (1980).

7. *Cantwell* v. *Connecticut*, 310 U.S. 296, 306 (1940). Accord, *e.g.*, *Hynes* v. *Mayor of Oradell*, 425 U.S. 610, 618–19 (1976).

8. But see *Hynes* v. *Mayor of Oradell*, 425 U.S. 610, 622 (1976) (identification requirement held impermissibly vague).

9. *E.g.*, *Staub* v. *City of Baxley*, 355 U.S. 313, 321 (1958); *Cantwell* v. *Connecticut*, 310 U.S. 296, 307 (1940); *Schneider* v. *New Jersey*, 308 U.S. 147, 164 (1939); *Lovell* v. *City of Griffin*, 303 U.S. 444, (1938).

10. *Sylte* v. *Metropolitan Gov't*, 493 F. Supp. 313, 319 (M.D. Tenn. 1980); *Cherris* v. *Amundson*, 460 F. Supp. 326, 328 (E.D. La. 1978); *Hillman* v. *Britton*, 111 Cal. App. 3d 810, 825, 168 Cal. Rptr. 852, 862 (1980).

11. *Village of Schaumburg* v. *Citizens for a Better Environment*, 444 U.S. 620 (1980).

12. See *Fernandes* v. *Limmer*, 663 F.2d 619 (5th Cir. 1981).

13. 415 F.2d 41 (5th Cir. 1969), *cert. denied*, 396 U.S. 1040 (1970).

14. The Fifth Circuit in *National Foundation* had noted that "[n]o consitutional right exists to make a public solicitation of funds for charity." *Id.* at 45. *Schaumburg*, however, proclaimed it to be "clear" that "charitable solicitations . . . are within the protections of the First Amendment." *Village of Schaumburg* v. *Citizens for a Better Environment*, 444 U.S. 620, 633 (1980). That this discrepancy went unmentioned in *Schaumburg* may be explained if the quoted sentence in *National Foundation* is considered to be dictum, that is, a statement of law unnecessary to the court's precise holding. Such a view of the Fifth Circuit opinion may well be defensible.

15. *Village of Schaumburg* v. *Citizens for a Better Environment*, 444 U.S. 620, 643 n.1 (Rehnquist, J., dissenting).

16. *National Black United Fund, Inc.* v. *Campbell*, 494 F.Supp. 748, 759-60 (D.D.C. 1980) (Parker, J.).

17. *Hillman* v. *Britton*, 111 Cal.App.3d 810, 825, 168 Cal. Rptr. 852, 862 (1980).

18. See generally Stevenson, *Key Legal Aspects of Schaumburg*, Philanthropy Monthly, May 1980, at 7, 8–9.

19. See, *e.g.*, *Follett* v. *Town of McCormick*, 321 U.S. 573 (1944); *Murdock* v. *Pennsylvania*, 319 U.S. 105 (1943).

20. *Walz* v. *Tax Comm'n*, 397 U.S. 664, 672 (1970). See *NLRB* v. *Catholic Bishop*, 440 U.S. 490 (1979).

21. See *Murdock* v. *Pennsylvania*, 319 U.S. 105 (1943).

22. See, *e.g.*, *Surinach* v. *Pesquera de Busquets*, 604 F.2d 73, 78 (1st Cir. 1979).

23. In *Fernandes* v. *Limmer*, 663 F.2d 619 (5th Cir. 1981), the court invalidated a percentage limitation provision of the Dallas-Fort Worth Airport solicitation ordinance similar to that in *National Foundation*, even while recognizing that after *Schaumburg*, "[t]he rebuttable nature of the presumption undoubtedly narrows the sweep of the ban. . . ." Grounding its decision in the "free exercise rights of religious minorities," but also somewhat cryptically referring as well to "religious and charitable organizations . . . whose unorthodox messages will inevitably yield less cost-effective solicitation results," the court ruled that the authorities may not "premise the simultaneous

admission of, for example, evangelical Baptists and the exclusion of Krishna devotees on the results of their fund solicitation efforts. . . ."

24. *Perlman* v. *Municipal Court (People)*, 99 Cal. App. 3d 568, 579, 160 Cal. Rptr. 567, 573 (1979).

25. *Hillman* v. *Britton*, 111 Cal. App. 3d 810, 825, 168 Cal. Rptr. 852, 862 (1980).

26. See *Perlman* v. *Municipal Court (People)*, 99 Cal. App. 3d 568, 579, 160 Cal. Rptr. 567, 573 (1979), But see *Hillman* v. *Britton*, 111 Cal. App. 3d 810, 825, 168 Cal. Rptr. 852, 862 (1980).

27. See *Fernandes* v. *Limmer*, 465 F. Supp. 493, 504–05 (N.D. Tex. 1979), aff'd, 663 F.2d 619 (5th Cir. 1981).

28. *Village of Schaumburg* v. *Citizens for a Better Environment*, 444 U.S. 620, 637-38 (1980) (footnote omitted).

29. Ill. Rev. Stat. ch. 23, Section 5102 (a) (Smith-Hurd 1968).

30. *Village of Schaumburg* v. *Citizens for a Better Environment*, 444 U.S. 620, 638 n.12 (1980).

31. See, *e.g.*, Maine Charitable Solicitations Act, Me. Rev. Stat. tit. 9, ch. 385 (1980 & Supp. 1981-1982) (effective Jan. 1, 1978); Minn. Stat. Ann. Sections 309.50-.61 (1980).
    The Minnesota statute contained its own twist which led to an additional constitutional contretemps. A 1978 amendment, 1978 Minn. Laws ch. 601, Section 5, included churches within the scope of the charitable solicitations act, but at the same time continued to exclude certain churches, those which received more than half their contributions from their members or parent organization. A federal appellate court has recently held this inherent interchurch discrimination to violate the establishment clause of the first amendment. *Valente* v. *Larson*, 637 F.2d 562 (8th Cir.). prob. juris. noted, 101 S. Ct. 3028 (1981). In so doing, the federal court followed the result reached by the North Carolina Supreme Court with respect to a similar statute of its own state. *Heritage Village Church and Missionary Fellowship, Inc.* v. *State*, 299 N.Ç. 399, 263 S.E.2d 726 (1980).

32. See, *e.g.*, *Surinach* v. *Pesquera de Busquets*, 604 F.2d 73, 78 (1st Cir. 1979); *Sylte* v. *Metropolitan Gov't*, 493 F. Supp. 313, 319 (M.D. Tenn. 1980); *International Soc'y for Krishna Consciousness* v. *City of Houston*, 482 F. Supp. 852, 863 (S.D. Tex. 1979), appeal docketed, No. 79-3879 (5th Cir. Nov. 30, 1979); *Fernandes* v. *Limmer*, 663 F.2d 619 (5th Cir. 1981).

33. *Lemon* v. *Kurtzman*, 403 U.S. 602, 612-13 (1971).

34. Kalven, *The Concept of the Public Forum*: Cox v. Louisiana, 1965 Sup.Ct.Rev. 1, 25.

35. *Cox* v. *New Hampshire*, 312 U.S. 569 (1941).

36. Kalven, *supra* note 4, at 26.

37. *Niemotko* v. *Maryland*, 340 U.S. 268, 282 (1951) (Frankfurter, J., concurring).

38. For an effort to do so a decade later, see *id.* at 282–83.

39. L. Tribe, *American Constitutional Law* 683 (1978).

40. *Schneider* v. *New Jersey*, 308 U.S. 146, 162 (1939).

41. *Martin* v. *City of Struthers*, 319 U.S. 141, 147 (1943).

42. Ely, *Flag Desecration: A Case Study in the Roles of Categorization and Balancing in the First Amendment*, 88 Harv. L. Rev. 1482, 1484-87 (1975).

43. *Village of Schaumburg* v. *Citizens for a Better Environment*, 444 U.S. 620, 637 (1980); *Cantwell* v. *Connecticut*, 310 U.S. 296, 306 (1940); *Schneider* v. *New Jersey*, 308 U.S. 147, 164 (1939).

44. *Martin* v. *City of Struthers*, 319 U.S. 141, 147-48 (1943). The continuing vitality of *Martin* was twice demonstrated last year. See *Troyer* v. *Town of Southampton*, 101 S.Ct. 522, aff'g *Troyer* v. *Town of Babylon*, 483 F.Supp. 1135 (E.D.N.Y. 1980); *Village of Schaumburg* v. *Citizens for a Better Environment*, 444 U.S. 620, 639 (1980).

45. The Court has declared that marginal cost in efficiency is irrelevant in a closely related context, regulation of expression by means of discretionary licensing systems in order to protect the same state interests such as privacy or order. "Frauds may be denounced as offenses and punished by law. Trespasses may similarly be forbidden. If it is said that these means are less efficient and convenient than . . . [deciding in advance] what information may be disseminated from house to house, and who may impart the information, the answer is that considerations of this sort do not empower a municipality to abridge freedom of speech and press." *Village of Schaumburg* v. *Citizens for a Better*

Environment, 444 U.S. 620, 639 (1980) (quoting *Schneider* v. *New Jersey,* 308 U.S. 147, 164, (1939)).

46. *Schneider* v. *New Jersey,* 308 U.S. 147, 163 (1939). Accord, *e. g. , Carey* v. *Brown,* 447 U.S. 455, 468 n. 13 (1980).

47. *Consolidated Edison Co.* v. *Public Serv. Comm'n,* 100 S.Ct. 2236, 2335 n.10 (1980).

48. L. Tribe, *supra* note 39. Accord, Kalven, *supra* note 4, at 30.

49. See *Talley* v. *California,* 362 U.S. 60 (1960) (anonymous handbills); *Kovacs* v. *Cooper,* 336 U.S. 77, 102 (Black, J., dissenting) (loudspeakers); *Martin* v. *City of Struthers,* 319 U.S. 141 (1943) (door-to-door canvassing); *Schneider* v. *New Jersey,* 308 U.S. 147 (1939) (handbills).

50. 408 U.S. 104 (1972).

51. *Id.* at 117–18 (footnotes omitted).

52. Kalven, *supra* note 4, at 28.

53. The example is taken from Stone, *Fora Americana: Speech in Public Places,* 1974 Sup. Ct. Rev. 233, 269.

54. See, *e. g. , Lehman* v. *City of Shaker Heights,* 418 U.S. 298, 304 (1974) (plurality opinion) (speculation that political advertising on municipal bus system could lead to greater loss of revenue from commercial advertisers).

55. The lower courts seem to assume that the burden rests upon the government, see, *e. g. ,* *Wright* v. *Chief of Transit Police,* 558 F.2d 67, 68 n.1 (2d Cir. 1977), and that a failure of proof justifies a decision for the challenger. Compare *Verrilli* v. *City of Concord,* 548 F.2d 262, 268 (9th Cir. 1977) with *Baldwin* v. *Redwood City,* 540 F.2d 1360, 1369 (9th Cir. 1976), *cert.* denied, 431 U.S. 913 (1977) (different rulings on similar ordinances in similar cities in same area because of evidence of governmental interests presented).

56. *Westfall* v. *Board of Comm'rs,* 477 F.Supp. 862, 871–72 (N.D. Ga. 1979).

57. *Citizens for a Better Environment* v. *Village of Olympia Fields,* 511 F. Supp. 104 (N.D. Ill. 1980); *Connecticut Citizens Action Group* v. *Town of Southington,* 508 F. Supp. 43 (D. Conn. 1980).

58. The International Society for Krishna Consciousness [ISKCON] has been in recent years a frequent litigator of first amendment issues and has generated more than forty published opinions since its first appearance in the reporters in a case involving a rather easy place restriction, a total exclusion from the Vieux Carré area of New Orleans. *International Soc'y for Krishna Consciousness* v. *City of New Orleans,* 347 F.Supp. 945 (E.D. La. 1972).

59. 101 S. Ct. 2559 (1981), rev'g 299 N.W.2d 79 (Minn. 1980).

60. See, *e. g. , International Soc'y for Krishna Consciousness* v. *Bowen,* 600 F.2d 667, 670 (7th Cir.), *cert.* denied, 444 U.S. 963 (1979).

61. All of the appellate courts which had previously considered the question had so held. *International Soc'y for Krishna Consciousness* v. *Barber,* 650 F.2d 430 (2d Cir. 1981); *Edwards* v. *Maryland State Fair & Agricultural Soc'y,* 628 F.2d 282 (4th Cir. 1980); *International Soc'y for Krishna Consciousness* v. *Bowen,* 600 F.2d 667 (7th Cir.), *cert.* denied, 444 U.S. 963 (1980); *International Soc'y for Krishna Consciousness* v. *Colorado State Fair & Indus. Exposition Comm'n,* 610 P.2d 486 (Colo. 1980), as had the Minnesota Supreme Court, *International Soc'y for Krishna Consciousness* v. *Heffron,* 299 N.W.2d 79 (Minn. 1980).

62. Restrictions based upon the subject matter of expression, *Consolidated Edison Co.* v. *Public Serv. Comm'n,* 447 U.S. 530 (1980), or upon its content, *Carey* v. *Brown,* 447 U.S. 455 (1980); *Police Dep't* v. *Mosley,* 408 U.S. 92 (1972), contravene the substantive aspect of the first amendment in the absence of a compelling state interest.

63. *Heffron* v. *International Soc'y for Krishna Consciousness,* 101 S.Ct. 2559, 2564-65 (1981).

64. *E. g. , Schneider* v. *New Jersey,* 308 U.S. 147, 160 (1939).

65. *Heffron* v. *International Soc'y for Krishna Consciousness,* 101 S. Ct. 2559, 2565 (1981). The Fair Manager's affidavit was not specifically mentioned, but the statistics were drawn from it.

66. *Id.* at 2571.

67. *Id.* at 2569-71.

68. *Id.* at 2593 (Blackmun, J., concurring in part and dissenting in part).

69. An effective oral advocate, especially one for an unpopular cause, can often draw a

crowd, while a literature distributor may well be cavalierly disregarded. Compare, *e.g.*, *Feiner* v. *New York*, 340 U.S. 315 (1951) (pushing, shoving, milling, crowd of 75 or 80 people attracted by street corner orator), with *Wolin* v. *Port of N.Y. Auth.*, 392 F.2d 83, 86 (2d Cir.), *cert.* denied, 393 U.S. 940 (1968) (peaceful leafletter did not cause any interference with traffic).

70. The many other public buildings and places that have been forced to accept the presence of literature distributors or solicitors in recent years do not seem to have been overwhelmed or inundated by large numbers of people seeking to exercise first amendment rights.

71. *Heffron* v. *International Soc'y for Krishna Consciousness*, 101 S. Ct. 2559, 2567 (1981).

72. For examples of employment of this device, see *International Soc'y for Krishna Consciousness* v. *Griffin*, 437 F.Supp. 666, 671 (1977) (Pittsburgh airports); Spokane County & City of Spokane, Wash., Joint Resolution and Ordinance para. 22 (1978).

73. *Heffron* v. *International Soc'y for Krishna Consciousness*, 101 S.Ct. 2559, 2567 (1981).

74. See L. Tribe, *American Constitutional Law* Section 12–21, at 691-92 (1978). Obviously, in a case in which this dictum is to be applied, some nice judgments as to the relevant audience, the definition of the forum, and the degree to which the primary purpose of the forum must be sacrificed to accommodate free speech must be made. The Court has provided no guidance whatsoever for the solution of these problems. In *Grace* v. *Burger*, No. 80-2044 (D.C. Cir. Sept. 8, 1981), the District of Columbia Circuit struck down a flat ban on First-Amendment activity on the grounds of the United States Supreme Court building. Since, unlike the Minnesota State Fair's booth rule, "[t]he statute at issue in this case does not merely limit the area of the Supreme Court grounds available for expressive activity," but rather prohibited it entirely, *Heffron* was explicitly distinguished. *Id.*, slip op. at 24 n.20.

75. *Heffron* v. *International Soc'y for Krishna Consciousness*, 101 S. Ct. 2559, 2567 (1981).

76. Some public entities appear to be willing to try, however. See, *e.g.*, Kansas State Fair Policies and Procedures, para. 1 (n.d.), invalidated in *Winslow* v. *Kansas Bd. of State Fair Managers*, No. 78-1374 (D. Kan. Sept. 4, 1981).

77. See note 62, *supra.*

78. *Heffron* v. *International Soc'y for Krishna Consciousness*, 100 S. Ct. 2559, 2567 (1981).

79. But see *Lamont* v. *Postmaster General of the United States*, 381 U.S. 391, 307 (1965) (imposition of affirmative obligation on listener to request access to information violates first amendment). In the fair context, the potential listener must affirmatively seek out the message since he must approach the booth in which the speaker is confined.

80. The development of the concept of the non-traditional public forum is recounted is Stone, *supra* note 53.

81. *Heffron* v. *International Soc'y for Krishna Consciousness*, 101 S.Ct. 2559, 2565 (1981) (quoting *Hague* v. *CIO*, 307 U.S. 496, 515 (1939)).

82. *Id.* at 2567.

83. See W. Neely, *The Agricultural Fair* 249 (1935) (Columbia University Studies in the History of American Agriculture No. 2).

84. See *Niemotko* v. *Maryland*, 240 U.S. 268, 282 (1951) (Frankfurter, J., concurring).

85. *International Soc'y for Krishna Consciousness* v. *Rochford*, 585 F.2d 263, 272 (7th Cir. 1978); *Chicago Area Military Project* v. *City of Chicago*, 508 F.2d 921, 925 (7th Cir.), *cert.* denied, 421 U.S. 992 (1975); *Kuszynski* v. *City of Oakland*, 479 F.2d 1130, 1131 (9th Cir. 1973); *Wolin* v. *Port of New York Auth.*, 392 F.2d 83, 89 (2d Cir.), *cert.* denied, 393 U.S. 940 (1968); *International Soc'y for Krishna Consciousness* v. *Wolke*, 453 F. Supp. 869, 872 (E.D. Wis. 1978); *International Soc'y for Krishna Consciousness* v. *Collins*, 452 F. Supp. 1007 (S.D. Tex. 1977); *International Soc'y for Krishna Consciousness* v. *Griffin*, 437 F. Supp. 666, 671 (W.D. Pa. 1977); *Moskowitz* v. *Cullman*, 432 F.Supp. 1263, 1266 (D.N.J. 1977); *International Soc'y for Krishna Consciousness* v. *Engelhardt*, 425 F. Supp. 176, 180 (W.D. Mo. 1977); *In re Hoffman*, 67 Cal. 2d 845, 849-50, 434 P.2d 353, 355-56, 64 Cal. Rptr. 97, 99-100 (1967) see *International Soc'y for Krishna Consciousness* v. *Eaves*, 601 F.2d 809 (5th Cir. 1979); *International Soc'y for Krishna Consciousness* v. *Lentini*, 461 F. Supp. 49 (E.D. La. 1978); *International Soc'y for Krishna Consciousness* v. *New York Port Auth.*, 425 F. Supp. 681 (S.D.N.Y. 1977).

86. *Grayned* v. *City of Rockford*, 408 U.S. 104, 115 (1972).

87. What else besides a fair is a limited public forum is open to speculation. Presumably,

the concept applies to those activities of the government that are themselves aimed at promoting the exchange of ideas. Under this analysis a school or a library would be a paradigm limited public forum. But *cf. Tinker* v. *Des Moines Independent Community School Dist.*, 393 U.S. 503 (1969); *Brown* v. *Louisiana*, 383 U.S. 131 (1966) (plurality opinion) (school and library, respectively, analyzed under conventional public forum standards).

88. In the first reported appellate decision after *Heffron* involving a non-traditional forum, the Fifth Circuit declared unconstitutional an ordinance of the Dallas-Fort Worth Airport that forbade literature distribution and solicitation inside the airport buildings, but allowed these activities to occur on the sidewalks abutting the terminals, subject to a permit requirement. *Fernandes* v. *Limmer*, 663 F.2d 619 (5th Cir. 1981). The court held that the terminal buildings did not constitute a "limited public forum" in the same ways as did the state fair in *Heffron:* "The airport . . . is a permanent, on-going concern, and its directors are not subject to the same pressures as is the [fair] in formulating short-lived, expedient regulations to ensure order." Equally important, the court placed significance in the fact that the airport had "not shown which, if any, areas are so congested" as was the fair in *Heffron.* The ordinance was thus "overbroad to the extent that it covers areas in which the [airport's] interest in pedestrian traffic control has not been shown to be substantial." If the *Fernandes* analysis is followed, it would seem that restrictions on expressive activity in fora with characteristics less unusual than those of a state fair will continue to be carefully scrutinized by the courts.

89. *E.g.*, *Wolin* v. *Port of N.Y. Authority*, 392 F.2d 83, 89 (2d Cir.), *cert.* denied, 393 U.S. 940 (1968).

90. 101 S. Ct. 3028 (1981) (order noting probable jurisdiction).

91. Minn. Stat. Sections 309.50-.61 (1980).

92. See *id.* Section 309.515(1)(a) (exempting charitable organizations which receive a total of less than $10,000 per year from the public).

93. *Id.* Section 309.515(1)(b).

94. *Valente* v. *Larson*, Civil No. 4-78-453 (D. Minn. Jan. 19, 1980).

95. *Id.*, 637 F.2d 562 (8th Cir. 1981).

96. *Id.* at 565 (quoting *Everson* v. *Board of Educ.*, 330 U.S. 1, 15 (1947); *Zorach* v. *Clausen*, 343 U.S. 306, 314 (1951)).

97. *Id.* at 566.

98. *Id.* The Court went on to hold the exemption provision invalid as well under the "three-prong" test elucidated by *Lemon* v. *Kurtzman*, 403 U.S. 602 (1971), and its progeny. In *Lemon* the Court held that a statute violates the establishment clause unless it meets each of three criteria, that it "have a secular legislative purpose," that its "principal or primary effect . . . be one that neither advances nor inhibits religion," and that it "not foster 'an excessive governmental entanglement with religion.'" *Id.* at 612-13. The Eighth Circuit in *Larson* found that the Minnesota statute failed to comply with the first and second requirement of *Lemon;* the court did not discuss the application of the third. *Valente* v. *Larson*, 637 F.2d 562, 566-69 (8th Cir. 1981).

99. See, *e.g.*, C. Antieau, A. Downey & E. Roberts, *Freedom from Federal Establishment* 132 (1964).

100. 401 U.S. 437 (1971).

101. 50 U.S.C. app. Section 456(j) (1976).

102. The draftees in *Gillette* were two: one whose "humanist approach to religions" required him to abstain from participating in the Vietnam war and another, "a devout Catholic," whose adherence to that faith's doctrinal distinction between "just" and "unjust" wars led to the same result. *Gillette* v. *United States*, 401 U.S. 437, 439–40 (1971).

103. The establishment clause holding of *Gillette* was overshadowed later the same year by the seminal decision in *Lemon* v. *Kurtzman*, 403 U.S. 602 (1971). See note 98, *supra.* Perhaps for this reason, the Court has not relied upon *Gillette* in any significant way. Commentary on the case has thus tended to focus more on its subject matter, the relationship between religion and the draft law, than on its effect on general first amendment doctrine. See, *e.g.*, G. Gunther, *Cases and Materials on Constitutional Law* 1602 (10th ed. 1980); Greenawalt, *All or Nothing At All: The Defeat of Selective Conscientious Objection*, 1971 Sup. Ct. Rev. 31.

104. *Gillette* v. *United States,* 401 U.S. 437, 451-52 (1971).
105. *Id.* at 452.
106. But *cf. Stone* v. *Graham,* 449 U.S. 39 (1980) (law requiring copies of Ten Commandments to be posted in schools had no secular purpose).
107. *E. g., Village of Schaumburg* v. *Citizens for a Better Environment,* 444 U.S. 620, 637 (1980).
108. But see note 92, *supra.*

OBTAINING INFORMATION FROM RELIGIOUS BODIES BY COMPULSORY PROCESS

1. *In re Weir,* 377 F.Supp. 919 (1974).
2. *U.S.* v. *Nixon,* 418 U.S. 683, 41 L.Ed. 1039 (1974).
3. *Gelbard* v. *U.S.,* 408 U.S. 41, 92 S.Ct. 2357 (1972).
4. *Branzburg* v. *Hayes,* 408 U.S. 665, 96 S.Ct. 2646, 33 L.Ed.2d 626 (1972).
5. *Smilow* v. *U.S.,* 465 U.S. F.2d 802 (1972).
6. *In re Subpoenas,* 77 Cr.Misc. # 45586 at 10 (1977).
7. *People* v. *Woodruff,* 272 N.Y.S.2d 786, 788-89 (1966).
8. *Surinach* v. *Pesquera de Busquets,* 604 F.2d 73 (1st Cir. 1979).
9. *U.S.* v. *Holmes,* 614 F.2d 985, 988 (5th Cir. 1980).
10. *U.S.* v. *Life Science Church of America,* 636 F.2d 221 (8th Cir. 1980).
11. *U.S.* v. *Freedom Church,* 613 F.2d 316 (1st Cir. 1979).
12. *EEOC* v. *Mississippi College,* 626 F.2d 477 (5th Cir. 1980).
13. *N.Y. Times,* Feb. 9, 1981, pages A-1 and A-12.
14. Policy Statement of CIA dated Feb. 11, 1976.
15. *Schneider* v. *State of N.J., Town of Irvington,* 308 U.S. 147 (1938).

GOVERNMENT RESTRAINT ON POLITICAL ACTIVITIES OF RELIGIOUS BODIES

1. I.R.C. Section 501(c)(3).
2. Treas. Reg. Section 1.501(c)(3)-1(c)(3).
3. Treas. Reg. Section 1.501(c)(3)-1(c)(3)(iv).
4. Rev. Rul. 64-195, 1964 C.B. 138.
5. Rev. Rul. 70-79, 1970-1 C.B. 127.
6. Treas Reg. Section 1.501(c)(3)-1(c)(3)(ii)—This definition is parallel to those in Sections 4945 and 4911.
7. Rev. Rul. 67-293, 1967-2 C.B. 185.
8. *Christian Echoes National Ministry, Inc.* v. *U.S.,* 470 F. 2d 849 (10th Cir. 1972), *cert.* denied, 414 U.S. 864 (1973) [hereinafter cited as *Christian Echoes*].
9. Treas Reg. Section 1.501 (c)(3)-1(c)(3)(ii).
10. *Roberts Dairy Co.* v. *Commissioner,* 195 F. 2d 948 (8th Cir. 1952).
11. *Christian Echoes,* 470 F. 2d at 854-55.
12. *Haswell* v. *U.S.,* 500 F. 2d 1133 (Ct. Cl. 1974), *cert.* denied, 419 U.S. 1107 (1975) [hereinafter cited as *Haswell*].
13. *League of Women Voters* v. *U.S.,* 180 F. Supp. 379 (Ct. Cl.), *cert.* denied, 364 U.S. 822 (1960) [hereinafter cited as *League*]; see also, *Kuper* v. *Commissioner,* 180 F. Supp. 379 (Ct. Cl. 1960).
14. Rev. Rul. 70-449. 1970-2 C.B. 112.
15. *Haswell,* 500 F. 2d at 1145.
16. Prop. Treas. Reg. Section 53.4945-2, 45 Fed. Reg. 229 (1980).
17. *Murray Seasongood* v. *Commissioner,* 227 F. 2d 907 (6th Cir. 1955).
18. *Haswell,* 500 F. 2d at 1147.
19. *Christian Echoes,* 470 F. 2d at 855; *Haswell,* 500 F. 2d at 1142.
20. *League,* 180 F. Supp. 379.
21. I.R.C. Sections 501 (h) and 4911, sometimes called the "Conable Amendment" after its sponsor, the Hon. Barber Conable (R-N.Y.), ranking minority member of the House Ways and Means Committee.
22. Section 53.4945-2(a)(5)(ii) of the regulations defines non-partisan analysis, study or

research in terms of presenting a full and fair exposition of the facts. This is the same language that was found to be unconstitutionally vague in *Big Mama Rag, Inc.* v. *U.S.*, 631 F. 2d 1030 (D.C. Cir. 1980).
23. I.R.C. Section 501(c)(3)
24. *Id.*
25. Treas Reg. Section 1.501(c)(3)-1(c)(3)(i), (v).
26. Treas Reg. Section 1.501(c)(3)-1(c)(3)(iii).
27. *Id.*
28. *Id.*
29. Rev. Rul. 67-71, 1967-1 C.B. 125.
30. Rev. Rul. 67-368, 1967-2 C.B. 194. Although this ruling applies to a Section 501(c)(4) organization, it is indicative of the thinking of the Service on political campaign activity.
31. Rev. Rul. 76-456, 1976-2 C.B. 151.
32. 1978-1 C.B. 153.
33. 1978-1 C.B. 154.
34. IRS Letter Ruling, Sept. 4, 1980.
35. 1980-41 I.R.B. 7.
36. See *Buckley* v. *Valeo*, 424 U.S. 1, 41(1976).
37. *Id.* at 41 n. 48.
38. *Id.* at 42.
39. Id. at 44 n. 52.
40. *Consol. Edison Co.* v. *Public Service Commission*, ____U.S.____, 100 S. Ct. 2326, 2333 (1980).

THE USE OF LEGAL PROCESS FOR DE-CONVERSION

1. L. Carroll, *Through the Looking-Glass*, ch. 5 (1872).
2. T. Patrick & T. Dulack, *Let Our Children Go!* 63 (1976).
3. Briggs, *Religious "Brainwashing" Dispute*, N.Y. Times, Apr. 9, 1977, at 8, col. 5.
4. Transcript of Proceedings, Information Meeting on the Cult Phenomenon in the United States, Washington, D.C., 59-60 (Feb. 5, 1979).
5. T. Patrick & T. Dulack, *op. cit;* Patrick has, however, been convicted as a result of his deprogramming activities. See, e.g., LeMoult, "Deprogramming Members of Religious Sects," *Fordham Law Review* 46:599, 628-29 (1978).
6. Meislin, *Carey Vetoes Bill to Help Parents Act Against Cults*, N.Y. Times, July 9, 1980, at B4, col. 5. The same thing occurred in 1981 with a bill, A. 7912-B, that was somewhat different in detail from the one described in the text, but no less objectionable.
7. A. 11122–A Section 1 (N.Y. Mar. 25, 1980).
8. *Katz* v. *Superior Court*, 73 Cal. App. 3d 952, 970, 141 Cal. Rptr. 234, 244 (1st Dist. 1977) (footnote omitted).
9. Martin, *Deprogramming Defended*, Liberty, May/June 1978, at 16, 16.
10. J. Acton, *Sir Erskine May's Democracy in Europe*, in The History of Freedom and Other Essays 4 (1907).

WHEN IS GOVERNMENTAL INTERVENTION LEGITIMATE?

1. See Engdahl, David E., "Soldiers, Riot and Revolution: The Law and History of Military Troops in Civil Disorders," 57 *Iowa Law Review* 1, 1971.
2. *Religious News Service*, March 15, 1976, May 9, 1977.
3. *Religious News Service*, June 5, 1979.
4. *Religious News Service*, February 25, 1981, p. 9.
5. *Religious News Service*, December 24, 1980.
6. See Worthing, Sharon L., "The State Takes Over a Church" in *Annals of the American Academy of Political and Social Science*, vol. 446, Nov., 1979, pp. 136ff.
7. This incident occurred at Faith Center Church, Glendale, Calif., *Los Angeles Herald-Examiner*, June 9, 1980, page A10.

8. See citations in Flowers, Ronald B., "Freedom of Religion versus Civil Authority in Matters of Health," *Annals, loc. cit.*, pp. 156ff.
9. *People* v. *Woody*, 394 F.2d 813 (1964).
10. See Flowers, *loc. cit.*
11. 98 U.S. 145, 1878.
12. 133 U.S. 333 (1890).
13. 341 U.S. 494 (1951).
14. *Davis* v. *Beason*, supra.
15. 268 U.S. 510 (1925).
16. *Griswold* v. *Connecticut*, 381 U.S. 479.
17. 319 U.S. 624 (1943).
18. *Minersville School District* v. *Gobitis*, 310 U.S. 586 (1940).
19. See comments on this case by Laurence Tribe, p. 36 above.
20. 366 U.S. 599 (1961).
21. 374 U.S. 398 (1963).
22. 406 U.S. 205 (1972).
23. 322 U.S. 78 (1944).
24. *Ibid.*
25. *Village of Schaumburg* v. *Citizens for a Better Environment*, 444 U.S. 620 (1980).
26. New York and California have the most stringent such statutes.
27. U.S. Constitution, First Amendment.
28. See Kelley, *Why Churches Should Not Pay Taxes*, N.Y., Harper & Row, 1977, chapter 6.
29. *U.S.* v. *Ballard, loc. cit.*
30. See p. 173 above and Whelan, Charles, chapter 5 above.
31. See text at note 7.
32. *Walz* v. *Tax Commission*, 397 U.S. 664 (1970), *Lemon* v. *Kurtzman*, 403 U.S. 602 (1971) and its progeny.
33. *Presbyterian Church* v. *Mary Elizabeth Blue Hall Memorial Presbyterian Church*, 393 U.S. 440 (1969).
34. *Watson* v. *Jones*, 13 Wallace 679 (1872) through *Hull Church*, loc cit.
35. *Kedroff* v. *St. Nicholas Cathedral*, 344 U.S. 94 (1952) through *Serbian Eastern Orthodox Diocese* v. *Milivojevich*, 426 U.S. 696 (1976).
36. *Maryland and Virginia Eldership* v. *Sharpsburg Church*, 396 U.S. 367 (1970) through *Jones* v. *Wolf*, 443 U.S. 595 (1979).
37. *Barr* v. *United Methodist Church*, 90 Cal. App. 3d 259 (1978), settled out of court.
38. Dissenting in *Everson* v. *Board of Education*, 330 U.S. 1.
39. *Lemon* v. *Kurtzman*, loc. cit.
40. *Catholic Bishop of Chicago* v. *NLRB*, 559 F.2d 1112 (1977), affirmed by U.S. Supreme Ct. on statutory grounds.
41. Kelley, *op. cit.*, ch. 5.
42. Hopkins, Bruce, *The Law of Tax-Exempt Organizations*, N.Y. John Wiley & Sons, 3d Ed., 1979, p. 134.
43. *Reynolds* v. *U.S.*, *loc. cit.*
44. *NAACP* v. *Alabama*, 357 U.S. 449 (1968), and its progeny, including *Gibson* v. *Florida* 372 U.S. 539.
45. See text at notes 33–37 above.
46. Excerpt from Reporter's Transcript of Proceedings in Superior Court of California, Los Angeles County, *People of State of California* v. *Worldwide Church of God*, February 21, 1979.
47. See text at notes 21–22 above.
48. 470 F.2d 849, 10th Cir., 1972, *cert.* denied, 414 U.S. 864 (1973).
49. *Ibid.*
50. See *Sherbert* v. *Verner, loc. cit.*, and *Speiser* v. *Randall*, 357 U.S. 513 (1958).
51. It is important to note, however, that Congress had occasion to consider the validity of *Christian Echoes* when it enacted the Tax Reform Act of 1976, and it explicitly declined to endorse that decision: "It is the intent of Congress that enactment of this section is

not to be regarded in any way as approval or disapproval of the decision of the Court of Appeals for the Tenth Circuit in *Christian Echoes, National Ministry, Inc.*, v. *United States*, 470 F.2d 849 (1972), or of the reasoning in any of the opinions leading to that decision." (I.R.C. § 504(c) note).

52. See Weithorn, Stanley, chapter 6, pp. 64 ff., above.
53. Acts of the Apostles, 5:39, RSV.